CHANGE AND DEVELOPMENT IN THE GULF

Also by Abbas Abdelkarim

PRIMITIVE CAPITAL ACCUMULATION

SUDAN – THE GEZIRA SCHEME AND AGRICULTURAL TRANSITION (*with Tony Barnett*)

SUDAN – CAPITAL, STATE AND TRANSFORMATION (*editor with Tony Barnett*)

Change and Development in the Gulf

Edited by

Abbas Abdelkarim
Senior Lecturer
Institute of Social Studies
The Hague

WITHDRAWN

LEBANON VALLEY COLLEGE LIBRARY

First published in Great Britain 1999 by
MACMILLAN PRESS LTD
Houndmills, Basingstoke, Hampshire RG21 6XS and London
Companies and representatives throughout the world

A catalogue record for this book is available from the British Library.

ISBN 0–333–73891–8

 First published in the United States of America 1999 by
ST. MARTIN'S PRESS, INC.,
Scholarly and Reference Division,
175 Fifth Avenue, New York, N.Y. 10010

ISBN 0–312–21658–0

Library of Congress Cataloging-in-Publication Data
Change and development in the Gulf / edited by Abbas Abdelkarim.
p. cm.
Includes bibliographical references and index.
ISBN 0–312–21658–0 (cloth)
1. Persian Gulf Region—Economic conditions. 2. Persian Gulf
Region—Economic policy. 3. Persian Gulf Region—Social conditions.
4. Persian Gulf Region—Politics and government. I. Abdelkarim,
Abbas, 1950–   .
HC415.3.C48   1998
338.9536—dc21   98–34976
                                                                CIP

Selection, editorial matter and Chapters 1 and 2 © Abbas Abdelkarim 1999
Chapters 3–11 © Macmillan Press Ltd 1999

All rights reserved. No reproduction, copy or transmission of this publication may be made without written permission.

No paragraph of this publication may be reproduced, copied or transmitted save with written permission or in accordance with the provisions of the Copyright, Designs and Patents Act 1988, or under the terms of any licence permitting limited copying issued by the Copyright Licensing Agency, 90 Tottenham Court Road, London W1P 9HE.

Any person who does any unauthorised act in relation to this publication may be liable to criminal prosecution and civil claims for damages.

The authors have asserted their rights to be identified as the authors of this work in accordance with the Copyright, Designs and Patents Act 1988.

This book is printed on paper suitable for recycling and made from fully managed and sustained forest sources.

10 9 8 7 6 5 4 3 2 1
08 07 06 05 04 03 02 01 00 99

Printed and bound in Great Britain by
Antony Rowe Ltd, Chippenham, Wiltshire

Contents

Notes on Contributors vii
List of Tables viii

Introduction and Background 1

1 Change and Development in the Gulf: an Overview of Major Issues 3
   Abbas Abdelkarim

2 Oil, Population Change and Social Development in the Gulf: Some Major Trends and Indicators 25
   Abbas Abdelkarim

PART I: Oil and the Economy: Dependence and Diversification 49

3 The State in Oil Rentier Economies: the Case of Bahrain 51
   Khalid M. Abdulla

4 Industrial Strategies and Change in the UAE during the 1980s 79
   Fatima S. Al-Shamsi

5 Diversification through Industrialization: the Saudi Experience 104
   Osama Saad Ahmed

PART II: Human Resources and Gender Relations 131

6 Population Policies in the Countries of the Gulf Cooperation Council 133
   Baquer Salman Al-Najjar

7 Overview of Major Issues in the Development of National Human Reources in the Gulf 151
   Adil Osman Gebriel

8 Women, Income Generation and Gender Relations in Rural Oman 164
   Charlotte Heath

9	The Saudis and the Gulf War: Gender, Power and the Revival of the Religious Right *Eleanor A. Doumato*	184

PART III: Political Change and Militarization: the Impact of the Gulf War 211

10	Post-War Kuwait and the Process of Democratization: the Persistence of Political Tribalism *Paul Aarts*	213
11	Arms, Oil and Security in the Gulf: a Tenuous Balance *Serge Herzog*	238

Index 260

Notes on Contributors

Paul Aarts, Department of Political Science, University of Amsterdam

Abbas Abdelkarim, Institute of Social studies, The Hague, The Netherlands

Khalid M. Abdulla, Department of Economics, University of Bahrain, Manama, Bahrain

Osama Saad Ahmed, Ministry of Labour and Social Affairs, Manama, State of Bahrain

Baquer Salman Al-Najjar, Department of Sociology, Manama University of Bahrain, Manama, Bahrain

Fatima S. Al-Shamsi, Department of Economics, University of United Arab Emirates, Al Ain, UAE.

Eleanor Doumato, Department of History, University of Rhode Island, USA

Adil Osman Gebriel, Consultant, Amsterdam, The Netherlands

Charlotte Heath, Department for International Development, London, UK

Serge Herzog, Ministry of Defence, Geneva, Switzerland

List of Tables

2.1 Crude oil production in selected years, by country
2.2 Proven published oil reserves as of 1 January 1990 and as of 1 January 1994, by country
2.3 Average annual government oil revenue of OPEC member Gulf Countries
2.4 GNP per capita in the Gulf, 1994
2.5 Some indicators of dependence on oil
2.6 Population by nationality in the Gulf countries
2.7 Number and percentage of non-nationals in the labour force in the Gulf
2.8 Some indicators of educational development in the Gulf
2.9 Gulf female/male gap in education
2.10 Percentage of women in selected occupations in three Gulf countries in 1990
2.11 Some indicators of health development
3.1 Oil production, reserves and crude production per capita for selected countries
3.2 The significance of oil exports to the Bahraini economy
3.3 Employees of the Bahrain oil sector as a percentage of total population
3.4 The significance of government employment in Bahrain
3.5 Bahrain: breakdown of the government budget
3.6 Bahrain: public expenditure on the infrastructure
3.7 Bahrain: the growth of government's wage bill
3.8 Bahrain government budget's public revenue by source
3.9 The significance of oil revenue and government expenditure to the economy of Bahrain
3.10 Government participation in domestic enterprises
4.1 GDP distribution between oil and non-oil sectors in the UAE
4.2 UAE GDP growth
4.3 Some important indicators of the UAE's manufacturing sector
4.4 Manufacturing value added and employment by emirate
4.5 Distribution of invested funds in the manufacturing sector, by emirate

List of Tables

4.6 Value added, gross fixed capital formation and employment in the UAE by manufacturing sector
5.1 Production of factories under the foreign capital investment system by industrial activity, Saudi Arabia
5.2 Industrial licences issued in Saudi Arabia in 1414 AH
5.3 Foreign participation in joint ventures in Saudi Arabia by nationality and industrial sector
5.4 Saudi exports by industrial origin
5.5 Saudi imports by economic category
6.1 National and non-national population in the Gulf, by gender
11.1 Geographic/demographic data of GCC states
11.2 Economic/military data of the Gulf states

Introduction and Background

1 Change and Development in the Gulf: an Overview of Major Issues
Abbas Abdelkarim

The major aim of this chapter is to introduce, link and put in context the different themes that the rest of the chapters of the book address. In doing so this chapter will attempt to capture and preliminarily assess some of the major socioeconomic and political changes and developments brought by oil, and to reflect on the major development challenges facing the countries of the Gulf.

'Gulf' is used in this book in reference to the countries that are members of the Gulf Cooperation Council (GCC), which are: Bahrain, Kuwait, Oman, Qatar, Saudi Arabia and the United Arab Emirates. The GCC was established in May 1981. Its constitution describes it as an organization for realizing and coordinating integration and cooperation in all economic, social and cultural affairs among its member countries. Despite not emphasizing politics/security, it is this main concern that brought these countries together. Both Iraq and Iran represented a political and military threat to the other countries of the Arab Gulf. The time of establishment of the GCC was chosen carefully, shortly after the start of the first Gulf War between Iraq and Iran. Had Iraq not been preoccupied with the war, it could have been difficult to exclude it from a cooperation council among the Arab states of the Gulf without risking an immediate political confrontation.

'Gulf War' refers to the 'Second Gulf War' after the occupation of Kuwait by Iraq.

The processes of change, stagnation and development in the Gulf viewed in this chapter are organized in three sections which correspond to the three parts of the book. In the first part the impact of oil in redefining the (redistributive) role of the state and in shaping economic policies and the business environment will be briefly outlined. Reducing dependence on oil is an endeavour of all GCC countries. Industrialization is one venue that has been explored by a number of them; this will also be dealt with in this part. Oil wealth brought spectacular changes in the population structure. In all of the Gulf countries the majority of the labour force are foreigners coming from all over the world. Attempts to develop population policies and the problems of national human resource development are introduced in Part II. In this same section two case studies of stagnation and change in gender relations in two Gulf country contexts will be examined. The last part deals with the impact of the Gulf War on internal political systems and on militarization. It will be shown that the Gulf War has initiated more political change in Kuwait than the rest of the GCC, and it increased military spending to such a problematic level that it may impede future economic development.

I. OIL AND THE ECONOMY: DEPENDENCE AND DIVERSIFICATION

The Gulf region (including, in addition to the present GCC countries, Iraq and Iran), according to Zahlan (1989), is one of the oldest continuously inhabited regions in the world. Dilmus, a flourishing civilization on the western coast of the Gulf which came into existence some five thousand years ago, was referred to in the poetry of Sumerians as 'Land of Paradise', 'Land of Living' and 'Home of the Gods' (ibid.: 1). Zahlan describes Dilmus, which covered most of eastern Arabia and present Bahrain, as a fertile land with abundant water supplies and a sophisticated irrigation system and agricultural activities. In addition to dates, Dilmus also produced pearls for the international market. These two products continued to become the major products of the Gulf region until the discovery of oil. The trading activities of Gulf people have been known for centuries. Ships from the Gulf regularly sailed all the way to India and China. Baghdad (in present-day Iraq) and Sohar (in Oman) were two important trading centres. On the eastern coast of the Gulf, Siraf was the first known major trading centre. Foreign powers had a strong presence in the region: first the Ottoman empire, and from

An Overview of Major Issues

the fifteenth century and for four centuries, the Western countries (Portugal first, followed by Holland and France, and later Britain).

Soon after the discovery of oil it became the major contributor to GDP and almost the only export commodity in the GCC countries. Gulf countries produced 23 per cent of the world total production of oil in 1993 and held 46 per cent of the world's oil reserves in January 1994. Saudi Arabia has more oil reserves than any other country in the world (26 per cent of the total) and Kuwait could continue production at its present level for years longer than any other country (see Chapter 2 of this book). These facts explain the strategic importance of the liberation of Kuwait and of the protection of Saudi Arabia for the Western countries (the largest consumers of Middle Eastern oil).

Production and exportation of oil set the Gulf economies on the road of internationalization and introduced profound economic and social changes. The primary initiator of these changes is the state. That the state is the primary recipient of oil income and that the economies of the Gulf significantly depend on this source of income and on the state expenditure made Mahdavy (1970) and Abdel-Fadil (1979 and 1987), respectively, introduce the terms 'rentier states' and 'rentier economies' to describe the various political and socioeconomic features that characterize the state and the economy of the Middle Eastern countries. Abdulla (Chapter 3) uses the concepts of 'rentier state' and 'rentier economy' to examine the impact of the various rentier features on the pattern of resource allocation and the economic behaviour in the state in Bahrain. Abdulla describes the oil rentier economies as those countries that receive a substantial amount of external oil rents on a regular basis. Endowed with huge oil rents, the state is not only independent of the domestic economy (does not need to resort to taxation as a source of income) but is set to play a leading role in it. In his study of the case of Bahrain, Abdulla concludes that the major features of the rentier state in Bahrain (and in the Gulf generally) are:

i) It distributes a significant part of oil rents among the national population through availing them of government employment and subsidizing a wide range of goods and

services, partly to enhance the population's standard of living and partly to secure loyalty;
ii) it uses much of its income in expanding infrastructure; and
iii) it participates in establishing a larger number of business enterprises whose behaviour (and the sustainability of their activities) depend largely on government expenditure.

As Abdulla (in this book) has argued, the rentier states of the Gulf have created and strengthened a national private sector. Members of the (new) class of entrepreneurs come from the old small merchant classes, tribal allies of the state, and from the growing elite groups. Support from the state includes (heavily) subsidized loans and other forms of subsidies and incentives. As an example of these in Saudi Arabia, the Saudi Industrial Development Fund (which had a capital of 5 billion US$ in 1995), among other institutions, provides concessionary loans to private investments. Electricity, water and agricultural inputs and machinery, among other production inputs, are heavily subsidized (*Middle East Review*, 1993/4). Azzam (1988) and EIU (1996) also give some examples of government subsidizing local industry and giving preferential treatment in government procurement and assistance in market research in support of national entrepreneurs.

The building of a sound industrial sector is regarded as strategic goal for securing future incomes from non-oil sources. Given this objective, industrialization has become a common agenda in the development plans of the Gulf countries. To achieve this objective of diversification, the GCC countries have diverted a sizable segment of revenues received from oil exports to finance ambitious programmes of industrialization. As a result, joint ventures with foreign partners were formed to import technology capable of utilizing oil and gas as feed stock for petrochemical industries (mainly for export). By 1985, according to the Gulf Organization for Industrial Consulting, there were 3,600 manufacturing enterprises operating in the region, with a total investment of $75 billion. The majority of these enterprises were engaged in import substitution products and depended mostly on imported skills and materials for their operation (Azzam, 1988).

An Overview of Major Issues

In spite of the huge financial investment in the industrial sector, studies on the process of industrialization in the Gulf, by advocates and critics alike, have tended toward negative conclusions. For those who advocated industrial development as a path out of colonial dependency toward greater Arab economic integration, there has been a disenchantment at the lack of progress and coordination among the Gulf countries. For those who want to see the Gulf industrial sector as an important source of national income and employment, there have been disappointments of varying degree.

Two works in this book analyse industrialization as a venue for diversification of the economy. Al-Shamsi (Chapter 4) examines industrial strategies in the UAE and Ahmed (Chapter 5) studies problems of industrialization in Saudi Arabia.

A major conclusion of Al-Shamsi is that manufacturing industry in the UAE was unable to attain rapid diversification of the economy. The role of industrialization in promoting a national labour force and skills, including indigenizing foreign technology and inducing economic, social and institutional changes, has not been attained.

According to Al-Shamsi a coherent industrial strategy can not be developed outside a coherent general development strategy. The UAE lacks an efficient strategy to channel funds into production-related projects; equally it lacks the political, social and administrative institutions capable of managing economic development and planning for industrialization. She asserts that given the characteristics of the UAE and other Gulf economies, the drive for industrial development will remain restricted unless it acquires a real regional dimension.

Ahmed's study (Chapter 5) of problems of industrialization in Saudi Arabia has come to similar conclusions as that of Al-Shamsi. His analysis finds that the industrial sector has remained a minor part of the Saudi economy, in spite of the huge investment oriented to it. Due to a number of internal and external constraints, its progress has been slow and often extremely costly, relative to the gains achieved by other developing countries, especially those in East and South-east Asia.

In view of the findings of these two studies, one may conclude that the industrial policies implemented in the UAE and Saudi Arabia since the 1970s have not been effective either in achieving the objective of diversification of income sources or in accomplishing industrial growth targets. The limited success of these policies may be attributed to the fact that they were carried out in the absence of: a comprehensive development strategy, including an appropriate economic management framework; a conducive socio-political environment; and proper industrial planning and appropriate selection of industrial projects and technology; all of which would induce a process of dynamic industrial growth to achieve the aim of diversification of the economy.

There have been very few attempts by countries of the GCC to seek reduction of their dependence on oil by developing other sectors than manufacturing. The agricultural production in Saudi Arabia is serving political rather than economic objectives and it survives only with heavy subsidies (Looney, 1990).

There have been no systematic plans and investments directed towards revitalizing and modernizing the fisheries sector, which not long ago in the history of the Gulf countries was the major occupation for a sizable segment of the population. In a sense Oman is an exception, not because it has gone back to fisheries, but because fisheries has not disappeared.

II. HUMAN RESOURCES AND GENDER RELATIONS

The social structure of the Gulf states is made up of 'Badu' (Bedouin) and 'Hadar' (settled people), both being tribally organized. Unlike most of the developing countries, underpopulation is the major economic development constraint in the post-oil period.

In a few decades, and as a result of a huge influx of migrants after the production of oil, the population and labour force structures of the Gulf changed drastically. In all Gulf countries the migrant labour force became dominant, and in some of them the majority of the population are nonnationals (see among others, Birks and Sinclair, 1980; Sirageldin et al., 1983, and Chapter 2 in this book).

Nevertheless, with the exception of Kuwait, none of the Gulf countries has formulated explicit population policies (see Galal-el-Din, 1983, and Russel and Al-Ramadhan,

1994). None has taken seriously such important issues a population imbalance, the potential increase of unemployment among national population and the question of job opportunities for coming generations. The work of Al-Najjar in this book (Chapter 6) addresses this very important policy issue facing the Gulf countries. Al-Najjar asserts that there is a lack of explicit policy concerning population at both the national and regional levels in the Gulf area. There exist a few regulations and rules which, usually, are only short-lived responses to present problems rather than well-studied long-range policies. For example, when the UAE was badly affected by the sudden decline in oil prices in 1983–6, it started sending 'un-needed' foreign labour back home in the hope that such a measure would alleviate domestic economic problems. More recently, when it started to gain back some of its economic strength, the UAE started recalling foreign labour. However, most importantly, political issues and concerns have been the determining factors underlying the changing attitudes of the Gulf governments towards the presence and employment of foreign labour. This was clear in their attitude towards Egyptians during the Nasser era and towards Palestinians in the late 1960s, and towards Shia of Iran, Iraq, Lebanon and elsewhere during the first years of the Iranian revolution in 1979. This was also clear during the Iran–Iraq war from 1980 to 1988 and more recently towards the Palestinians, Jordanians, Iraqis, Sudanese and Yemenis since the Iraqi occupation of Kuwait. In other words, politics and security rather than economics were and still are the main determinant of attitudes to the presence and employment of foreign labour. This political factor also applies to the manipulation of the national population, where the decision to increase the number or the power of specific groups is a response to internal power struggles between various ethnic and tribal groups or to external threat.

Despite the continuous call for a significant reduction in the migrant population, the need for them will continue for years to come. The social welfare of the region as well as the interest of the property owner and merchant classes require their presence.

The dependence of Gulf economics on a foreign labour force does not arise only from the small size (and youthful structure) of their population base, but also from scarcity of skilled manpower. Shortage of skills has affected all the Gulf countries. In all of them, except possibly Bahrain, the lack of technical, professional and management skills (at all levels) is very acute (see among others, Birks and Sinclair, 1980; Sirageldin et al., 1983; Al-Misnad, 1985). Some authors discuss the negative attitudes towards work generally and especially towards work involving physical effort (see for example Looney, 1994, Fergany, 1984, and Chapter 7 in this book). The roots of these negative attitudes are to be sought in the 'welfare state' policies. The 'welfare policies' are mechanisms (of the rentier economy) for redistribution of part of the oil revenue to nationals. These policies make it possible for nationals to participate in activities that have either a secured income (e.g. government employment) or extremely high profitability, without contributing much (or any) to productive work. In fact, the educational system has become geared towards preparing nationals for this 'luxury' rather than for productive employment (Fergany, 1984). Exposing these and other problems facing national human resource development in the Gulf, Gebriel (Chapter 7 below) argues that it is imperative that Gulf countries should use various social and educational institutions to work on changing the negative social values and attitudes toward manual and technical jobs. He further contends that the availability of financial resources and the presence of a joint venture system in various economic sectors (which can allow transfer of technology and skills) represent a unique opportunity for the Gulf countries to improve the educational and skill profile of their people. Another factor discussed in Gebriel's work which could lead to a decrease in the need for migrants is technology. Importation, adaption, and use of (more) capital-intensive technology could lead to a reduction in dependency on foreign labour if those who will operate, adapt and develop it are primarily nationals. Gebriel, however, points out that the current weakness and inappropriateness of the educational system and research and development (R&D) is hindering the creation and development of national skills and indigenous technological capabilities.

Gebriel also addresses the (socially and culturally motivated) problem of low female participation in the labour force. He asserts that changes in the organization of work (such as allowing part-time employment for women) and the creation of suitable sociocultural environment should be initiated to allow a higher participation of women in the work force. This could be one of the most effective ways to reduce the dependence on migrant labour.

Unlike the many studies which tackle women's participation in the labour force and conclude implicitly or explicitly that the historically defined sociocultural and religious structures of the Gulf countries impede the fuller utilization of women's human resource (see for example Shah, 1986; Ghanem, 1992; Seikaly, 1994), Webster (1986) notes that oil and 'development' have increased women's withdrawal from the labour force. Before oil, seclusion of women was an ideal that was only available to the very wealthy. After oil the majority of women have lost their former economic roles and have been confined to the stereotype of 'respectable seclusion'.

The position and roles of women have normally been addressed from the angle of their economic activity; i.e. participation in the labour force (notable exceptions in past research include Eikleman, 1984; Wikan, 1982; Webster, 1991). Two works in the present book, Heath (Chapter 8) and Doumato (Chapter 9) go beyond women's role in the labour market to address the rather under-researched topic of gender relations in the Gulf.

Heath (Chapter 8) addresses some aspects of gender relations in rural Oman by examining the ways in which two rural women's groups, 'badu' (Bedouin) and 'hadhar' (settled), have responded to a government initiated income generation project. Heath concludes that the two groups of women have been able to use the project to move (social) boundaries and pursue autonomy. The semi-secluded and semi-masked Bedouin women were more able (than the unsecluded and unmasked village women) to respond to opportunities that led to changes in those boundaries. The project allowed the Bedouin women access to a legitimate interaction with a formal/wider world that would not have been (easily) attainable without it. Through the study of a weaving project and of gender relations (in conflict or cooperation), and issues of patriarchy and subordination in the two Bedouin and village communities, she concludes that rural women have goals which they want to achieve in the context of their lives. That the achievement of these goals may be dependent on 'patriarchal bargains' and acceptance of male dominance may be difficult for development agencies to understand.

Doumato (Chapter 9) examines the ideology of 'ideal islamic womanhood' in Saudi Arabia and the impact of the Gulf War on it. The idealized woman is a wife and mother. Her place is within the family and men are her protectors. The Saudi rule is responsible for upholding the islamic moral value of protecting women within the family under the guardianship of men. This ideology emanates not only from religious scholars and conservative writers, but is an integral component of state institutions and policy in Saudi Arabia.

The Saudi king's alignment with the USA during the Gulf War and his initiative for women's participation in civil defence work have led to an expectation of a decline in religious-conservative influence. This did not happen, because the ideology of 'ideal islamic woman' has always been a component of paramount importance to the myth of national identity from which the Saudi monarchy draws its legitimacy. Doumato asserts that the ideal islamic woman is more pronounced during times of political instability – the mosque seizure of 1979 and the women's driving demonstration of 1990 (after the invasion of Kuwait). Support for the patriarchal family and 'traditional values' is taken as support for stability (read, continuity of the present sociopolitical structure).

III. POLITICAL CHANGE AND MILITARIZATION: IMPACT OF THE GULF WAR

The most common constraint on the development process in the Gulf countries is the lack of a reliable democratic political system and an administrative structure to support the development efforts. According to Keith and Anne McLachlan (1989), there is political uncertainty and fear of violent change. Citizens are reluctant to commit their capital to long-term ventures and wherever possible make safer investments in the developed world. In a day-to-day context,

An Overview of Major Issues 13

many nationals and immigrants fail to identify with current political policies. Lack of democracy, rigidly centralized management structures, corruption and other forms of inefficiency affect, slow down, all economic and social development projects.

During the invasion of Kuwait by Iraq, a number of Gulf governments promised political change, implying relatively more participation (see the Annex to this chapter). In Saudi Arabia, UAE, Oman and Bahrain this meant an introduction of 'consultative councils' which have no legislative or executive powers. The exception was Kuwait. To what extent Kuwait is an exception and to what extent the Gulf War has impacted on political change is examined by Aarts in Chapter 10 of this book.

Kuwait and Bahrain are the only two Gulf countries with some aborted democratic experience prior to the Gulf War (again, see the Annex to this chapter). The war and liberation from the Iraqi forces, argues Aarts, have opened the way for more pluralist policies, limited as they may be, and have politicized the Kuwaitis in a way that might not otherwise have occurred. The system of political tribalism (which is the basic form of social organization of the state in the Gulf) has been stretched to its limit. The invasion and the inability of the Kuwaiti ruling family to guarantee external security has undermined the legitimacy of the regime, which can no longer be dependent only on its traditional tribal allies for support. Under pressures from opposition elite and political groups, and seeing no way out, the Kuwaiti regime has opted, or has been forced, to broaden the democratization process and to take some initial steps to change the relations between the state and citizens. However, these changes, as Aarts stresses, should not be overstated.

The sense of danger engendered by the invasion of Kuwait in 1990 has put defence and security problems in the forefront of challenges facing the GCC countries. The response was to beef up their defence spending. Reflecting the sensitivity of the governments of the GCC countries over the size of defence spending, accurate official data on military expenditures are not readily available. Nevertheless it can still be shown from available data that after the Iraqi invasion of Kuwait, Gulf countries have increased their spending. According to Herzog (Chapter 11 in this book), military spending of the GCC countries rose by 50 per cent between 1992 and 1993 and accounted for 9.35 per cent of the GDP. In Saudi Arabia, for instance, defence spending accounted for about 34 per cent of total expenditure in the Five Year Plan (1990–5) (EIU: 1996). The Kingdom has purchased military aircraft, defence equipment and weaponry of all sorts from the West in recent years, involving huge sums of money and providing payment in crude oil in some cases (AOGD: 1996). Saudi Arabia has turned into a leading world importer of high-tech weaponry.

As Herzog notes, it is clear that the potential military threat by either Iraq or Iran can hardly be met with Gulf countries alone. While possessing huge financial and military hardware resources, the GCC countries lack the political will to pool these resources to minimize external dependence on protection. Herzog further contends that the acquisition of modern military hardware by the GCC countries has brought and exacerbated a number of problems. Increased military spending is taking place at times of depressed oil revenues. It is compounding the shortage of technically skilled people (as it increases the demand for such people to operate the sophisticated modern weapons). Because of the lengthy operational life of modern weapons acquired, post-war military spending is also augmenting the dependence of the GCC countries on supplier states and their politics. In addition, military procurement in the Gulf countries, due to internal conflicts, is suffering from massive diseconomies of scale, duplication and non-standardization. Herzog rightfully concludes that the post-war fever to purchase high-tech weapons potentially hinders economic development and the endeavour to diversify away from dependence on oil.

ANNEX: SOME NOTES ON THE HISTORY OF THE GULF STATES

This annex draws on Halliday (1975), Europa (1991 and 1995) and Zahlan (1989).

1. Bahrain

The present state of Bahrain consists of 35 islands with a total area of 691 square kilometres. Causeways link Bahrain, the principal island, with two other islands and with Saudi Arabia. The first known foreign occupation of Bahrain was by the Portuguese in the period 1521–1602. Bahrain had also been subjected to occasional Iranian rule until the year 1783, when the Utub tribe of Saudi Arabia expelled the Iranians and established the independent Bahrain.

Facing Iranian and Ottoman threats, the Sheikh of Bahrain signed a protection treaty with the British in 1861. In 1880 the Sheikh further undertook not to enter into any relations with any other foreign government without the consent of the British. Bahrain practically came under British administration through advisers appointed by the British government. This continued even after 1913 when Britain and Turkey signed a convention acknowledging Bahrain's independence.

In January 1970 substantial administrative and political reforms were adopted. A twelve-member Council of State was established from Bahrainis and headed by the ruler's brother. British advisers, previously with considerable political and administrative influence, were turned into civil servants. In August 1971, Bahrain was proclaimed a full independent state. The Council of State became the Council of Ministers and Sheikh Isa, the ruler, took the title of Amir. The actual power rests with the Amir and his (Al-Khalifa) family.

Sixteen months after independence, elections were held for a Constituent Assembly. In December 1973 the Constituent Assembly passed a new constitution and paved the way to an elected National Assembly. In less than two years from that, in August 1975, the National Assembly was dissolved by the Amir with the allegation that it was hindering the functioning of the government. Bahrain's first democratic exercise had not continued for long before being aborted. Twenty months after the second Gulf war (November, 1992) the Amir announced the establishment of a new consultative council. Having very limited powers, the council was not received enthusiastically. It has not been able to absorb the unrest among the Shi'ite population which continues to date.

2. Kuwait

The area of the state of Kuwait is 17,818 square kilometres. Kuwait city is the capital.

No history is recorded on the area around Kuwait before the beginning of the eighteenth century when a segment of Anaiza tribe of Arabia settled there. The new settlers appointed a sheikh, founder of the present Sabah dynasty, to administer their internal affairs and external dealings with the Ottoman government. In 1765 the population of the town of Kuwait was estimated at 10,000 persons living on sea trade, fishing and pearling.

The Kuwaitis were not under direct Ottoman adminstration, but they paid tributes in recognition of the Turkish general dominion over the mainland. With an increasing influence of the Turks in the second half of the nineteenth century, Sheikh Abdullah bin Sabah al-Jabir accepted the title of commandant under the Turkish governor of Basra.

Kuwait relations with the British government started when the East India Company diverted most of the trade of Basra to Kuwait as a result of the Persian occupation of Basra in 1776–9. Toward the end of the nineteenth century the British were alarmed by the rising political influence of the Germans and the Turks due to the proposed Berlin–Baghdad railway. On the other hand, the then Sheikh of Kuwait, Mubarak, wanted independence from the Turks. He and the British government signed a treaty in 1899 in which the British were granted exclusive presence in Kuwait. In return, Mubarak was granted protection and 15,000 pounds a year. In 1961 the 1899 treaty was cancelled and Kuwait was declared an independent state. Shortly after independence, Abdul-Karim Qasim of Iraq claimed sovereignty over Kuwait. British troops were called to assist by the Kuwaiti Amir. Arab League forces then came to replace the British. In 1963 a new Iraqi government recognized Kuwait's independence.

The first Kuwaiti democratic experience was six months after independence, when twenty members of a Constituent Assembly were elected (the rest being the appointed ministers). After drafting the constitution, a national Assembly was elected in January 1963. The franchise was limited to male, 'first class' citizens (defined as those who can prove Kuwaiti ancestry from before 1920). No political parties were allowed.

Since its establishment, the National Assembly had been suspended twice: 1976–81 and 1986–92, on the ground that it was delaying legislation and hindering the functioning of the government, among other things.

The consecutive cabinets have always been headed by the heir apparent. Ministers have always been appointed by the Amir and key cabinet posts have been largely held by members of the royal family and other prominent, royal family-allied families.

In August 1990 Iraq invaded Kuwait. The Iraqi government refused to abide by the United Nations resolutions demanding the withdrawal of Iraqi troops. An American-led coalition forced the Iraqi troops out of Kuwait in March 1991. The Kuwaiti government returned with the promise of making some political reforms including the restoration of the National Assembly.

In October 1992 a new National Assembly was elected. A new 'national unity' government was appointed by the Amir. The new cabinet included members of the left- and right-wing 'opposition' groups, who secured 31 out of the 50 seats of the assembly. In June 1994 the Assembly passed legislation allowing sons of naturalized Kuwaitis to vote. Women are still excluded despite their protests and campaigns.

3. Oman

With a total area of 300,000 square kilometres, Oman is the second largest Gulf country. It has a long coastline of over 1,600 kilometres on the Indian ocean.

In contrast to Bahrain and Kuwait, Oman has a long history. It was one of the first countries to be converted to Islam (in the seventh century AD). In the eighth century, Omanis established their own Islamic state: Imamate. During this independent Imamate a number of main cities prospered, and Sohar developed into the largest city in the Arab world in the tenth century.

The Portuguese arrived in the last quarter of the sixteenth century and established themselves primarily on Sohar and Musaqat. A strong Omani Imam expelled them from Oman in 1650. Regaining their command of the sea around them, the Omanis managed to turn away the Portuguese from the East African coast; from Mogadishu, Mombasa and Zanzibar, in 1730. Not long after this, the Omani influence in East Africa was weakened as a result of civil war in Oman. Said Bin Sultan (who ruled between 1804 and 1856) revived Omani interest in Zanzibar. The dynasty he founded there ruled until the revolution in 1964.

During the reign of Said bin Sultan, strong relations with the British were established. British domination effectively started in the mid-nineteenth century. Britain never admitted that Oman was a colony; it claimed it was only 'assisting' Omani rulers under obligations of treaties. A number of UN resolutions starting from 1960 demanded the end of all forms of British domination. However, it was only in 1971, a year after Sultan Qaboos came to power, as a result of military coup against his father, that Oman became a member of the UN.

In 1965, during the rule of Sultan Said bin Taimur (Qaboos's father) a guerrilla war broke out in Dhofar province led by the Popular Front for the Libration of the Occupied Arab Gulf and Dhofar Liberation Front. Sultan Qaboos managed in 1975 to control the rebellion with the assistance of Iranian troops and other forms of assistance from Saudi Arabia, Jordan and the UAE.

Despite some reforms in the economy during the period of Qaboos, compared to the rule of his father, political power remained unchanged – totally concentrated in the hands of the Sultan. The Sultan is assisted by ministers appointed by him. During the invasion of Kuwait, Qaboos promised some political reforms in the form of a consultative council. In 1992 he announced the formation of a 59 (later increased to 80) member Consultative Council. Women were promised the right to vote. The council has no legislative power. However, ministers have to present statements to and have to answer questions by the Consultative Council.

4. Saudi Arabia

In addition to its geographical significance, occupying 2,240,000 square kilometres (four-fifths of Arabia) and bordering all other Gulf states (and three other Arab countries), Saudi Arabia is also the largest Gulf country in terms of population.

The first recorded urban settlement in what now constitutes Saudi Arabia is Mina Kingdom in the south-west, which is believed to have been established in the twelfth century BC. Other known early kingdoms were Sabaa and Himuarite, lasting until the sixth century AD.

From pockets of small settled civilizations, Arabia after Islam expanded its domination within a century (from the second half of the seventh century) from Spain to northern India. However, with the weakening of the Caliphate in Baghdad to which the political centre of gravity shifted from Hijaz in the west of Arabia, where Islam was born, the large Islamic state started to disintegrate.

Another religiously inspired movement, this time coming from Najd in the centre of Arabia, united a large part of Arabia. The religious reforming Wahhabi movement, named after a militant preacher called Mohammed ibn Abd al-Wahhab (1703–92), found adequate political support in a coalition of tribes led by the Saudi tribe. This coalition conquered a large part of Arabia by the beginning of the nineteenth century. Its further expansion was limited by the British, who dominated what are now Bahrain, the UAE, Oman and Yemen, and the Ottoman empire, which was by then exercising power over north-west Arabia. Not long after this and as a result of campaigns by the Ottoman Empire, and Egypt acting in the name of the Ottoman Sultan, Wahhabis were driven out from Mecca and Medina (in the west) in the first half of the nineteenth century and were replaced by the Hashemite Sharif Hussien, a dependent of the Ottoman empire. In 1890 the Wahhabis (and their leaders, the Saudi family) lost control over central and eastern Arabia.

In 1902 the Saudis and their followers set out to hit back. Led by Abdel Aziz ibn Saud, coming from exile in Kuwait, they captured Riyadh and the provinces of eastern Arabia. By 1925 they turned the Hashemites out of the western provinces. In 1926 Abdel Aziz proclaimed himself King of Hijaz (western Arabia) and in 1932 declared the whole territory under the Saudi control, united under the name of Kingdom of Saudi Arabia.

King Abdel Aziz succeeded in crushing internal opposition and dealt with clashes with British occupied territories in the north (Jordan and Iraq) and the south-west (Yemen). The British government recognized the Saudi government in 1927.

During the late 1930s and the Second World War, the kingdom lost its major source of revenue – the Muslim pilgrimage. Standard Oil of Los Angeles (a US company), having already discovered oil in the kingdom, managed to raise financial assistance from the US government to help Abdel Aziz out of his economic crisis of the 1940s.

Abdel Aziz was succeeded by his son Saud in 1953. Saud's brother, Faisal, replaced him as Crown Prince. A struggle over executive power between the King and the Crown Prince ended in the exile of the former. During this period the ideas of Saudi reformers like Prince Tilal and Abdullah Tariqi, first Saudi oil minister, found expression. Some economic and social reforms were made during Faisal's rule, which also consolidated Saudi Arabia's relations with the US. Saudi Arabia's external position; within the Arab League and Islamic countries was also changing primarily because of its growing economic position. A temporary storm in Saudi–US relations took place after the Arab–Israeli War of 1973 when Saudi Arabia joined an OPEC embargo on petroleum supplies to several Western countries, including the USA. Within less than a year after that, the USA and Saudi Arabia signed an economic and military cooperation agreement.

King Faisal was assassinated by one of his nephews in 1975. He was succeeded by his brother Khalid, who was succeeded seven years later by Fahad. While the position of Saudi Arabia has been strengthened considerably in the region in the 1970s and 1980s as a result of its expanding economic power and its relations with the West, its internal political structure remains unchanged. The country continues to be under the rule of one family and in conditions of severe social and political repression. During and after the occupation of Kuwait, some opposition by organized (primarily underground) Muslim fundamentalist groups has been noted.

5. Qatar

The state of Qatar occupies a territory of 11,437 square kilometres. Doha, the capital, contains more than half of the population.

Archaeological discoveries found evidence of habitation as early as 4000 BC. However, recorded history goes back only to the eighteenth century, when Qatar was dominated by the ruling family of Bahrain. Qatar was annexed to the Ottoman empire in 1872. When the latter left during the First World War, the British moved much as they had in the rest of the Gulf: by recognizing a local ruler, Sheikh Abdullah Al-Thani, and signing with him treaties that secured British domination.

When the British withdrew, the ruler of Qatar attempted to enter into a federation with Bahrain and the present UAE. As a result of disagreement on terms of the union, the ruler, Sheikh Ahmed Al-Thani, announced himself Amir and Qatar became an independent state in 1971.

Less than six months after independence, Sheikh Khalifa, by then the prince and cousin of the Amir, succeeded in deposing Sheikh Ahmed in a palace coup and declared himself Amir of the country.

The Amir enjoys absolute power. He is assisted by a council of ministers (headed by him) and an advisory council. He appoints ministers and allows elections of members of the advisory council by a limited suffrage. The way the Amir has been handling government affairs was criticized in a petition by 50 leading Qatari citizens in 1992. They demanded political, economic and educational reforms. The Amir responded with a government reshuffle. Three years later (in 1995) he was deposed by his son, Sheikh Hamad Bin Khalifa, who became the Amir.

6. The United Arab Emirates (UAE)

The UAE is a union of seven emirates: Abu Dhabi, Dubai, Sharijah, Ras Al-Khaimah, Umm Al-Qaiwain, Ajman and Fujariah. Their total area is 77,700 square kilometres.

Not much is known about the scattered lower Gulf sheikhdoms prior to the coming of the Europeans to the Gulf. People of the lower Gulf were leading a nomadic life, but they were also dependent on the sea: fishing, pearling, trading (including slave trade) and also pirating. Piracy (by both Europeans and Arabs) was widespread in the Gulf from the seventeenth to the early nineteenth centuries.

In 1820, Britain signed a treaty with the Arab tribes of the Gulf to suppress piracy and slave trade. In a further treaty in 1835 (referred to as a maritime truce) the sheikhs agreed not to engage in any form of hostilities by sea during the pearl-diving season. This was further developed in 1853 into a permanent agreement. The Gulf coast, previously named the 'Pirate Coast', was then changed to the 'Trucial Coast'. The British government, through its forces in the region, supervised the agreement. With the aim of excluding other European powers, Britain signed separate treaties with Trucial rulers similar to those with Bahrain and Qatar, in which the rulers undertook not to enter into any form of relationship with a foreign government other than Britain. Rulers of the Trucial states also accepted that the British government was to settle their disputes and to fix state boundaries.

A Trucial council made of seven rulers was formed in 1952 with the aim of establishing a federation in the future. A federation including Bahrain and Qatar was negotiated before the departure of the British. However, these two states opted not to enter the United Arab Emirates when it was founded in December 1971. Sheikh Zayed, the ruler of Abu Dhabi, was elected by the Supreme Council (composed of the rulers of the emirates) as the President of the UAE. A 40-member Federal National Council, the role of which is advisory, was also established. In both this Council and the Council of Ministers a balance of power between the emirates has always been kept.

While the individual emirates enjoy some autonomy, the federal government is responsible for central economic planning, health, education, defence, agriculture, national roads and telecommunications. The more wealthy emirates, Abu Dhabi and Dubai, contribute 50 per cent of their oil revenue to the federal budget.

Federal power remains in the hands of the Supreme Council of Rulers and its President, who also appoints ministers. The Vice-President (ruler of Dubai) is also Prime Minister. At the individual emirates level, and outside the federal government's direct responsibilities, the ruler has absolute powers.

REFERENCES

Abdul-Fadil, M. (1979), 'The Pure Oil-rentier States: Problems and Prospects of Development', in *Oil and Arab Cooperation*, vol. 3 (in Arabic).
Abdul-Fadil, M. (1987), 'The Macro-behaviour of Oil-rentier States in the Arab Region', in Beblawi, H. and G. Luniani (ed.), *The Rentier States*, Croom Helm, London.
Arab Oil and Gas Directory (AOGD) (1996), *Saudi Arabia: Industry and Development*, AOGD, Arab Petroleum Research Centre, Shelburne.
Azzam, T. Henry (1988), *The Gulf Economies in Transition*, Macmillan Press Ltd, Basingstoke.
Birks, J. S. and Sinclair, C. A. (1980), *International Migration and Development in the Arab Region*, ILO, Geneva.
Eikleman C. (1984), *Women and Communities in Oman*, New York University Press, New York.
The Economist Intelligence Unit (EIU) Country Profile (1996), *Saudi Arabia Country Profile 1995–96*, The Economist Intelligence Unit Ltd, London.
Europa (1991 and 1995), *The Middle East and North Africa 1973/4, 1990/1 and 1995*, Europa Publications Limited, London.
Fergany, N. (1984), 'Manpower Problems and Projections in the Gulf', in Azhary, M. S. (ed.), *The Impact of Oil, Revenues on Arab Gulf Development*, Croom Helm, London.
Galal el-Din, M. E. (1983), 'Population and Labour Policies from a Development Perspective', in Fergani, N. (ed.), *Foreign Labour in Arab Gulf Countries*, Centre for Arab Unity Studies, Beirut.
Ghanem, S. M. A. (1992), *Industrialization in the United Arab Emirates*, Avebury Ashgate Publishing Limited, London.
Halliday, F. (1975), *Arab Without Sultans*, Vintage Books, New York.
International Journal of Middle East Studies, vol. 26, 569–87.
Looney, E. R. (1990), 'Economic Development in Saudi Arabia, the Consequences of the Oil Price Decline', *Contemporary Studies in Economic and Financial Analysis, Economic and Financial Analysis*, vol. 66.
Mahdavy, H. (1970), 'The Patterns and Problems of Economic Development in Rentier States: the Case of Iran', in Cook, M. (ed.), *Studies in the Economic History of the Middle East*, Oxford University Press, Oxford.
McLachlan, Keith and Anne (1989), *Case Studies in the Developing World: Oil and Development in the Gulf*, John Murray.
Middle East Review (1993/4), 19th edition, Kogan Page and Walden Publishing, London.

Al-Misnad, S. (1985), *The Development of Modern Education in the Gulf*, Ithaca Press, London.

Russel, S. S. and Al-Ramadhan, M. A. (1994), 'Kuwait's Migration Policy Since the Gulf Crisis', *International Journal of Middle East Studies*, vol. 26.

Seikaly, M. (1994), 'Women and Social Change in Bahrain', in *International Journal of Middle East Studies*, vol. 26.

Shah, N. M. (1986), 'Foreign Workers in Kuwait: Implications for the Kuwaiti Labour Force', *International Migration Review*, vol 20, no.4.

Sirageldin, I. et al. (1983), *Manpower and International Labour Migration in the Middle East and North Africa*, Oxford University Press for World Bank, Oxford.

Webster, R. (1986), 'Human Resource in the Gulf', in Netton, I. R. (ed.), *Arabia and the Gulf: from Traditional Societies to Modern States*, Barnes and Noble, Lanham, Md.

Webster, R. (1991), 'The Al Wahiba: Bedouin Values in an Oil Economy'. *Nomadic People*, vol. 28.

Wikan, U. (1982), *Behind the Veil in Arabia*, Johns Hopkins University Press, Baltimore.

Zahlan, R. S. (1989), *The Making of the Modern Gulf States: Kuwait, Bahrain, Qatar, The United Arab Emirates and Oman*, Unwin Hyman, London.

2 Oil, Population Change and Social Development in the Gulf: Some Major Trends and Indicators
Abbas Abdelkarim

In terms of both pace and depth, the economic and social changes that have been brought by the discovery and exportation of oil in the Gulf Arab states are unparalleled in the modern history of any other region in the world. In a few decades, the economic and demographic structures of these countries have changed completely. From pockets of scattered communities in the desert and small coastal towns relying for their livelihood on animal husbandry, fishing, pearling and sea trade, oil has transformed the Gulf countries into 'modern' ones – with modern cities, infrastructure and social services. The Gulf has been changed in less than three decades from a population-push to a principal population-pull region.

This chapter provides a short account of the role of oil in the Gulf countries and exposes some of the major changes in their population, labour force and progress in social development during the post-oil period.

ROLE OF OIL IN THE ECONOMY

Oil Production and Reserves

Bahrain was the first Gulf state to produce crude oil, followed by Saudi Arabia. In 1938, Bahrain was producing 22,000 barrels per day and Saudi Arabia, just starting, produced 2,200 barrels daily (Europa 1973/4: 75). Other Gulf countries joined in the second half of the 1940s and 1950s.

In 1970, just before the oil price boom, the Gulf countries together produced 8.345 million barrels a day: 18 per cent of

Table 2.1 Crude oil production in selected years (millions of barrels per day)

Countryc	1970	1980	1989	1993
Bahrain	0.075	0.050	0.043	0.055
Kuwait	2.735	1.425	1.600	1.950
Neutral Zone*	0.505	0.535	0.400	n.a
Oman	0.330	0.285	0.390	0.780
Qatar	0.370	0.470	0.390	0.500
Saudi Arabia	3.550	9.990	5.260	8.695
United Arab Emirates	0.780	1.705	2.000	2.975
Gulf Total	8.345	14.460	10.088	14.955
Middle East & North Africa Total	18.820	22.380	19.895	23.240
World Total	47.800	62.590	63.560	65.075
Gulf as % of World	(18)	(23)	(16)	(23)
MENA as % of World	(39)	(36)	(31)	(36)

Note: * The Neutral Zone is shared equally between Kuwait and Saudi Arabia.
Source: Europa, *The Middle East and North Africa* 1973/4, 1981/2 and 1995.

the world's total production of crude oil (Table 2.1). In the same year, all Middle Eastern and North African (MENA) countries – including the Gulf – made up 39 per cent. During the 1970s the world production of oil expanded considerably: 31 per cent more in 1980 compared to 1970. During the same period, Gulf countries increased their production by 73 per cent. Hence, their share in the world's total production moved up to 23 per cent, while that of the MENA countries dropped to 36 per cent.

While the world produced crude oil in 1989 more or less at the same level as 1980, Gulf production declined from 14.46 to 10.088 millions barrels per day (from 23 per cent to 16 per cent of the world total). This decline was made possible by the country quota system adopted by OPEC (of which the largest four Gulf countries are members). With the interruption of oil production in Kuwait and Iraq during the occupation of the former by the latter (August 1990 to March 1991), Saudi Arabia and the other Gulf countries raised their production considerably. This high rate of production (compared to the 1989 level) continued after the liberation of Kuwait. In fact Kuwait also joined the others by increasing its production by 22 per cent in 1993 compared to 1989. The Gulf countries together were producing oil in 1993 at the same high rate of 1980. This increase was meant to compensate for the Iraq's share: since the occupation, it could not produce for the international market due to UN sanctions. The increase mode the Gulf countries, especially Saudi Arabia, better able to pay for the cost of the Gulf War of 1991.

The strategic importance of the Gulf (and MENA) countries in the oil business is even more explicit when we view their share in oil reserves (Table 2.2). The Gulf states accounted for 46 per cent (MENA for 70 per cent) of the world's proven published reserves in January 1994. The Gulf could produce for 125 years (from 1990) at the level of production of 1989 and 85 years (from 1994) at the level of production of 1993. Corresponding figures for the world as a

Table 2.2 Proven published oil reserves as of 1 January 1990 and as of 1 January 1994 (thousand million barrels)

Country	Reserves		Years of Production at	
	1990	1994	1989 level	1993 level
Bahrain	0.1	0.07	9	5
Kuwait	94.5	96.5	162	136
Neutral Zone[*]	5.2	n.a	35	n.a
Oman	4.3	4.7	20	17
Qatar	4.5	3.7	32	21
Saudi Arabia	255.0	261.2	133	84
United Arab Emirates	98.1	99.6	134	92
Gulf Total	461.7	465.8	125	85
Middle East & North Africa Total	694.6	704.4	96	75
World Total	1,011.8	1,009.0	44	43
Gulf as % of World	(46)	(46)		
MENA as % of World	(69)	(70)		

Note: [*] The Neutral Zone is shared Between Kuwait and Saudi Arabia.
Source: Europa, *The Middle East and North Africa*, 1991 and 1995.

whole are 44 and 43 years respectively. Saudi Arabia has more oil reserves than any other country in the World (26 per cent of the world's total) and Kuwait could continue production for years longer than any other country in the world (162 years from 1990 at 1989 production levels). These facts alone explain why the liberation of Kuwait and protection of Saudi Arabia were of paramount importance to the USA and other Western countries.

Government Oil Revenue

Much of the economic and social development in the Gulf countries since the 1950s and 1960s has been the result of oil revenues received by governments. That this source of revenue is extracted from subsoils and is exhaustible, and that revenues received make a premium of scarcity (protected through alliances and cartels), has led a number of scholars to call such revenue 'economic rent'. Perhaps the first scholar to specifically address the impact of economic rent on Middle Eastern oil exporting countries was Mahdavy (1970) in the case of Iran. More elaborate and wider-ranging works on the subject are collected in Beblawi and Lunciani (1987). Thomas Stauffer, cited in K. and A. McLachlan (1989), estimated that the depletion of oil (that is, oil revenues are created from a decreasing asset; producing more reduces the amount that can be produced in the future) and the scarcity premium contributed about 60 per cent of total oil income in the early 1980s.

Oil revenue in the Gulf has gone through three different periods: (a) a relatively slow but continuous growth resulting mainly from increased production from the 1960s to the early 1970s; (b) a period of enormous rises in oil prices that multiplied revenues a number of times from the early 1970s to the mid-1980s; and (c) a period of retreat of the price from very high levels back to the levels of the early 1970s.

Table 2.3 shows the change in the average annual government income for four Gulf countries (all OPEC members) over the period 1966–91 at four-year intervals between 1966 and 1989 and at two-year intervals for the last period, 1990–1. In the period 1982–5, all four Gulf countries attained their highest level of income. This period is taken as a base.

Table 2.3 Average annual government oil revenue of OPEC member-gulf countries (1963–91) (millions of USD)

Country	1966–9	1970–3	1974–7	1978–1	1982–5	1986–9	1990–1
Kuwait	751	1,687	8,125	9,780	14,415	7,246	3,450
	(5.2)	(12)	(56)	(68)	(100)	(50)	(24)
Qatar	105	294	1,813	3,668	4,173	1,765	2,100
	(2.5)	(7)	(43)	(88)	(100)	(42)	(50)
Saudi Arabia	901	3,417	31,875	44,419	81,296	18,187	44,300
	(1.1)	(4)	(39)	(54)	(100)	(22)	(55)
U.A.E.	137	604	6,625	13,098	14,978	8,743	17,550
	(0.9)	(4)	(44)	(87)	(100)	(58)	(117)

Notes: Figures include income from refined products and gas liquids, except Saudi Arabia, which excludes natural gas liquids from 1980 onward. Figures for Kuwait and Saudi Arabia include equal share revenue from the Neutral Zone. Figures for the UAE include only Abu Dhabi until 1972; thereafter they include other Emirates as well as Dhubai and Sharjah. Figures in brackets refer to revenue as percentage of the base period (1978–81).
Source: Europa, *The Middle East and North Africa*, 1973/4, 1982/83, 1991 and 1995.

In the period 1966–9 to 1982–5, the four Gulf countries achieved an unprecedented level of oil income growth. The slowest among the four, the government of Kuwait, was growing at an average compound rate of 28 per cent (multiplying its revenue 19 times in 16 years). Qatar, Saudi Arabia and the UAE were accomplishing average annual growths of 36 per cent, 46 per cent and 48 per cent respectively. The UAE, during this period, multiplied its government oil revenue by 110 times!

The four-year period that followed the peak (1986–9) showed steady decline in the revenues realized by Gulf governments. The Saudi government endured the fastest decline, achieving in the period 1986–9 only 22 per cent of its income level in the base period, but still gaining a handsome 18 billion USD on average annually. The UAE suffered least, maintaining its income level at 58 per cent of the base year in the period 1986–9. Oil revenue attained in the subsequent two years (1990 and 1991) on an annual average

Table 2.4 GNP per capita in the Gulf, 1994

Country	GNP per capita (USD)
Bahrain	7,460
Kuwait	19,420
Oman	5,140
Qatar	12,820
Saudi Arabia	7,050
United Arab Emirates	21,430

Note: For the UAE, the figure is for the year 1993.
Source: World Bank, *World Development Report*, 1995 and 1996.

basis was much higher, except for Kuwait (which stopped production for part of the two years). Saudi Arabia's government in this last period (of Table 2.3) was able to achieve two and a half times its income in the period 1986–9, but still only 55 per cent of the level of the base period, 1978–81. The UAE was able to exceed its 1978–81 average annual income in the period 1990–1.

Oil income placed three Gulf states (the UAE, Kuwait and Qatar) in the high income group countries as classified by the World Bank (the three countries attained, respectively, a GNP per capita of USD 21,430, 19,420 and 12,820 in 1994 – Table 2.4). The other three countries, Bahrain, Saudi Arabia and Oman (where GNP per capita income was, respectively, 7,460, 7,050 and 5,140 in 1994 – ibid.), are placed in the upper-middle income group of countries.

Dependence on Oil

Size of government income from oil does not in itself indicate the prominence of this commodity in the economies of the Gulf. To this end, relative share of oil in the GDP and in total exports is a relevant indicator and is shown in Table 2.5.

Despite the lower level of oil income, oil contribution to the GDP was not less than 29 per cent in any Gulf countries in 1989. In countries like Kuwait and the UAE its share was as high as 47 per cent and 48 per cent respectively.

The dependence of the Gulf economies on oil becomes more apparent when its share in the total exports is considered. None of the Gulf countries exported any non-oil commodities (or services) for more than 13 per cent of their total exports in 1989. Kuwait's non-oil exports, for example, represented only 4 per cent of its total in the same year. A closer look into the composition of the small fraction of non-oil exports reveals that it is largely composed of commodities production which is related to oil (e.g. petrochemicals) and/or re-exportation of goods, mainly by non-nationals to their own home countries. Taking into account these and other impacts of oil on the economy, K. and A. McLachlan (1989), estimate that 78 to 86 per cent of the Kuwait national income originated from oil in the late 1980s. Oil revenues have also been used for investment abroad which generates income.

Production and exportation of oil set the Gulf economies on the road of internationalization. In a short period, the Gulf countries became heavily dependent on external markets. Exports developed into a significant component of the national income and imports constituted a fundamental segment of final consumption. Table 2.5 shows that the share of

Table 2.5 Some indicators of dependence on oil, and the internationalization of Gulf economies – 1989

Country	% Share of oil in GDP	% Share of oil in total export	Total exports as % of GDP	Total imported goods as % of total final consumption
Bahrain	31	87	36	52
Kuwait	47	96	49	39
Oman	44	87	51	42
Qatar	34	92	37	–
Saudi Arabia	29	91	32	34
United Arab Emirates	48	91	53	57

Note: The year 1989 has been selected as a benchmark because oil production in subsequent years was affected by the Gul War.
Sources: World Bank, *World Development Report 1991* and *World Tables 1991*. World of Information, *The Middle East Review 1992*. Oman Development Council, *Statistical Year Book 1990* (in Arabic).

exports in the GDP ranges between 32 per cent (Saudi Arabia) and 53 per cent (UAE) in 1989. Higher levels of income also changed consumption structure and patterns. A great deal of the consumer goods demanded are imported. Imported goods made up 34–57 per cent of the total final consumption of the Gulf states in 1989.

The vulnerability of dependence on oil revenues was clear when the oil price collapsed after the rises of the 1970s and early 1980s. Gulf countries were unable to adjust expenditure quickly: some of them financed their current expenditure from reserves and, later, especially in the cases of Saudi Arabia and Kuwait after the Gulf War, from borrowing (see McLachlan, 1989; Europa, 1995; *The Economist* Intelligence Unit, 1996).

INTERNATIONAL MIGRATION AND CHANGE OF POPULATION AND LABOUR FORCE STRUCTURE

Migration to the Gulf has wide-reaching economic and demographic consequences and is quite distinct from other modern migrations in the world. In a few decades, the population and labour force of the Gulf have changed drastically. In all Gulf countries the migrant labour force became dominant, and in some of them the majority of the population are non-nationals. International migration to this region involved migrants from many regions of the world, from over 100 countries, and across a wide spectrum of professions.

Modern, oil-associated migration to the Gulf started first in Bahrain and Kuwait in the 1940s and then extended to the rest of the Gulf. Oman is the last Gulf country to join as net labour-receiving (it was for some time labour-sending).

Importation of labour was for some Gulf countries (Bahrain, Kuwait, Qatar and the UAE) the only way forward for economic growth, as they had an excess of capital and an acute shortage of labour at all skill levels (Birks and Sinclair, 1979). Another reason for the high dependence of the Gulf countries on foreign labour is the low labour force participation rates of the national population: 21 per cent in Saudi Arabia, 18 per cent in Kuwait, 17 per cent in the UAE, 25 per cent in Oman and Bahrain, and 19 per cent in Qatar (Looney, 1991: 122).

Phases of Migration

It is important to note from the outset that population and labour force data in the Gulf is largely based on various estimations made by national, regional and international organizations. Kuwait is the only country that has regularly undertaken censuses, with a gap of five years in the period 1955 to 1985. This was interrupted after the occupation of the country in 1990. Bahrain also had population censuses with a gap of ten years (the latest was in 1991).

Three phases of labour migration to the Gulf can be distinguished. The first started in late 1940s to early 1950s and extended to the early 1970s. This phase featured a relatively steady and continuous flow of migrants. A majority of the migrants, in the Gulf generally but not in each of its countries, are believed to have been Arabs (see among others Birks and Sinclair, 1979 and Sirageldin et al., 1983). Having no accurate estimates of the numbers of the migrant population in Saudi Arabia at the end of phase one (Table 2.6), we can roughly estimate the total non-national population in the Gulf at 1–1.25 million in 1970.

The second phase started in the early 1970s with the large increase in oil price and revenues, and ended in the early 1980s. In this phase, the rate of inflow of migrants was very high. In five years, from 1970 to 1975, the number of non-national population doubled and once again doubled in the following five years (1975–80), to reach 4.5 million persons. The non-national labour force increased in 1980 to 262 per cent of its total number in 1975 (Table 2.7).

The second phase also witnessed a change in the rate of inflow of economically active migrants from the two major ethnic groups: Arabs and Asians. In some Gulf countries more Asians were employed than Arabs, even before the start of this phase. However, in all of them, the rate of increase of Asians was higher than that of Arabs during this period, and hence, the ethnic composition of the migrant labour force was increasingly changing to the advantage of the Asians (see below).

The third phase of labour migration started in the early 1980s at the time of the retreat of oil price and revenue. Flow of migrants started to slow down. The average annual

Table 2.6 Population by nationality in the Gulf countries (1970–94) (thousands)

Country	1970 N	1970 M	1970 T	1975 N	1975 M	1975 T	1980 N	1980 M	1980 T	1985 N	1985 M	1985 T	1994 N	1994 M	1994 T
Bahrain	178	38	216	214	68	282	238	112	350	274	157	431	346	204	550
Kuwait	347	391	738	472	523	995	566	792	1358	681	1016	1697	671	949	1620
Oman	558	42	610	651	160	811	730	270	1000	816	494	1310	1511	538	2049
Qatar	46	65	111	65	115	180	85	175	260	105	284	389	129	403	532
Saudi Arabia	–	–	–	6089	927	7016	7206	2382	9588	7789	3451	11240	13053	5127	18180
UAE	101	119	220	197	459	656	263	780	1043	434	1239	1673	628	1522	2150
Total				7688	2252	9940	9088	4511	13599	10099	6641	16740	16338	8743	25081

Notes: N = National, M = Migrants, T = Total.
Sources: Al-Sabah (1989), Compiled from different regional and national sources (in Arabic). UN-ESCWA (1995), *Demographic and Related Socio-economic Data Sheets*, No. 8.

Table 2.7 Number and percentage of non-nationals in the labour force in the Gulf (1970–90) (thousands)

Country	1975	1980	1985	1990
Bahrain	38.7	78.3	100.5	132.0
	(46)	(57)	(58)	(51)
Kuwait	217.6	392.6	551.7	731.0
	(70)	(78)	(81)	(86)
Oman	103.3	170.5	335.7	442.0
	(54)	(59)	(69)	(70)
Qatar	57.0	106.3	155.6	230.0
	(83)	(88)	(99)	(92)
Saudi Arabia	474.7	1734.1	2621.8	2878.0
	(32)	(59)	(65)	(60)
United Arab Emirates	234.0	470.8	683.8	805.0
	(84)	(90)	(90)	(89)
Total	1125.3	2952.5	4417.3	5218.0
	(47)	(65)	(70)	(68)

Note: Figures between brackets are percentages.
Source: UN-ESCWA (1992), *Survey of Economic and Social Development in ESCWA Region*.

compound rate of growth of both the non-national population and non-national labour force between 1980 and 1985 was 8 per cent. Consequently, their numbers grew to 6.6 and 4.4 million respectively (in 1985 the non-national labour force was 150 per cent of its level in 1980).

Post-1985 data suggests continuation of the decline in net increase of migrants. Between 1985 and 1990 the average annual rate of inflow of the migrant population was only 3.3 per cent (compared to 8 per cent in the preceding 5-year period). The migrant labour force increased annually by 31 per cent in the period 1985–94.

It is debatable whether the post-Gulf War period represents a new, fourth phase for the whole of the Gulf. It is certainly a new phase for Kuwait. Several hundred thousand migrants left the country during the occupation. The Kuwaiti government expelled the remaining Palestinians (whose number before the occupation was in the range of 300 thousand) after its return in 1991. A segment of the migrants from other nationalities returned to Kuwait after the libration. There are indications that this replacement is favouring Asians (single or without family). The number of total migrants in 1994 was significantly less than its number before the occupation. In other Gulf countries post-invasion, changes in migrant population and labour force patterns are less profound. In Saudi Arabia three to four hundred thousand Yemenis (out of more than one million stock) and a smaller number of Palestinians left after the occupation of Kuwait. There are no signs of change in the features of the third phase in other countries of the Gulf: the slowing down of demand is continuing and ethnic composition of migrants is dominated by Asians.

Changes in Origin of Migrants

The first flow of migration to the region in the late 1960s and early 1970s was dominated by Arab migrants (71.2 per cent). South and south-east Asians comprised 19.8 per cent, Americans and Europeans made about 2 per cent and the rest came from Iran, Turkey and Africa (Birks and Sinclair, 1979: 25).

Although by 1975 some of the construction projects were completed, the labour market attracted new migrants. This was due to (a) the departure from the region of Iranians and Iraqis attracted by development in their own countries, and (b) the growing social and personal services and industrial sectors. Major labour-sending countries (Egypt, Jordan and Yemen) failed to match labour requirements and could not keep pace with the increasing demand for labour in GCC countries. As a result of that, according to Serageldin et al. (1983: 48), GCC countries started the importation of labour from outside the Arab World, mainly from Asia. However, this is not the whole story. As Kritz and Keely (1981) among others point out, political reasons have extensively influenced the importation of Asian labour. Gulf countries favoured temporary workers from Asian, non-Arab countries to reduce dependence on Arab workers. Unlike most of the Asian workers, migrants from Arab countries, who come from different social and political systems from those of most of the Gulf countries, and who have a common language and culture with that of the national population, can influence the latter politically. This was highly undesirable to the ruling families in the Gulf. With the first oil price drop in the late 1970s another major factor increased the tendency to favour Asian workers: the lower wages that Asian workers were, and are, prepared to accept. The percentage of Arab migrants dropped to 30.1 from 65.0 between 1975 and 1985, while the percentages of South Asian (India, Pakistan, Bangladesh and Sri Lanka) and East Asian (Philippines, Thailand, Indonesia and others) rose to 43.0 per cent and 20.3 per cent respectively (Addleton, 1992: 522). Gulf countries since then have ceased publishing data on the region of origin of the migrants, but indicators show that the trend of increasing dependence on Asian workers has not been reversed.

Dependence on Non-national Labour Force

The most striking characteristic of the internationalized Gulf labour markets is that the migrant workers have become the dominant labour force. The earliest available estimate for the whole of the Gulf is for the year 1975 (Table 2.7). In that year, it was estimated that 47 per cent of the total labour force was non-national. This proportion escalated, during the years of high labour demand associated with high-level oil income, to 65 per cent in 1980. The enhancement of the proportion of the migrants in the total labour force of the Gulf as a whole has not been checked during the early years of the decline of the new flow of migrants in 1980s. In 1985, about 70 per cent of the working population were non-nationals. However, post-1985 data suggests that the proportion of migrant labour force is on the decline: 68 per cent in 1990.

The degree of dependence on migrant labour force varies among the different countries in the Gulf, and their position in this respect changed unevenly during the years shown in Table 2.7. The non-national labour force was lowest in Saudi Arabia in 1975 (32 per cent). Thereafter Bahrain hosted relatively fewer migrant workers than the rest (in 1994 51 per cent of total labour force were non-national). Qatar and the UAE represent the extreme case of dependence on migrant labour: between 88 and 92 per cent in the period 1980–94. Saudi Arabia's immigration of foreign labour between 1975 and 1980 increased at a relatively very high rate (average annual increase of 30 per cent). The non-national labour force stock changed from 475,000 to 1.73 million between 1975 and 1985.

The degree of dependence on migrants also varies in different sectors and professions. Below are some examples.

1) The total Qatari labour force was estimated in 1985 at 85,750, of whom only 16,250 were nationals. EIU (1996) estimates for 1995 put the size of the labour force at 120,000, with a roughly similar proportion of expatriate workers. Of the non-Qataris in the labour force, approximately 75 per cent were Asians. In 1994 the government began to insist (legislation has been implemented) that Qataris be recruited to senior jobs in both the public and the private sectors. The first graduates from the University of Qatar, for example, were given top jobs in government ministries despite their lack of experience. Because many Qataris (as in any other Gulf country) are reluctant to enter technical or manual jobs, the government has paid salaries to students entering industrial training courses. Qatari women tend to be employed only in teaching and nursing (EIU, 1996: 37).

2) According to 1995 estimates, expatriates formed 50 per cent of the Bahraini labour force (the labour force totalled 260,000), mostly from India, Pakistan and South-east Asia. There are comparatively few non-Bahraini Arabs in the work force as Bahrain has enforced very stringent entry requirements for other Arab nationals. In 1995 Bahraini nationals accounted for just 29 per cent of those employed in the private sector, a proportion almost unchanged from 1986, despite the government's commitment to increasing their ratio. Asian expatriates hold 70 per cent of private-sector jobs and are seen as a more flexible alternative to Bahrainis because of wage differentials and the legal difficulties involved in dismissing nationals (EIU, 1996: 11).

3) In Saudi Arabia in 1991 Saudis occupied 50 per cent of professional and technical posts and 73 per cent of clerical jobs, while unskilled jobs were mostly performed by foreigners (World of Information-MER, 1995: 97).

4) In 1986 Oman's labour force was estimated at 467,000. Only 167,000 of those were nationals, less than 36 per cent of

the total. By 1993 there were just over 484,000 expatriates representing some 67 per cent of the total labour force. Most of the foreign labour force came from the Indian subcontinent. More than 90 per cent of these immigrants were employed in the private sector. By the end of 1991 only 31 per cent of the work force in the private sector was Omani. The number of expatriates in the private sector rose by 6.8 per cent in 1990, 27.4 per cent in 1991 and 19.8 per cent in 1992 (EIU, 1995: 15).

Although the non-national labour force has become the dominant one since some time between 1975 and 1980, the non-national population in the Gulf as a whole has never overshadowed the national one. In 1985, the migrant population represented 40 per cent of the total (in comparison with a migrant labour force of 70 per cent of the total in the same year). While in 1994 non-nationals made up only 35 per cent of the total Gulf population, in three countries (Kuwait, Qatar and the UAE) the majority of the population have become non-nationals since 1970 (Table 2.6).

SOCIAL DEVELOPMENT

Oil revenue has placed three of the six Gulf countries covered in this study in the high income group of industrial economies. The other three attain 40–50 per cent of the GNP per capita of this group. This section, through the use of some indicators, attempts to explore to what extent been has oil wealth translated into social (human resources) development.

Educational Development

Compared to many other developing countries, education in the Gulf started to expand late. Bahrain was the pioneer among the Gulf countries; its gross primary school enrolment ratio was as high as 99 per cent in 1970 (Table 2.8). Bahrain continues to be a leading Gulf country in educational attainment, surpassed at present only by Qatar, the tertiary enrolment of which is higher than in many industrial countries.

The literacy rate of the Gulf countries is not much better (in three it is worse) than the average developing countries:

Table 2.8 Some indicators of educational development in the Gulf

Country	Adult literacy rate 1970	Adult literacy rate 1990	Primary school enrolment ratio (gross) 1970	Primary school enrolment ratio 1992	Secondary school enrolment ratio (gross) 1970	Secondary school enrolment ratio 1992	Tertiary enrolment ratio 1980	Tertiary enrolment ratio 1992	Enrolment ratio for all levels (% age 6–23) 1970	Enrolment ratio for all levels 1992
Bahrain	–	77	99	110	51	85	–	–	583	75
Kuwait	54	73	89	94	63	82	11	14	–	–
Oman	–	35	3	100	–	57	0	6	280	61
Qatar	–	82	–	96	–	85	–	24	605	78
Saudi Arabia	9	62	45	78	12	46	7	14	363	50
UAE	–	55	93	118	22	69	2	10	445	73

Notes: Some of the figures are for years other than shown, and some are estimated figures. Primary enrolment for Qatar is net.

Sources: UNDP, *Human Development Report 1995*. World Bank, *World Development Report 1995*.

68 per cent. The reason is to be found not only in the relative lateness of educational expansion, but also in the educational background of the immigrant population, a relatively large segment of which is illiterate.

The enrolment ratio for all levels (age 6–23) in all the Gulf countries, except Saudi Arabia, was higher than the average of the developing countries in 1992. A country like Oman, in which education virtually developed only from 1970, had an enrolment ratio of 61 per cent for all levels in 1992. The growth of the enrolment ratio in Oman in primary (and secondary) education was remarkable, perhaps unprecedented. In 22 years the primary enrolment ratio went up from as low as 3 per cent in 1970 to 100 per cent in 1992. Following rapid development in the last few years the number of schools went up from three schools with 900 pupils before 1970 to 920 schools with more than 453,000 pupils and more than 20,000 teachersby 1993/4. The effort devoted to female education has risen considerably and there are now 379 schools for girls, compared with only 47 in 1974/5, as well as 134 mixed schools. In 1992/3 girls accounted for over 47 per cent of the total number of pupils attending primary and secondary levels in government schools. Official figures say the primary education enrolment ratio is now estimated to be 100 per cent for males and 96 per cent for females. In 1990 the pupil–teacher ratio in primary schools was 28 and in secondary schools 16 (EIU, 1995: 9).

Bahrainis are comparatively well-educated, with an adult (aged 15 and above) literacy rate in 1992 of 83.5 per cent. In 1990, the year for which the most recent figures are available, the ratio of pupils to teachers in primary schools was 19, while in secondary schools it was 14. At least 20 per cent of adults have completed secondary or higher-level education. By 1986 there were 139 state schools, but the number has since increased with the revival of development plans following the 1990–1 Gulf war (EIU, 1996: 7).

By 1991 there were 796 schools in the UAE catering for some 403,000 pupils, which represents remarkable growth for a country where there was virtually no education system before 1971. About two-thirds of these schools were government-run; the rest were private. The central government spends about 15 per cent of its budget on education. The

UAE has the highest level of female literacy in the Arab world at 68 per cent. Overall literacy rose from 43.5 per cent in 1975 to 77.7 per cent in 1992. Primary schools now register 100 per cent enrolment and female college admissions have risen to 75 per cent. The UAE also has one of the lowest pupil-to-teacher ratios in the world. In 1990 there were 13 pupils for every teacher in secondary schools and 18 in primary schools (EIU, 1995: 17).

In spite of the dramatic headway the GCC countries have made in education, the education system adopted by the Gulf has not been the type of system most suited to the needs of such rapidly developing countries. It was found in 1985 that only 18 per cent of the total required manpower at the professional and technical level and 27 per cent of the required sub-professional manpower were provided by the national labour force (Al-Tuhaih, 1986: 128).

Technical and vocational education and training is considered markedly inferior to general academic education, which is the only means of achieving a university place (Birks and Sinclair, 1979: 305). Several new technical and vocational institutes have been opened to attempt to draw nationals to fill posts now held by foreigners. Enrolment, however, is well below expectations. Status, prestige and tradition play a major role in the failure to attract students into the technical/vocational streams. A technical or vocational degree is viewed as dead-ending in a job strictly involving manual labour (George and Patrick, 1986: 169 and Roy, 1992: 478). Another reason that technical education has been less popular among Gulf youth according to al-Misnad (1985: 131–2) is that the region adopted plans in structuring its technical and vocational education applicable to other developing countries whose social and economic circumstances were different from those of the Gulf states.

The female–male gap in education (Table 2.9) has narrowed down considerably. In primary and secondary enrolment in 1990, Kuwaiti and Qatari females were doing as good as their male counterparts, and in the UAE the secondary enrolment for girls was higher than for boys. The number of females in tertiary education was higher than males in three countries: the UAE, Qatar and Bahrain in 1990. The female/male ratio in tertiary education in the UAE was the highest in

Table 2.9 Gulf Female–Male Gap in Education
(Index: Male = 100)

Country	Adult literacy 1970	Adult literacy 1990	Mean years of schooling 1990	Primary enrolment 1970	Primary enrolment 1990	Secondary enrolment 1970	Secondary enrolment 1990	Tertiary enrolment 1970	Tertiary enrolment 1990
Bahrain	58	87	67	81	100	70	100	59	113
Kuwait	66	91	79	73	93	60	92	53	100
Oman	–	–	22	18	94	0	79	0	71
Qatar	84	99	93	77	98	96	99	87	213
Saudi Arabia	34	66	26	49	81	28	95	12	79
UAE	33	99	101	63	100	46	108	24	269

Notes: Primary school, age 6–11 years; secondary school, age 12–17; tertiary school, age 18–23.
Source: UNDP, *Human Development Report 1992*.

the world (264 per cent); and Qatar (213 per cent) was the third highest in 1990. The UAE's lead in female education in the Gulf is also reflected in the mean years of schooling; a female/male per cent of 101. The same ratio for Saudi Arabia is 26 per cent. Unfortunately, women's attainment in the field of education has not (yet) been translated equally into socio-economic empowerment. Table 2.10 shows that the participation of women in the occupational category of administration and managerial workers in three countries (for which data is

Table 2.10 Percentage of women in selected occupations in three Gulf countries in 1990

Country	Administrative and managerial workers	Professional technical and related workers	Clerical and sales workers	Service workers
Kuwait	5.2	36.8	18.9	46.0
Qatar	0.9	26.8	6.3	26.6
United Arab Emirates	1.6	25.1	7.6	24.5
East Asia	11.4	45.0	39.5	–
OECD	25.7	46.3	53.7	57.1

Source: UNDP, *Human Development Report 1995*.

available) in 1990 ranged between 0.91 per cent (in Qatar) and 5.2 per cent (in Kuwait), while their proportion in the professional and technical occupational groups was (much) better, ranging from 25.1 per cent (in the UAE) to 36.8 per cent (in Kuwait). While these three countries enjoy comparable GNP per capita and close to comparable educational status (including the education of women) to that of OECD countries, women are still at a distance from the labour market generally and particularly from higher level jobs.

Roy (1992) cites the case of Saudi women as an example of the gap between manpower requirements and educated resources in the Gulf. Although Saudi women, by 1980, accounted for over one-third of all nationals attending college and universities, they are denied – with few exceptions, such as teaching – participation in the labour force. Roy (1992: 482) then asks, what is the logic of educating them?

Health Development

Table 2.11 shows an impressive record of achievement in health in the Gulf. Life expectancy at birth, an indicator chosen by the Human Development Report and World Development Report as the main indicator of health, rose considerably between 1960 and 1992 in all the six Gulf

Table 2.11 Some indicators of health development

Country	Life expectancy at birth		Infant mortality rate (per 1000 live births)		One-year-olds immunized (%)		Population with access to health services (%)
	1960	1992	1960	1992	1981	1990	1985–93
Bahrain	55.5	71.6	130	18	55	84	100
Kuwait	59.6	74.9	289	18	65	95	100
Oman	40.0	69.6	214	30	18	95	96
Qatar	53.0	70.5	145	20	31	81	–
Saudi Arabia	44.4	69.7	170	29	42	94	97
UAE	53.0	70.8	14.5	19	38	85	99

Sources: UNDP (1992 and 1995), *Human Development Report 1992 and 1995*. World Bank (1991a) *World Development Report 1991*.

Some Major Trends and Indicators

countries. Longevity in the least of them is 94 per cent of the average of the North (the industrial countries). In Kuwait it is higher.

Infant mortality was reduced from a range of 130 to 214 per 1,000 live births in 1960, to 18 to 20 in five Gulf countries, and to 30 in Oman in 1992. The whole of the populations of Bahrain and Kuwait and almost the whole in the UAE, Saudi Arabia and Oman (99 per cent, 97 per cent and 96 per cent respectively) have access to health services.

Gulf countries have invested heavily in healthcare. In the Kingdom of Saudi Arabia, for example, the provision of health and social services accounted for 17.9 per cent of planned development expenditure in both the fourth and fifth five-year plans. The nominal value allocated to health and social services in the annual budgets has declined from SR 14bn (USD 3.8bn) in 1992 to SR 13bn in 1995, but as a percentage of total budgetary expenditure the amount has risen from 7.7 per cent to 8.6 per cent respectively. There are now over 170 hospitals and more than 1,700 primary health centres, and 98 per cent of the population have access to these facilities (EIU, 1996: 24).

Kuwait has the highest life expectancy among the Gulf states, followed by Bahrain and the UAE (Table 2.11). The patient/doctor ratio in Kuwait in 1986 was 572, which can be compared to a ratio of 425 in West Germany in the same period (Raffer and Salih, 1992: 231).

Concluding Notes on Social Development

Compared to their past and also to other countries the Gulf countries have realized remarkable achievements in a relatively short time in education and health. However, to stop at this level of comparison is not enough. Another important aspect of comparison would be how much of the available resources have been diverted to social development in comparison to other uses. This chapter is in no position to assess in a meaningful way comparative use of oil resources in the Gulf countries (an attempt has been made by Fergani, 1985). However, one simple indicator could point to whether social (human resource) investment could have been expanded (and hence development accelerated). This indicator is military expenditure as a percentage of combined education and health expenditure. This in the years 1988–90 was as follows: Bahrain (134), Kuwait (83), Oman (268), Saudi Arabia (177), the UAE (174), and for Qatar no data was available (UNDP, 1992).

It appears from this that four out of five Gulf countries spend (much) more on defence than on the educational and health sectors combined. The Gulf countries' relative military expenditure exceeded by far those of the industrial countries, the same indicator of which for the same period was 28 per cent. A country like Oman spent more than two and a half times as much on defence as on education and health combined. The 'impressive' record of progress in education and health shown above looks less impressive when one assesses it in the light of what could have been done if the military expenditure (or a large segment of it) could have been directed to a more efficacious purpose.

REFERENCES

Addleton, J. (1992), 'The Impact of the Gulf War on Migration and Remittances in Asia and the Middle East'. *International Migration Review (IMR)*, vol. 29, no. 4, 1991.

al-Misnad, Sheikha (1985), *The Development of Modern Education in the Gulf*. Ithaca Press, London.

Al-Tuhaih, Salem M., (1986), 'The Vicious Cycle of Manpower in Kuwait'. In *Workforce Management in the Arabian Peninsula: Forces Affecting Development*, eds G. S. Roukis and P. J. Montana, Greenwood Press, Westport.

Beblawi, H. and Lunciani, G. (eds) 1987) *The Rentier State*, Croom Helm, London.

Birks, J. S. and Sinclair, C. A. (1979), 'The International Migration Project: An Enquiry in the Middle East Labour Market'. *International Migration Review (IMR)*, vol. 13, no. 1.

Birks, J. S. and Sinclair, C. A. (1980), *International Migration and Development in the Arab Region*, ILO, Geneva.

Demery, L. (1983), 'Asian Labour Migration to the Middle East: An Empirical Assessment'. *International Social Science Journal*, vol. 35, 1983.

The Economist Intelligence Unit (EIU) (1995), *Country Profile: Oman and UAE. The Economist* Intelligence Unit Limited, London.

The Economist Intelligence Unit (EIU) (1996), *Country Profile: Qatar, Bahrain and Saudi Arabia*. The Economist Intelligence Unit Limited, London.

Europa (1973, 1974, 1982, 1991 and 1995), *The Middle East and North Africa 1973/74, 1981/82, 1990 and 1995*, Europa Publications Limited, London.

Fergani, N. (1985), *The Lost Opportunity: A Inquiry into Whether Arab People are Progressing towards their Objectives* (in Arabic), Centre for Arab Unity Studies, Beirut.

Kritz, M. M., Keely, C. B. and Tomasi, S. M. (eds) (1981), *Introduction to Global Trends in Migration: Theory and Research on International Population Movements*, Center for Migration Studies, New York.

Looney, E. Robert (1991), *Factors Affecting Employment in the Arabian Gulf Region, 1975–85. Population Bulletin of ESCWA, 1991*. Population Studies, no. 81, New York, USA. UN Economic and Social Commission for Western Asia, Oman, Jordan.

Mahdavy, H. (1970), 'The Patterns and Problems of Economic Development in Rentier States: the Case of Iran'. In *Studies in the Economic History of the Middle East*, ed. M. Cook, Oxford University Press, Oxford.

McLachlan, Keith and Anne (1989), *Case Studies in the Developing World: Oil and Development in the Gulf*, John Murray Limited, London.

Raffer, K. and Salih, M. (1992), *The Least Developed and the Oil-rich Arab Countries: Dependence, Interdependence or Patronage?* Macmillan, London.

Roy, A. Delwin (1992), 'Saudi Arabian Education: Development and Policy'. *Middle Eastern Studies*, vol. 28, no. 3, July 1992; Frank Cass, London.

Roukis, G. S. and Montana, P. J. (1986), 'Development and Human Resources Management in the Arab Oil Rich States'. In *Workforce Management in the Arabian Peninsula: Forces Affecting Development*, eds Roukis and Montana.

Serageldin, I. et al. (1983), *Manpower and International Labour Migration in the Middle East and North Africa*, Oxford University Press for World Bank, Oxford.

UNDP (1992, 1995), *Human Development Report 1992 and 1995*, UNDP, New York.

UN-ESCWA (1992), *Survey of Economic and Social Development in ESCWA Region*, UN Economic and Social Commission for Wester Asia, Oman, Jordan.

UN-ESCWA (1995), *Demographic and Related Socio-Economic Data Sheets, No. 8.*, UN-ESCWA, Oman, Jordan.

World Bank (1991a, 1995, 1996), *World Development Report/ 1991, 1995 and 1996*, Oxford University Press – published for the World Bank, Oxford.

World Bank (1991b), *World Tables 1991*, John Hopkins University Press – published for the World Bank, Baltimore and London.

World of Information (1990, 1992 and 1995), *The Middle East Review*, The World Information, UK.

Part I
Oil and the Economy: Dependence and Diversification

3 The State in Oil Rentier Economies: the Case of Bahrain
Khalid M. Abdulla

INTRODUCTION

The theoretical articulation of the concepts 'rentier states' and 'rentier economies' took place only recently. In 1970, H. Mahdavy introduced the concept of 'rentier states' to desig nate a situation under which the state's dependence on external rents (that have very little to do with the productive effort of the society as a whole) is predominant. While Mahdavy concentrates largely on the state without establishing the important ties with the economy, Abdel-Fadil and Beblawi put greater emphasis on the economy, and define the concept of 'rentier economy' as an economy substantially supported by the rents that accrue from abroad.

The economies of the Arab Gulf oil exporting countries significantly depend on the expenditure of the state which is the principal recipient of the external oil rents, hence the term 'oil rentier economies'.

The rentier economy thesis attempts to explain the emerging pattern of development in oil exporting countries by: (i) establishing the various political and socioeconomic features that characterize them as oil rentier economies; (ii) examining the impact of the various rentier features on the pattern of resource allocation and the economic behaviour of the state, firms and individuals. In doing so, it further attempts to highlight the various problems that are likely to hinder the growth and development of such economies in the long run.

In this paper we will focus our attention on the nature and the economic behaviour of the state in oil rentier economies in general and Bahrain's experience in particular.

THE OIL RENTIER ECONOMY

The nationalization of the oil industry in the early 1950s enabled the Iranian government to appropriate a larger share of the rents that previously accured to the oil companies. During the five years after 1955, Iran's oil revenue amounted to almost twice that of the 38 years before 1952.[1] This enabled the Iranian government to embark on large public expenditure programmes without resorting to taxation.

The magnitude of the oil rent was so significant that it enabled the government to become the dominant factor in the economy through the expenditure side of the budget. Discussing the impact of the increasing role of the government in the economy – through the use of oil rent – on the pattern of economic development in Iran, Mahdavy first introduced the concept of 'rentier states' to designate a situation under which the economy's (and the state's) dependence on external rent is predominant. Hence, he defines the rentier states as 'those countries that receive on a regular basis substantial amounts of external rent'. The external rent is in turn defined as 'rentals paid by foreign individuals, concerns or governments to individuals, concerns or governments of a given country'.[2] Looking at oil revenues from a different perspective, Abdel-Fadil argues that the external nature of such rent stems from the fact that the size of rent received by producing countries is determined by a number of interrelated external economic factors – including the world demand for oil and the bargaining position of the oil producers as a group rather than those of individual countries. Because it is mainly the external factors rather than the domestic cost factors that determine the size of the rent, such rent is described as external.[3]

While Mahdavy emphasizes the geographical origin of the rent, Abdel-Fadil concentrates on the forces that generate rent. We feel that it would be sound to adopt both analyses since they complement each other.

The quadrupling of oil prices in the early 1970s enabled a small cluster of oil exporting countries to acheive extraordinary wealth based on oil rent rather than on the productive capacity of their citizens. This led to a renewed interest in the concept of 'rentier states'. Social scientists from different disciplines attempted to provide a better understanding of the rentier phenomenon. In doing so, particular aspects of the rentier economies were emphasized and a number of theoretical issues were resolved. This section aims at consolidating the different contributions in this area in order to provide a more comprehensive view of the rentier economy and to provide a framework within which the case of Bahrain can be examined.

In discussing the rentier states, two approaches can be distinguished. The first concentrates exclusively on the state without establishing the important ties with the economy. The other approach 'put[s] greater emphasis on the economy, and defines the concept of 'rentier economy', which is either an economy substantially supported by expenditure from the state, while the state itself is supported from rent accruing from abroad; or more generally an economy in which rent plays a major role. A rentier state is then a subsystem associated with a rentier economy'.[4]

Clearly, the first approach falls short of serving our purpose in analysing the nature and the consequences of the interaction between the state and the different sectors in such an economy. As a result we are inclined to follow the alternative approach, where 'the state becomes the main intermediary between the oil sector [the rent generating sector] and the rest of the economy'.[5]

In an attempt to define the main elements of the rentier economy in oil producing countries, Beblawi starts by noting that there is no pure rentier economy, and that every economy has some elements of rent. Following Mahdavy's proposition, he then defines the rentier economy as an economy where external rent predominates.

Emphasizing the importance of the external origin of rent to the concept of the rentier economy, Beblawi argues that 'The existence of an internal rent, even substantial, is not sufficient to characterise a rentier economy, though it could indicate the existence of a strong rentier class or group. A pure internal rent can not be sustained without the existence of a vigourous domestic productive sector. In such a case, a rentier class is only one face of the coin, the other face would be a productive class. Internal rent is no more than a situation of domestic payment transfer in a productive economy. An external rent on the other hand can, if substantial, sustain the economy without a strong productive domestic sector, hence the epithet of a rentier economy.'[6] The dependence on external rent in a way high lights two features of such an economy: first, the limited domestic productive capacity of the rentier economy in areas other than the rent producing industry; second, the enclave nature of the oil industry, where, its direct integration – the vertical and horizontal linkages – with the other sectors of the economy is minimal.

The oil industry, while being responsible for most of the society's income, employs a limited number of the population because of the capital intensive technology it uses. This leads to the conclusion that in such rentier economies 'the creation of wealth is centered around a small fraction of the society; the rest of the society is only engaged in the distribution and utilisation of this wealth'.[7]

In the rentier state – as a special case of rentier economy – the rent received from the exports of the rent producing sector is concentrated in the hands of the state, which establishes the links between the rent generating sector and the rest of the economy through the expenditure side of the budget. Countries that exhibit these characteristics include the GCC states, Libya, Iran, Iraq and Algeria.

Having established the main features of the rentier economy, we will now focus on issues related to the nature and main functions of the state in such economies.

THE STATE IN AN OIL EXPORTING RENTIER ECONOMY

The significance of the role of the state in the economy stems from the fact that the state is the principal recipient of external rent. This enables the state to play a crucial role in both the diffusion of oil rent among the population and determining the fabric of the society. Hence, the state is at the centre of the analysis of oil rentier economies.

The oil exporting rentier economy is seen as 'a hierarchy of layers of rentiers, with the state or the government at the top of the pyramid, acting as the ultimate support of all other rentiers in the economy'. With the state being the principal rentier, the different social and economic interests are organized in such a manner as to capture as much of government rent as possible.[8]

The majority of the Arab oil countries are of tribal origin. Discussing the role of the state in such countries, Beblawi relates the attitude of the modern state to the long triabal tradition of securing loyalty and allegiance through the distribution of favours. Hence, he argues that 'The conventional role of the state as provider of public goods through coercion – mainly taxation – is now blurred in the Arab oil states by its role as a provider of private favours through the ruler's benevolence. Public goods and private favours have thus gone together in defining the role of the state.'[9]

The distribution of government rent among the population takes place through several channels. The Kuwaiti government initiated a system whereby the state buys private land at prices that are much more than their market value. Later, the same system was adopted by some other Gulf states.

A major outlet for dispersing oil revenues is government employment. Citizens regard recruitment in the state apparatus as a legitimate aspiration. Assuming a social obligation to ensure the employment of their citizens, governments find that the easiest route is to create large bureacracies to fulfil such aspirations.

The huge expansion in the provision of public goods and services – particularly in the areas of health, education, housing and social services – represent an important tool of redistributing oil rent among the population. The standard and quality of such public goods and services are considered to be adequate, and in some countries comparable to those of the industrial countries. Furthermore, the prices of basic foods, electricity, water, gas and petrol are heavily subsidized and maintained well below the opportunity cost of production.

The development and expansion of the infrastructure absorb a large share of government expenditure. Such projects are concentrated in the field of construction, to facilitate immediate consumption needs. A sizable proportion of government revenues is spent on lavish highways, airports or housing schemes, rather than more directly on increasing the domestic productive capacity by building factories. An underlying reason for such programmes is that 'public works yield high immediate political results...and the results are visible for all to see'.[10]

With virtually no direct taxes, the government budget is reduced to an expenditure programme. The absence of direct taxes, while freeing the government from any need to share power (no representation without taxation), reduces the redistributional power of fiscal policy. In such rentier economies one can merely speak of a distribution policy.

The huge oil rents enable the state to increase its involvement in the economy by expanding the public sector. The government becomes the prime mover of the economy while the role of the private sector declines relatively. This gives rise to a phenomenon that can be described as *étatisme*.

Marxist class analysis was based on the study of societies which were engaged in agriculture and/or manufacturing for their subsistence. Such societies were perceived to be based on class exploitation as a means of extracting surplus value. The state emerged as a tool of the dominant class to organize and regulate class exploitation.

The rentier states deviate from the above thesis in two ways: First, the surplus value (rent) is generated in the international market because of the monopolistic position of oil producers as a group. Second, the relations of production are not centred around the exploitation of one class by another; rather, the society makes its living through exploiting natural resources.[11]

With economic activities centred around the use and distribution of the external rent, the economy can be described mainly as a consumption or distribution economy.[12] Since oil production is effectively controlled by the state, the term 'dominant class' is confined to the state (the ruling families). The dominant class's power is based on the appropriation of extractive rent; hence it is described by Longuenesse as a 'rentier aristocracy'.[13]

By appropriating the external rent on the hand and distributing it locally on the other, the state acquires the function of a mediater between the outside world and the inside. referring to such role, Villie described the dominant class (the state) as a 'functional class'.[14]

Being the main source of social and economic power, the state, through its public expenditure, investment policies and policies affecting the distribution of rent, is capable of shaping the emerging social stratification. In other words, the social stratification is determined by the relation of the different groups with the state rather than by production relations.[15]

The position of individuals and groups in the social strata can be defined by the closeness to the source of rent (the state). Thus, the society is seen as being structured principally around the rent, and the social stratification is regarded as a function of its distribution.

Delacroix argues that in distributive states challenges to the ruling elite are based strictly on moral considerations. He further argues that since class cannot be an organizational base for such challenges, alternative structures of social solidarity will then have to be activated. He suggests that such challenges would arise from the traditional tribal, ethnic and religious structures.[16] The events of 1978 in Saudi Arabia, the Islamic revolution in Iran, and more recently the events in Algeria seem to confirm this conclusion.

BAHRAIN AS AN OIL RENTIER ECONOMY

Oil rentier economies are defined as economies that depend on external oil rent as the main source of income. Table 3.1 shows that compared to other oil producing countries, Bahrain's oil production is very modest. Moreover, it can be deduced that the Bahrain's field reserves, which are estimated at 170 million barrels, will be exhausted by the mid-1990s should production continue at the present level – about 15 million barrels per annum.

The relative significance of oil production to the different oil producing countries as measured by the per capita daily oil production, indicates that despite the fact that Bahrain's oil production is modest, its significance for Bahraini society is relatively high because of the limited size of population. Based on the information in Table 3.1, one may conclude that, given the size of population, oil production in Bahrain is of greater importance than in a number of OPEC member countries such as Iraq, Iran, Venezuela or Libya.

Table 3.1 Oil production, reserves and crude production per capita for selected oil producing countries (1984)

Country	Oil Production, thousand barrels day (b/d)	Proven crude oil reserves (m.barrels)	Crude oil production per capita
Algeria	695	9000	0.033
Bahrain	112	170[a]	0.279
Indonesia	1280	8650	0.001
Iran	2032	58874	0.044
Iraq	1221	65000	0.079
Kuwait	1160	92710	0.709
Libya	957	21100	0.264
Nigeria	1388	16650	0.014
Saudi Arabia	4079	127415	0.368
Venezuela	1696	28028	0.101

[a] excluding Abu-Saafa field, for which information is not available.
Sources: Table 3.8, in the Appendix to this chapter; Organization of Petroleum Exporting Countries (OPEC), *Annual Statistical Bulletin*, 1985; Organization of Arab Petroleum Exporting Countries (OAPEC), *Eleventh Annual Statistical Report*, 1984; International Monetary Fund (IMF), International Financial Statistics, Yearbook, 1988.

The extent of the economy's dependence on oil is further illustrated by Table 3.2 The figures reveal the paramount importance of oil as the major source of income.

As revenues from oil exports – which take the form of external rent – are received by the government (Table 3.8), the impact of oil rents on the domestic economy is realized through the government's expenditure of such income. Thus, the government becomes the main intermediary between the oil sector and the rest of the economy.

In Bahrain, the emergence of the oil industry took the form of a transplant of an advanced technology by a foreign concern into an economically undeveloped (traditional) society. In the absence of any modern industry, almost all of the oil sector's inputs, apart from the unskilled labour and services, had to be imported from abroad either directly by the oil company or through local merchants.

Table 3.2 The significance of oil exports to the Bahraini economy, 1970–90

Year	Oil exports as % of commodity exports	Oil exports as % of total exports	Oil exports as % of GDP	Oil exports per capita (US$)
1970	61.9	59.8	35.4	390.4
1975	64.2	62.0	35.4	1467.4
1980	78.1	66.6	34.0	3470.4
1985	76.6	53.5	30.4	2819.8
1990	58.4	–	29.5	2283.3

Notes: Exports include re-exports.
Oil exports and exports in general exclude the Share of Saudi Crude refined in Bahrain
Source: World Bank, Bahrain – Current Economic Position and Prospects, 1973 and 1978; IMF, Bahrain – Recent Economic Developments, 1979, 1983 and 1988; Bahrain Monetary Agency, Quarterly Statistical Bulletin, vol. 5, no. 4, 1979; Bahrain Ministry of Finance and National Economy, The National Accounts 1982–8; Bahrain Central Statistical Organization, *Statistical Abstract* 1990.

Compared to the size of the oil industry's operations and revenues, the employment opportunities it created were limited because of the highly capital intensive technology it uses.

Table 3.3, indicates that the role of the oil sector in providing employment opportunities diminished over time both in absolute and relative terms, as a result of the increase in the size of population and labour force on one hand, and the application of more labour saving techniques on the other. In 1988 less than one per cent of the population were involved in generating an income that supported the whole economy.

EXTERNAL OIL RENTS AND THE ROLE OF THE STATE IN THE ECONOMY

The state's revenue during the pre-oil era consisted mainly of the various types of taxes, fees and dues collected by the governing authorities. Customs duties which reflected the

Table 3.3 Employees of the Bahrain oil sector as a percentage of total population and the economically active population

Year	(1) Oil sector employees	(2) Total pop.	(3) (1) as % of (2)	(4) Economically active pop.	(5) (1) as % of (4)
1959	8,817	143,135	6.2	46,955	18.8
1965	6,940	182,203	3.8	53,274	13.0
1971	4,310	216,078	2.0	60,301	7.1
1981	4,715	350,798	1.3	146,133	3.2
1986	4,554	445,676	1.0	172,441	2.6
1987	4,517	457,601	1.0	187,815	2.4
1988	4,441	473,296	0.9	192,909	2.3

Sources: Annual *Statistical Abstract* (several issues) Population Census 1971 and 1981; Central Statistical Organization, 'Population Projection for the State of Bahrain', January 1985.

level of trading activities represented the main revenue item. The rest came from taxes on palm cultivation and pearl diving, and a variety of administration fees. Thus, the size of public revenues was to a large extent related to the level of domestic economic activities.

An important outcome of oil production and export was that the external oil rent dominated the fiscal sources and freed the state from the need to raise income domestically. Under such circumstances, the size of the state (income, expenditure) is not tied to its domestic base, rather it is linked to the economic base of the oil importing countries via the international oil market. The implication for the nature of the state's function in the economy is that instead of being involved in raising income through taxing productive activities and reallocating such incomes, the state, relying on its appropriation of external oil rent, assumes an allocative and distributive role only.

A common view among the classical political economists from Adam Smith through Karl Marx is that the state is ultimately determined by the socioeconomic category, not a determinant of it. The Keynesian model, where the above view is modified, assigns only short run functions to the state, usually through policies designed to alter the level of aggregate demand and supply.[17] The execution of such policies involves heavy reliance on taxes on national incomes or production, an item absent or of little significance in the oil rentier economies.

Because of its appropriation of an income that is external to the national economy, the state in an oil rentier economy enjoys a considerable degree of autonomy. Moreover, through its expenditure on various consumption and development activities, it exerts a great influence in determining the long-term pattern of growth and development.

The above discussion provides an insight into the underlying basis of the state's emergence as the prime mover of the economy in Bahrain.

While oil income dominated government revenues soon after it was first exported in 1935 (Table 3.8), its full impact on the economy was not realized till after the quadrupling of oil prices during 1973/4, when the magnitude of oil rents reached unprecedented levels. In 1974 oil revenues were more than three times those of 1973, and the nominal GDP more than doubled as a result of the sharp rises in oil prices (Table 3.9).

The magnitude of oil rents at the disposal of the government soared dramatically after 1974 as a result of the following developments: (i) oil prices quadrupled; (ii) the goverment had a 60 per cent equity participation in oil production in 1975, while by 1980 the remaining share of oil production and 60 per cent ownership of the refineries were secured.

In addition, the government received a significant amount of non- repayable grants from more affluent neighbouring countries such as Saudi Arabia and Kuwait. During the period 1977–86 foreign grants amounted to BD 426 million – representing 31.9 per cent of the non-oil revenues.[18]

While the material bases of the rentier state in Bahrain were strengthened by the above developments, the National Assembly was dissolved in 1975, leaving the government to enjoy a considerable freedom in disbursing the rising oil rents. Parliamentary democracy was replaced by a traditional court 'democracy' where individuals and groups lobby the rulers directly in seeking gains or to alleviate grievances.

Through its expenditure of large rentier incomes, the state placed itself at the centre of economic activity, with the rest of economy organizing itself in such a way as to capture as much of the oil rents as possible. Thus, through its rising expenditure, the government started to transform the whole economy into a rentier one.

In independently and directly controlling the production and export of oil (the society's major source of income) the rentier state in Bahrain deviates from the Marxist proposition of the state acting as a tool of the dominant class regulating class exploitation. Furthermore, in such an economy the exploitation of natural resources replaces class exploitation as a means of extracting surplus value. Such surplus value is appropriated through the international trade mechanism and takes the form of external rent. The external oil rents are injected into the economy through government expenditure on numerous development projects, direct and indirect transfers, and government employment. Thus the state in Bahrain, rather than appearing as a coercive-exploitative class, assumes an allocative and distributive function.

While the growth in the oil sector was mainly due to the increase in internationally determined oil prices (Bahrain is not a member of OPEC), and thus can be regarded as exogenous to the Bahraini economy, the growth in the non-oil sector was largely influenced by government expenditure of the rising oil rents. The largely oil-financed government spending exerts a direct influence on the non-oil sector through public expenditure on goods and services, and an indirect one through the spill-over effect arising from a Keynesian multiplier-accelerator mechanism.

The postulated strong relationship between the government expenditure of oil rents and the non-oil sector is illustrated by the following two econometric equations:

$$\text{NOGDP} = B + B_1 G; B_1 > 0 \tag{1}$$

$$(\text{NOGDP}_t/\text{NOGDP}_{t-1}) = B + B_2(G_t/G_{t-1}) +$$
$$B_3(\text{NOGDP}_{t-1}/\text{NOGDP}_{t-2}); B_2 > 0, B_3 > 0 \tag{2}$$

The first equation estimates the non-oil sector as measured by the non-oil GDP (NOGDP), to be a linear function of the total government expenditure (G), where government expenditure itself is largely dependent on oil rents. The second equation attempts to model the growth of the non-oil sector. In addition to the changes in the total government expenditure, a lagged expression of the growth in the non-oil GDP is included to account for the spread effects, i.e. the additional rounds of oil rents circulation.

Using the available time-series data for the period 1970–1988 (current prices), the following results were obtained:

$$\text{NOGDP} - 1.7 + 2.54G \qquad R^2 = 0.989$$

$$(36.62) \qquad F = 1341$$

$$(\text{NOGDP}_t/\text{NOGDP}_{t-1}) = -0.377 + 0.322(G_t/G_{t-1})$$

$$(6.32) \qquad R^2 = 0.807$$

$$+0.587(\text{NOGDP}_{t-1}/\text{NOGDP}_{t-2}) \qquad F = 41.57$$

$$(6.53) \qquad \text{D.W.} = 2.17$$

(values in parentheses are t statistics)

The econometric results confirm the relationship specified in equations (1) and (2), where the expansion in non-oil activities was assumed to be determined by the government expenditure of oil rents. Both regressions yielded high adjusted R^2 values. The coefficients of determination are statistically significant at a 0.05 level of significance, and the F values are higher than the critical F values at the 95 per cent probability level.

As the amount of oil rents in the hands of the government increased sharply after 1973, its traditional role as the builder of the infrastructure and the provider of public goods and services increased dramatically. In addition, the state assumed the role of an entrepreneur whereby it actively participated in establishing a large number of domestic business enterprises (Table 3.10).

The underlying objective of such enterprises was the provision of certain goods and services at reasonable prices, the diversification of the production structure and sources of foreign earnings, and the generation of employment opportunities.

However, the most significant development during the oil boom period was the state's assumption of the role of an allocative agent, whereby it distributed part of oil rents to its citizens through government employment and direct and indirect transfers with the aim of enhancing their material well-being and ensuring allegiance and loyalty.

Table 3.4 indicates a significant expansion in government employment during the period after the 1973/4 oil price rise. In 1988, about one-quarter of the total labour force was absorbed by the government sector.[19] And while wages and salaries absorbed only 22 per cent of total government expenditure in 1974, by 1988 the figure had risen to 51 per cent.

The above figures can be partially explained by the extent of government services in the economy and partially by the fact that public sector employment was not related to the actual workload, rather it represented an important channel for distributing oil rents among the national population. In this regard, Serageldin et al. suggest that:

> Wages were often paid to sinecured employees more as a right of nationality than in return for particular services. Nationals of the oil-exporting states have never really been required to compete in the modern labour market on economic terms. They have effectively gained a 'rent' from being nationals of the Gulf oil-producing states, their remuneration being quite divorced from marginal productivity.[20]

The creation of a welfare state, i.e. the free provision of public goods and services such as health and eduation, is an important tool for distributing oil rent among the population. Furthermore, the prices of basic foodstuffs, electricity, water and petrol are heavily subsidized and maintained well below the opportunity cost of production.

The rapid expansion in the Bahraini economy during the oil boom period (1974–85) created vast opportunities for investment and employment. Government legislation was geared toward ensuring that most of the oil rent diffused into the economy through goverment expenditure and trickled down into the hands of Bahrainis. Thus the practice of most professions and trades was restricted to Bahrainis, and foreign companies operating in Bahrain had to have a Bahraini citizen as a sponsor or a partner. Such legal

Table 3.4 The significance of government employment in Bahrain, 1974–90

Year	Size of government employment	Wages and salaries (BD millions)	Wages and salaries as % total gov. expenditure	Wages and salaries as % of current expenditure
1974	12305	21.1	22.0	28.1
1975	14060	29.7	24.4	65.8
1976	14887	38.9	19.1	44.1
1977	15959	55.1	21.2	47.1
1978	17592	69.4	24.3	50.6
1979	18856	85.0	28.7	54.2
1980	20463	108.8	31.5	56.9
1981	20836	126.2	33.1	54.8
1982	22972	150.7	31.9	50.5
1983	23683	171.4	32.2	55.4
1984	24583	200.0	37.1	61.0
1985	25089	209.4	41.2	61.0
1986	25606	221.4	46.5	65.8
1987	25702	229.3	50.4	66.6
1988	26199	245.8	51.0	65.2
1990	27795	271.4	50.6	65.4

Note: wages and salaries in current prices.
Sources: Ministry of Finance and National Economy, Financial Planning and Budgeting Affairs, Statistical Data (n.d); Civil Service Bureau; Central Statistical Organization, *Statistical Abstract* (various issues).

restrictions gave rise to a purely rentier function of sponsor, *al-Kafil*. This is a national who permits expatriates to engage in various economic activities under his name, in return for a share of proceeds (rent).

THE IMPACT OF FALLING OIL RENTS ON THE ROLE OF THE STATE IN THE ECONOMY

During the mid-1980s, a number of factors led to the dramatic fall in oil prices. Mainly, these were: (i) the shift in OPEC's policy from defending the price to defending their share of the market, a consequence of which was an overproduction by OPEC members in excess of their respective quotas; (ii) the indusrial countries (who represent by far the largest oil consumers) succeeded in limiting their demand for oil through conservation measures and by shifting to alternative sources of energy; and (iii) the increase in non-OPEC oil production – between 1978 and 1988 the non-OPEC oil producers (the most important of which are the United Kingdom, Mexico, China, Norway, and what previously comprised the Soviet Union) increased their production by about 7.4 million barrels per day.[21]

The combined effect of the above factors was that oil supplies increased at a rate unmatched by the rate of increase in demand, creating an oil glut that put downward pressure on the price of oil. As a result, the price of crude oil decreased to $13.5 per barrel in 1986 and has continued at a relatively low level (compared to early 1980s price levels).[22] Moreover, future oil prices are forecasted to remain relatively low.[23]

Table 3.1 shows Bahrain oil production and reserves to be very modest. Bahrain's oil output comprises production from the onshore Bahrain field and one half of the liftings from the offshore Abu Saafa field (which is shared with Saudi Arabia). Production from Bahrain's field is expected to dwindle in the near future and cease by the turn of the century. Information about the Abu-Saafa field's reserve is unavailable.

It can be deduced from the above that the relative significance of future oil rent intakes would suffer a considerable deterioration, and this signals the demise of the oil rentier economy in Bahrain.

The government as the principal and initial receipient of the external oil rents is set to be the first to suffer from declining oil rent intakes. The impact of declining oil rents on the economy at large is brought about as a result of changes in government spending capacity and its level of intervention in the economy.

In 1974, following the first oil boom, oil rents accounted for 84 per cent of total government revenues, to decrease gradually thereafter to represent around 70 per cent by the early 1980 (Table 3.9). However, as oil prices fell sharply during the second half of the 1980s the relative significance of oil rents declined sharply to account for only 52.3 per cent of the total government revenue by 1988 (Table 3.5).

Table 3.5 shows the impact of falling oil prices and the subsequent decrease in the oil rent intakes on the budget financing in last decade.

As oil rents decreased, government revenues from non-oil sources – mainly import duties and non-tax revenues in the form of fees and charges for services proivided by government agencies and foreign grants – increased in significance.

Attempting to face the increasing budget deficit the government introduced several revenue raising measures. These included the introduction of an airport departure charge, a medical charge to expatriates using public health services, and changing the structure of customs duties. In financing the growing budget deficit, the government resorted to withdrawals from the reserves and to borrowing. With continuous borrowing difficult to sustain in the long run, broadening the government's revenue base is considered an urgent necessity. It is only a matter of time until the government resorts to some form of taxation.

We have already obtained an insight into the government's likely response to the falling oil rents, as the persistent budget deficit has forced the government to review its expenditure policies accordingly.

Table 3.5 indicates that due to the downward rigidity of many current expenditure items, manpower remuneration in particular, the impact of a squeeze on government revenues was borne mainly by capital expenditures. This explains the significant cuts in capital expenditure as government revenues declined. Such an outcome implies that the state's role as a builder of infrastructure will be among the most adversely affected by the falling oil rent intakes. This is made clear by Table 3.6, which shows a systematic reduction in infrasturcture expenditures during the period that witnessed a continuous fall in oil rent income.

In addition to the restrictions imposed by falling oil rents, the government's future capacity to spend on new structural projects is expected to be further limited by the need to allocate an increasing sum of finance toward the maintenance of the already established infrastructure.

Table 3.5 Bahrain: breakdown of the government budget (BD millions)

Year	Government revenue Oil BD	%	Non-Oil BD*	%	Total	Government expenditure Capital BD	%	Current BD	%	Total	Budget surplus or deficit (-)
1981	398.5	73.7	142.1	26.3	540.0	150.0	39.3	231.4	60.7	381.4	159.2
1982	401.9	72.4	152.9	27.6	554.8	174.8	37.1	296.1	62.9	470.9	83.9
1983	328.5	67.9	155.5	32.1	484.1	222.0	41.8	309.0	58.2	531.0	−46.9
1984	354.4	69.3	157.0	30.7	511.5	209.0	39.6	319.3	60.4	528.3	−16.8
1985	374.0	70.4	157.4	29.6	531.4	164.3	33.0	333.2	67.0	497.5	33.9
1986	246.1	57.9	178.9	42.1	425.0	140.2	29.4	336.3	70.6	476.5	−51.5
1987	247.1	57.9	180.0	42.1	427.1	110.4	23.4	344.4	75.7	454.8	−27.7
1988	209.9	52.3	191.4	47.7	401.3	105.1	21.8	377.1	78.2	482.2	−80.9
1989[a]	–	–	–	–	422.7	105.0	21.3	389.0	78.7	494.0	−71.3
1990[a]	–	–	–	–	432.1	125.0	23.1	415.0	76.9	540.0	−107.9

* including grants; [a] budgeted
Source: Central Statistical Organization, Statistical Abstract, 1988, 1987.

Table 3.6 Bahrain: public expenditure on infrastructure, 1984–90 (current prices) BD millions

Year	1984	1985	1986	1987	1988	1989	1990
Infrastructure expenditure	165.9	129.2	99.2	87.4	88.4	76.4	74.7

Source: Central Statistics Organization, *Statistical Abstract*,1990.

Another aspect of the government's role in its oil rentier economy that one can expect to be affected by the falling oil rents is the government's assumed responsibility as distributive agent. In Bahrain, the government fulfils such responsibility mainly through government employment and to a lesser extent via direct and indirect transfers.

Our earlier analysis showed that government employment, rather than being related to the actual workload, acted as an important channel for distributing part of the oil rents among the national population. However, the weakening oil prices since the early 1980s led to a review of such policy. In attempting to curb this practice a government sponsored study envisaged various measures, the most important being : eliminating any duplication in the work of the different government departments or establishments, shifting government employees from departments with excess labour to those suffering from a shortage to avoid new recruitment, paying more attention to training as a tool to increase productivity in government bureaucracies and thus reducing the need for new recruitment, and the adoption of a system encouraging the early retirement of government employees.[24]

The implementation of the above policies tied the increases in government employment to the real requirements of expansions in government activities.

A direct outcome of such a development was a curb on the rate of increase in the government's wage bill. Table 3.7 shows rises in the government wage bill throughout the period 1985–90 to be substantially lower than those of the pre-1985 period.

Table 3.7 Bahrain: the growth of government's wage bill, 1980-90 (Current Prices)

Year	1980	1981	1982	1983	1984	1985	1986	1987	1988	1989	1990
Government wages	108.8	126.2	150.7	171.4	200.0	207.0	221.4	229.3	245.8	258.2	271.4
% Growth	–	16.0	19.4	13.7	16.7	3.5	7.0	3.6	7.2	5.0	5.1

Source: Central Statistical Organization, *Statistical Abstract* (various issues).

As the rationalization policies are implemented more effectively, future rises in government employment are expected to be further restricted. Such rises are expected to be limited to levels necessitated by additional expansion in the major government activities, especially health, education, and utilities such as water and electricity. Should labour productivity rise sufficiently, new recruitment may be unnecessary. This, in effect, signals the government's abandonment of government employment as a channel for oil rent distribution in response to falling oil rent intakes.

Moreover, the termination of food subsidies is envisaged within 3 to 5 years; and other forms of transfer such as indirect subsidies to electricity and water are expected to cease in future, as a government report envisaged the operation of such utilities on a commercial basis.[25]

Among the far-reaching implications of the falling oil rents was the change in the government's attitude toward its direct involvement in economic activities. Thus, the previous policy of active participation in a wide range of economic activities was reversed in favour of the privatization of government owned/controlled enterprises. The new government policy is summarized by the Undersecretary for the Ministry of Development and Industry as 'to privatise whenever possible and to give as much incentives as possible'.[26]

The government's privatization initiative was partly motivated by the general argument in favour of privatization, i.e. that the private sector runs enterprises in a more efficient manner, but mainly by its need to raise funds to finance future expenditure on development projects. On the other hand, the privatization scheme provides alternative investment opportunities to a private sector which suffered from a decline in its traditional activities of trading and contracting due to the general slowdown in Bahrain's economy, which in turn occurred as a result of lower oil prices.

In May 1990 the government's 42 per cent stake in the Bahrain Hotels Company was floated on the stock exchange. In late 1990 a team of Amercian experts was advising the government on the best way to privatize various industrial establishments, with plans already under way to privatize the first of such establishments – Bahrain Aluminium Extrusion Company (Balexco). The first stage of Balexco privatization aims at selling 60 per cent of the government's share to the factory's customers, with the sale of the remaining 40 per cent to follow at a later stage.

On the other hand, a government sponsored study envisaged the running of some government utilities on a commercial basis, and the contracting of some aspects of their operations to the private sector. The possibility of privatizing the electricity and public transport services in the long run is anticipated.

It can be deduced from the above that the future trend will be characterized by an enhancment of the private secor's role in the economy, associated with a relative marginalisation of the role of the public sector as the government seems to abandon its distributive role and to drastically diminish its involvement in economic activities. The long-term implication of the private sector's, assumption of an increasing role in resource allocation, is a change in the country's political economy, with government influence on the running of the economy diminishing significantly while the private sector gains in prominence. As a consequence, the private sector is expected to exert an increasing influence on government legislation, at first through informal lobbying and, in the more distant future, through formal political participation via a parliamentary democracy.

CONCLUSION

The oil rentier economies were defined as those countries that receive substantial amounts of external oil rents on a regular basis. In such economies the vast oil revenues accrue directly to the government. This means that huge amounts of funds are made available for the government to spend without resorting to taxation. According to Katozian, this 'transforms the techno-economic autonomy of the oil sector in to the socio-economic autonomy of the state'.[27] Thus, endowed with the huge oil rents, the state is not only independent of the domestic economy but it is rather set to play a leading role in the economy.

Bahrain exhibits the features of oil rentier economies. The pattern of governments expenditure of oil rent is characterized by: (i) the distribution of a significant part of oil rent among the population through government employment, the provision of public goods and services, and the subsidizing of a wide range of commodities partly to enhance the population's standard of living and partly to secure allegiance and loyalty; (ii) devotion of government capital expenditure mainly to expanding the infrastructure; and (iii) active participation of government in establishing a large number of business enterprises.

The forecast of Bahrain's future oil rent intakes indicates the possibility of a remarkable deterioration in the relative significance of the external oil rents to the Bahraini economy.

The consequence of such a development are already manifested, as the declining oil rents since the mid-1980s have led to persistent budget deficits and stimulated a revision of the government's assumed role in the economy. The government in Bahrain assumed the roles of a builder of infrastructure, an allocative agent, and an entrepreneur. While continuing its vital role in improving and expanding the infrastructure, the government increasingly departed from its other roles due to the constraints imposed by falling oil rents. As a consequence, the private sector is expected to exert a significant influence on economic activities, with the role of the public sector being relatively marginalized.

NOTES

1. Issawi, C., and Yeganeh, M., *The Economics of Middle Eastern Oil*, Connecticut: Greenwood Press, 1977, Table 39, p. 129.

2. Mahdavy, H., 'The patterns and problems of economic development in rentier states: the case of Iran", in M. Cook (ed.), *Studies in the Economic History of the Middle East*, London: Oxford University Press, 1970, p. 428.
3. Abdul-Fadil, M., 'The pure oil-rentier states: problems and prospects of development', in *Oil and Arab Cooperation*, vol. 3, 1979, p. 37 (in Arabic).
4. Beblawi, H. and Lunciani, G. (eds) *The Rentier State*, London: Croom Helm Ltd., 1987, p. 11.
5. Abdul-Fadil, M., 'The macro-behaviour of oil-rentier states in the Arab region', in H. Beblawi and G. Lunciani, op. cit., p. 83.
6. Beblawi, H., 'The rentier state in the Arab world', in H. Beblawi and G. Lunciani, op. cit., p. 51.
7. Ibid.
8. Ibid., p. 53.
9. Ibid.
10. Seers, D., 'The mechanism of an open petroleum economy', Yale Univeristy Economic Growth Centre, paper no. 47, 1974.
11. See Delacroix, J., 'The distributive state in the world system', *Studies in Comparative International Development*, 1980, vol. 8, no. 3, pp. 3–21.
12. Longuenesse, E., 'Petrolium rent and class structure in the Gulf countries', *Mediterranean People*, 1984, vol. 26, p. 148.
13. Ibid.
14. Vieille, P., 'Petrole et classes fonctionnelle: le cas de L'Arabie Seoudite', *Mediterranean People*, 1977, vol. 1, pp. 153–193.
15. Longuenesse, E., op. cit., p. 156.
16. Delacroix, J., op. cit., p. 11.
17. Looney, R. E., *Economic Origins of the Iranian Revolution*, New York: Pergamon Press, 1982, pp. 100–101.
18. International Monetary Fund, *International Financial Statistics*, Yearbook, 1988.
19. Bahrain Ministry of Finance and National Economy, *The Study of Labour Market*, 1988, p. 30 (in Arabic).
20. Serageldin, I., et al., *Manpower and International Labour Migration in the Middle East and North Africa*, New York: Oxford University Press, 1983, p. 27.
21. Organization of Arab Petroleum Exporting Countries (OAPEC), *Secretary General Fifteenth Annual Report*, 1988, p. 17.
22. Ibid., p. 12.
23. Gulf International Bank, *Economic & Financial Report*, vol. 5, no. 4, April 1990.
24. Bahrain Ministry of Finance and National Economy, *The Report of the Strategic Options Committee, Part I*, 1986, p. 52 (in Arabic).

25. Ibid., pp. 48 and 53.
26. *The Middle East*, no. 184, February 1990, p. 32.
27. Katozian, H., *The Political Economy of Development in the Oil Exporting Countries: An Analytical Framework*, unpublished paper, University of Kent, 1975, p. 5.

APPENDIX TABLES

Table 3.8 Bahrain government budget's public revenue by source, 1935–70[a] (BD Thousand)

Year[b]	Customs	Interest	Other revenue	Total	Oil revenue	Grand total
1935	69	–	8	77	57	134
1936	87	–	8	95	69	164
1937	106	3	8	117	316	434
1938	100	10	10	120	354	474
1939	103	16	15	134	323	457
1940	87	22	26	135	355	490
1941	78	40	28	145	297	443
1942	88	30	18	136	262	399
1943	140	27	33	200	271	471
1944	204	28	39	271	279	550
1945	245	53	39	339	300	639
1946	273	30	53	356	311	667
1947	352	50	75	477	390	867
1935/47	1,932	316	360	2,608	3,590	6,189
1947/48	459	45	69	573	459	1,032
1948/49	590	62	75	727	492	1,219
1949/50	604	57	100	761	938	1,699
1950/51	816	66	105	987	1,534	2,521
1951/52	973	90	133	1,196	2,010	3,206
1952/53[k]	1,389	148	204	1,741	4,148	5,889
1954	1,065	192	163	1,420	5,250	6,670
1955	1,222	234	648[c]	2,104	4,255	6,359
1935/55[j]	9,050	1,210	1,857	12,117	22,676	34,793
1956	1,289	293	4,016	1,983	5,252	7,235
1957	1,380	335	267	1,982	5,256	7,238
1958	1,274	351	280	1,905	5,933	7,838
1935/58	12,993	2,189	2,805	17,987	39,117	57,104
1959[e]	1,442	406	367	2,215	5,030	7,245
1960[d,e]	1,584	433	365	2,382	5,287	7,669
1961[e]	1,684	–	327	2,011	5,211	7,222
1962[e]	1,500[f]	–	590[f]	2,090	5,410	7,500
1963[e]	1,900	–	350	2,250	5,379	7,629
1964[e]	2,085	–	342	2,427	5,856	8,283
1965[e]	2,115	–	450	2,565	5,903	8,468
1966[e]	2,269	–	1,232	3,501	7,851	11,352
1967[e]	2,431	–	2,207	4,638	7,761	12,399

Table 3.8 (*Cont.*):

1968[e]	2,593	–	3,307[g]	5,900	8,071	13,971
1969[e]	2,818	–	2,550[h]	5,368	9,661	15,029
1970[e]	3,184	–	5,491[i]	8,675	9,612	18,287
1935/70	38,598	3,028	20,383	62,009	120,149	182,158

[a] Excluding revenues of public bodies.
[b] Until 1952 the Bahrain government budget was assessed according to the Muhammadan calendar.
[c] Includes His Highness's grant to public protection (BD 50,000) and a drawing from the reserve fund (*Annual Report*, 1955, p. 90).
[d] This is the last year in which the Bahrain budget included reserve fund interest.
[e] Oil revenue excluding the allocation to the privy purse.
[f] Budget estimation.
[g] Includes BD 2 million transferred from the reserve fund to meet the budget deficit.
[h] Includes BD 1.1 million transferred from the reserve fund to meet the budget deficit.
[i] Includes BD 3.8 million transferred from the reserve fund to meet the budget deficit.
[j] *Annual Report*, 1955, p. 5.
[k] 16-month.

Source: Al-Kuwari, A. K., *Oil Revenues in the Gulf Emirates*, Essex: Bowker Publishing Company Ltd., 1978, Appendix 4.1, pp. 86–9.

Table 3.9 The significance of oil revenue and government expenditure to the economy in Bahrain (BD millions)

Year	Oil revenues	Total government revenue	Oil revenue as % of gov. revenues	Government expenditure	GDP at current market prices	Govt. expenditure as % of GDP
1970	9.8	19.9	49.3	18.3	115.4	15.7
1971	11.2	22.3	50.0	22.7	124.2	18.2
1972	12.0	23.0	52.3	22.1	133.1	16.6
1973	13.8	38.0	36.3	32.8	147.1	22.3
1974	104.1	123.7	84.1	95.8	313.0	30.6
1975	111.6	137.5	81.2	121.8	425.9	28.6
1976	157.0	201.8	77.8	203.2	599.7	33.9
1977	181.6	262.8	69.1	259.4	777.2	33.4
1978	192.7	308.1	62.5	285.5	915.0	31.2
1979	214.8	311.0	69.1	296.3	1029.2	28.8
1980	319.8	455.2	70.3	345.2	1344.1	25.7
1981	398.5	540.0	73.7	381.4	1359.0	24.7
1982	401.9	554.8	72.4	470.9	1370.8	28.1
1983	328.6	484.1	67.9	531.0	1404.4	37.8
1984	354.5	511.5	69.3	528.3	1468.5	36.0
1985	374.0	531.4	70.4	497.5	1392.9	35.7
1986	246.1	425.0	57.9	476.5	1198.2	39.8
1987	247.1	427.1	57.9	454.8	1191.8	38.2
1988	209.9	401.3	52.3	482.2	1262.9	38.2

Sources: Confidential Report on Bahrain, 1973 and 1978; Ministry of Finance and National Economy, Financial Planning and Budgeting *Statistical Data*, (n.d); Ministry of Finance and National Economy, Economic Affairs, *The National Accounts, Statistical Abstract* (various issues).

Table 3.10 Government participation in domestic enterprises

Companies	Govt's share of equity (%)
Aluminium Bahrain	57.9
Arab Shipbuilding and Repair Company	18.8
Bahrain Aluminium Extrusion	100.0
Bahrain Atomisers International	51.0
Bahrain Cinema and Film Distribution Company	16.0
Bahrain Flour Mills Company	65.0
Bahrain Hotels Company	42.4
Bahrain National Gas Company	75.0
Bahrain National Oil Company	100.0
Bahrain-New Zealand Trading and Stores Company	51.0
Bahrain Petroleum Company	60.0
Bahrain Ship Repairing and Engineering Company	2.0
Bahrain Telecommunications Company	36.7
Bahrain Tourism Company	27.8
Delmun Poultry Company	15.0
General Poultry Company	100.0
General Trading and Food Processing Company	20.0
Gulf Air	25.0
Gulf Aluminium Rolling Company	20.0
Gulf International Bank	—
Gulf Petrochemical Industries Company	32.3
Housing Bank	100.0
National Bank of Bahrain	49.0
National Building Materials Company	—
National Hotel Company	10.0
National Import and Export Company	10.0
National Poultry Company	40.0

Source: IMF, *Bahrain Recent Economic Development*, 1983 and 1988.

4 Industrial Strategies and Change in the UAE during the 1980s
Fatima S. Al-Shamsi

INTRODUCTION

The development policy of the United Arab Emirates is characterized by unique aspects which differentiate it from development policies and growth strategies in other developing countries. The opportunity provided in the oil era has contributed significantly to the structural transformation of the economy of the UAE. However, with the knowledge that oil supplies are not ever-lasting and that the exhaustion of the main source of income is anticipated, diversification away from oil became their paramount objective. The deterioration in the international oil market in the 1980s and the consequent decline in oil revenue made diversification more imperative and urgent, not only for long-term national economic development but also for current expenditure.

Accordingly, diversification has been given priority and the major development objectives have been to: sustain high growth rates, transform the economy from oil dependent to a diversified and self-sustained economy, secure other sources of income for the post-oil era, and generate productive employment for domestic labour.

The UAE's access to abundant capital and cheap energy provides an important base for its industrial development. Limitations imposed by a shortage of human resources and the narrowness of a natural resource base (e.g. agriculture), as well as the availability of financial resources, identified hydrocarbon-based industrialization as a pattern for industrial development. The public sector plays a predominant role in this strategy due to the fact that oil revenues accrue to the governments.

The investigation carried out through this paper will be aimed at examining the viability and effectiveness of the UAE's industrial strategy in attaining the objective of building a sound base for industrial development that favours diversification, structural change, transformation, self-sustaining growth and economic development.

THE ECONOMY OF THE UAE: AN OVERVIEW

Economic Structure

The United Arab Emirates (UAE) is a capital-rich state. High per capita income is a result of the fact that a small population (1,908,800 in 1991) enjoys a great amount of oil revenue.

Following the sharp increase in oil prices in 1973, the economy registered a rapid growth in real terms. The highest growth was registered in 1980 when GDP rose by 26.6 per cent in real terms. Nevertheless, with the drop in oil prices after 1981, a period of recession set in and real GDP fell by 7.8 per cent in 1982 (Table 4.1).

After a recovery in 1984, GDP continued to fall, markedly in 1986. By 1987 and as a result of a recovery in oil prices, the economy started to progress. There was a slowing of GDP growth in 1988 due to a drop in oil exports. This was followed by a significant growth in GDP in 1989 and 1990 as indicated in Table 4.2.

GDP per capita in real terms grew at an annual rate of 2.2 per cent during 1975–80. But the decline in oil revenue after 1980 resulted in a significant decline at an annual rate of 5.5 per cent during 1980–5. Estimation for 1986 indicated that a further reduction of 27 per cent from 1985 was registered. Oil GDP is the main contributor to total GDP. Real growth in oil GDP followed the same pattern as the whole GDP, and in 1986 there was also a significant drop in oil GDP.

There is no doubt that the hydrocarbon sector has been the driving force behind the substantial economic growth, providing the basis upon which significant economic progress can be undertaken. However, the issue of diversification became pressing, especially in the wake of the deterioration in the oil market in 1980. The process of diversification can

Table 4.1 GDP distribution between oil and non-oil sectors, 1975–1986 (million Dh/constant 1980 prices)

	1975	1976	1977	1978	1979	1980	1981	1982	1983	1984	1985	1986
GDP	53054	61437	71956	70506	88059	111470	115688	106607	100867	105406	102804	80345
Real GDP growth %	n.a.	15.8	17.1	−2.0	24.9	26.6	3.8	−7.8	−5.4	4.5	−2.5	−21.8
Oil GDP	35820	39456	41658	37622	52504	70532	65242	53181	44930	46955	45270	25320
Growth %	n.a.	10	5.6	−9.7	39.6	34.3	−7.5	−18.5	−15.5	4.5	−3.6	44.1
Non-Oil GDP	234	21981	30298	32884	35555	40938	50446	53426	55937	58451	57534	55075
Growth %	n.a.	27.5	37.8	8.5	8.1	15.1	23.2	5.9	4.7	4.5	−1.6	−4.3
GDP per capita*	94.5	89.2	82.6	74.8	89.1	105.4	100.7	87.4	82.1	82.2	79.1	57.4

* Thousand Dh

Sources: UAE Ministry of Planning, *National Accounts of the UAE*, Abu Dhabi, 1985. IMF, *UAE Recent Economic Development*, 1988.

be noticed from the continuing increase in the share of the non-oil sector in GDP at the expense of the decreasing share of the oil sector in the period 1981–6 (see Table 4.1). However, the oil sector picked up again and its growth exceeded the non-oil sector in the years 1989 and 1990 (Table 4.2).

Table 4.2 GDP gowth, 1987–90 (billion Dh/current prices)

	Oil Value	Oil Growth %	Non-oil Value	Non-oil Growth %	GDP Value	GDP Growth %
1987	32.5	24.1	53.8	3.1	86.3	9.9
1988	30.0	−7.7	58.0	3.9	88.3	2.0
1989	39.1	30.3	62.8	8.3	101.9	13.8
1990*	57.6	47.3	66.4	5.7	124.0	21.7

* Estimated.

Sources: Emirates Industrial Bank (EIB), *Journal of the EIB*, vol. 4, no. 2, Abu Dhabi, February 1988. Arab Monetary Fund, *Unified Arab Economic Report*, Abu Dhabi, 1992. UAE, Ministry of Planning (Estimation), 1991.

An Overview of the UAE'S Manufacturing Sector

The manufacturing sector's share of total capital formation reached its peak in 1982 (40.4 per cent), compared with 19.5 per cent in 1975. Thereafter, its share declined considerably to 21.7 per cent in 1986. Most government investments have been channelled to large-scale oil-based industries (36 per cent of the total) and to construction related materials (steel, aluminium, cement, etc.; 42 per cent of the total).

Between 1928 and 1982 the sector registered rapid growth averaging 78 per cent per annum, which is mostly due to the growth of oil-based industries. However, despite its rapid growth its contribution to GDP was only 8.1 per cent in 1982 and 9.7 per cent in 1984, dropping to 8.6 per cent in 1989. MVA at 1980 prices grew at an annual growth rate of 54.8 per cent during 1975–80, fell to 17.6 per cent during 1980–85 and was estimated to have grown at only 1 per cent during 1985–90 (Najjar, 1991: 6). The total labour force in the manufacturing sector was 34,000 in 1978. In 1981 the total labour force was 47,786 (an increase of 40.5 per cent), and in 1985 it totalled 61,534.

INDUSTRIALIZATION: GOALS, PLANS, STRATEGIES AND POLICIES

Goals and Objectives

Industrialization objectives are based on the desire to create a viable and modern economy with the purpose of diversifying the source of national income and of ensuring continued growth to secure per capita income after oil depletion. Accordingly, in 1972 federal laws assigned to the Federal Ministry of Finance and Industry the principal role regarding industrial affairs, and in 1979, the ministry introduced the first industrial law that specifically considers the industrialization issue in the UAE. It provides a basic legal framework for industrial development in the country. It identifies the bodies responsible for regulating industrial activities, issuing industrial licences, executing industrial projects and monitoring their performance. From the voluminous articles of the law, and recent federal initiatives regarding industrial activities, the perceptible and implicit official objectives of industrialization in the UAE can be identified as follows.

- Preparing a productive base to reduce the economic vulnerability of near total dependence an oil revenue, and increasing the contribution of the industrial sector to GDP.
- regarding industrialization as a propulsive force towards economic diversification that generates significant production linkages after the manifest failure of the petroleum sector to generate such linkages.
- encouraging the expansion of manufacturing activities that can effectively increase national income and provide a source of foreign exchange.
- exploiting the substantial comparative advantage, arising out of low-cost energy and feedstock, by encouraging hydrocarbon-based industries to attain optimal use of available natural resources.

- enhancing government participation in large-scale, capital-intensive projects and encouraging private investment in productive joint venture activities.
- restraining pure foreign capital investment and promoting joint venture investment in activities that require advanced technology and are highly competitive in international markets.
- encouraging local labour force participation in industrial activities, by stipulating that national management of projects and national labour be not less than 25 per cent of the total in each project.

Although the law laid down broad guidelines that aimed to regulate and promote industrial activities in the country as a whole, it fails to organize, coordinate and draw a clear framework for industrial development. Many factors contribute to its continuing failure. The weakness of the law is inherent in its lack of inclusiveness. It exempts all projects in which the government has a share, and all the local governments plans regarding the oil industry and related matters. Moreover, the industrial law has ignored the specific sectoral goals that are fundamental for any sectoral development. The projects' economies of scale, labour and technological requirements, and research and development needs, as well as the sectoral linkage effects, market size and relations with neighbouring countries' specific projects have not been identified and taken into consideration. However, the law's contradiction of the local authorities, the individual affairs of each emirate, is the main cause of its weakness and failure.

Plans and Policies

Planning economic and social development, including the framing of trade and commercial policies, formulating unified tax, customs and tariff policies and specifying a clear incentive and subsidy policy, are all necessary for a comprehensive and internally consistent industrial strategy. Thus, the Federal Ministry of Planning prepared an outline of a comprehensive five-year development plan for 1980–5. The plan specified the need for a coherent industrial strategy and it laid down the fundamental principles of UAE industrial development.

More precisely, it identified the general aims of the industrial strategy, and specified the sectoral objectives and the means of attaining such objectives. Moreover, it identified investment priorities at sectoral level and proposed substantial incentives to encourage such investment.

A central feature of the industrial strategy in this plan was the great emphasis on large-scale capital-intensive and oil-based industries. To guarantee the effective execution and performance of the plan's programme and to guide and regulate all industrial activities, the plan recognized the need for establishing permanent and effective authoritative bodies and institutions responsible for industrial affairs all over the country, specialized vocational and technical training centres, specialized research and development institutions as well as specialized financial bodies. However, it is noteworthy that the plan was not officially approved, most of its recommendations were not implemented, and its proposed activities have not been undertaken. The reasons why the plan was not approved and implemented are many. The individual emirates did not want to lose 'sovereignty' over matters such as planning of industrial investment. Lack of unanimity among the individual emirates on the development goals and strategy, accompanied by the multiplicity of bureaucratic bodies which complicate policy formation and coordination, and the contradiction among the emirates regarding financing the federal budget has severe effects on economic policy-making and implementation. 'Economic development efforts in the UAE, therefore, continue without a common framework and duplication of major investments in various emirates has taken place, leading to over capacities and wasteful uses of resources' (World Bank, 1983: p. 52).

Industrial Strategies

In the UAE, where it is hard to speak of a comprehensive development strategy for the country as a whole, speaking of an explicit, well-defined industrial strategy is meaningless. In fact, the autonomy of each emirate regarding its natural resources as well as the autonomy of the oil sector lie behind the ineffectiveness of any federal body that is established to promote and control industrial affairs. Accordingly, each emirate has appointed its own authoritative body and set up a specialized department for industrialization purposes.

Two poles of industrialization strategy have emerged. The first concerns investments in capital-intensive export-oriented (EOI) and hydrocarbon-based industries, and the second involves investment in small-scale mostly import-substituting production (ISI). Export-oriented, hydrocarbon-based industrialization has been regarded as an important option available for oil-rich emirates such as Abu Dhabi and Dubai. Gas processing, petroleum refining and other downstream activities were perceived as sources of increased value added to crude oil exports whilst providing a solid base for industrialization. In this regard, foreign consultants have been invited to prepare plans and feasibility studies for the perceived strategy. Presently there are two oil refineries, LNG and LPG plants (natural gas and petroleum gas respectively), and a nitrogen fertilizer plant in Abu Dhabi, as well as two other LPG plants in Dubia and Sharjah.

Iron, steel and aluminium smelting are the kind of export-oriented industrial projects gaining importance in the UAE in view of the availability of cheap energy. As mentioned previously, most of these projects have been undertaken by the two wealthiest emirates (Abu Dhabi and Dubai), and their governments provide a package of incentives to these projects, consisting of easy access to government funds, heavily subsidized gas for energy and feedstock, free or nominally priced utilities such as water and electricity, and well-developed infrastructure facilities. However, there is almost no information available regarding the costs, revenues and profits of all these projects, stifling further analysis of their viability and financial and economic returns. According to the World Bank, none of these ventures is profitable in a normal commercial sense, or economically viable in a narrow sense (World Bank, 1983: 40).

It is also noteworthy that most of the output of the export-oriented projects consists of intermediate and semi-finished products and is directed mainly to industrialized countries. Forward-linked industries have not been developed. Their dependence upon imported capital equipment and, in some cases, imported raw materials has created few backward linkages. In addition they employ foreign labour, management, expertise and foreign advanced technology. Thus, EOI has created foreign enclaves, has not contributed significantly to diversification, has contributed little to the formation of a national trained labour force and has not contributed to technological transformation or linkages with other sectors. Furthermore, its concentration in the two wealthiest emirates has probably exacerbated regional imbalance. The future of such activities would be precarious when oil reserves are depleted.

On the other hand, an import substitution industrial strategy (ISI), at least for certain industries, has also been adopted in the UAE. However, this strategy has not been a major policy in practice. Apart from some government-owned cement plants and some other projects undertaken by Abu Dhabi's government, most import-substitution projects have been small- scale, established in response to the expanding demand for consumer goods. Government intervention to implement such strategy has been at a low level. The scope for import substitution was found in bulky products such as cement, packaging and piping, and some consumer products such as food processing and packing, beverage bottling, stationary and printing, and machinery repair and assembly. Presently, there are nine large-scale, capital- and energy-intensive projects and some 650 medium and small establishments engaging 10 persons or more (IMF, 1988: 16). Most of the 650 establishments were undertaken in response to the expansion of the construction industry, which encouraged investment in building materials (concrete moulding, cement bags, bricks, steel pipes, steel reinforcing, rods, etc.). The increased demand for consumer goods encouraged the production of these products at home (especially industries with comparatively low domestic value added such as packaging and beverage bottling). There was also investment in plastic and chemical products (detergent, cleaning products, paints and varnish) which satisfied the expanding household demand as well as that of the construction sector during the boom period. In fact the domestic markets for the products of these industries are 'now saturated and there seems to be a shortage of industrial investment opportunities' (ibid.: 16). This means that the 'easy stage' of import substitution has been exhausted. It is noteworthy that most import substituting or non-oil projects are small-scale, labour-intensive and owned by the private sector, except in Abu Dhabi, where the public sector has long been active in this area.

It is also worth noting that entrepreneurs with 'industrialist intuition' do not exist in the UAE. Thus, the prominent merchants group handles most of the import substitution projects. For this group, whose prosperity is derived from trade and commercial activities, the most favoured import substitution projects are those which are related to and linked with such activities. Accordingly, the decision to invest has favoured short-run, rapid profit accrual activities. This in part accounts for the reluctance by merchant industrialists to accept planning and project coordination, and inhibits attempts to regulate and organize foreign trade activities for industrial activities' benefit. Since 1980, the condition of import substitution activities has deteriorated due to shrinking local demand for many goods and services, and lack of any protective policy which puts the products of the infant industries in direct competition with foreign products. This is partly due to the fact that 'import substitution industrial strategy has been characterised by spontaneity, disorganisation and lack of planning and feasible study' (Abdulla, 1985: 254), and mostly due to the fact that most such activities have been trapped in the easy stage – 'The easiest areas for import substitution have already been exploited' (World Bank, 1983: 82).

Policies to Promote Industrialization

In the UAE, a clearly defined and comprehensive policy that identifies a package of measures and instruments to accelerate industrial growth and encourage private sector participation has not materialized. Although the UAE's 1979 industrial law envisaged a general framework for manufacturing incentives, the programme lacks comprehensiveness, applicability and effectiveness. The incentive programme recognized by the law is only applicable to small-scale privately owned projects, leaving the incentive issue of state owned projects undefined and within the authority of local governments. This has resulted in variation in dealing with different manufacturing projects at the country level, as well as at the level of each emirate. There has been a bias in favour of state owned versus privately owned prefects, and in favour of projects located in oil rich emirates against others in poor emirates.

The absence of any information regarding the nature and size of incentives to state owned projects hinders the desire to evaluate the performance of these activities on an economic basis. In fact, these projects, while they were given preferential treatment, have not been subject to the same financial and market discipline as the private sector projects. The only federal government institution that was established to carry out and handle incentive measures via low interest loans to private sector manufacturing projects is the Emirates Industrial Bank. However, its role has been restricted by its relatively small lending capacity, and its activities have been modest. In practice, cheap rental land or building space in well-equipped industrial estates with subsidized utilities is the most utilized incentive measure in the UAE. However, this measure is a privilege accorded only to private investors in the two wealthiest emirates of Abu Dhabi and Dubai, where well-developed industrial sites are located. This situation in turn discriminates against industrial projects in the poorer emirates. In fact, it is not only subsidy to the private sector in Abu Dhabi and Dubai that is more pronounced than in the remaining emirates, but the local governments of the two emirates have duplicated with better conditions and subsidies similar government projects existing in the northern emirates.

It is noteworthy that subsidies provided in the industrial zones are not confined to manufacturing activities. Trade, commercial and service activities are also eligible for these subsidies. Given the preference of private investors for trade and commerce, this has produced an adverse impact on attracting private capital. Although the industrial law recognized other forms of incentive measures, the real application and adoption of these measures have not been undertaken. The law failed to provide a minimum level of protection to infant industries, and thus made local products subject to fierce competition from well-developed imported manufactured products. Failure to provide an export subsidy that may cover market development and higher risk costs has resulted in local products being less competitive in the international market. The tariff exemption on imported machinery, equipment, raw materials and semi-finished products as well as exports, implied no effective subsidy, given the fact that tariff and customs duties for all products is low, ranging between 2 and 4 per cent.

Generally speaking, the absence of a clearly defined and comprehensive incentive policy that is appropriate to the changing circumstances and business environment in the region, coupled with the lack of properly equipped and qualified institutions to implement, follow up and evaluate the performance of the manufacturing projects, have created circumstances in which the effectiveness of any incentive system in directing the flow of investment funds to industrial growth, product specialization, international competitiveness and industrial research/innovation has been perhaps considerably diluted (Mohyaddin: 1984: 61). The UAE's support to domestic industry, with the exception of state owned projects, has been very low and ineffective compared with that in other Gulf states.

STRUCTURE AND PERFORMANCE OF THE MANUFACTURING SECTOR IN THE UAE

Growth and Structural Change

Measuring structural change in manufacturing is usually pursued by using two measures – value added or net output expressed in monetary terms – and the quantity of one of its inputs (labour) expressed in physical terms (Devine et al., 1976: 61). Applying these to the manufacturing sector in the UAE may not give a reliable indication of the sector's structure. This is attributable to many factors, the most important of which are the lack of sufficiently reliable information regarding industrial activities and absence of sufficient data-collecting institutions at both federal and local level; the interaction and overlapping of industrial and commercial activities; the contradiction between federal and local government data-collecting bodies; and unwillingness on the part of establishments to reveal data concerning their production, capital costs, revenues and profits. However, using available information we will trace the development of the manufacturing

Table 4.3 Some important indicators of the UAE's manufacturing sector (million Dh/1980 prices)

	1975		1980		1985	
	Value/no.	% of total	Value/no.	% of total	Value/no.	% of total
Number of establishments	423	–	658	–	–	–
GDP	471.9	0.9	4191	3.8	9443.0	9.2
Gross fixed capital formation	3012.8	19.5	9983	30.0	9938.9	n.a.
Production value	1163.7	1.9	6900	5.1	18810.5	13.9
Value Added	472.1	0.1	4191	3.8	9329.6	9.3
Employment	17205.0	5.9	47573	7.2	61534.0	6.3

Sources: Ministry of Planning, Economic and Social Development in the UAE for 1975–83, Abu Dhabi, 1987. Ministry of Planning, National Accounts for UAE, 1973–84, Abu Dhabi,1985. Ministry of Finance and Industry, Industrial Directory, Abu Dhabi, 1988.

sector in the UAE with the aim of clarifying some of its characteristics. Table 4.3 presents an overview of the manufacturing sector based on output, capital investment and employment data.

The table shows that although industrialization, apart from some traditional manufactures, is a recent phenomenon (starting in the early 1970s), the manufacturing sector has experienced rapid growth.

In fact, the pattern of this expansion has been unsteady, in part due to the fluctuation in government economic policies. It is apparent that an expansionary pattern has occurred between 1975 and 1980, reflecting the growth in oil revenues and the government's emphasis on the industrialization process. Consequently, all principal indicators have risen significantly. For example, in this period, average annual growth in manufacturing value added and GDP was 64 per cent and 54 per cent respectively, and 27 per cent in gross fixed capital formation. This rapid growth may be attributed to many factors. The most important of these are the expansion in the construction industry and the infrastructure base, the tremendous increase in population, and the adoption of major hydrocarbon-related projects.

It is also worth mentioning that the relatively moderate expansion (17 per cent) in employment might be consistent with the government's desire to promote capital-intensive industrial activities.

Over 1980–5 there was a slowdown in the expansion of industry. Compared with the earlier period, there was moderate expansion in the manufacturing share of GDP, production value and value added (17 per cent, 22 per cent, 17 per cent respectively).

Interestingly, there has been a decline in fixed investment. This may be attributed to a number of factors. One is the completion of the initial phase of infrastructure development. Second is the change in attitudes to new investment proposals (World Bank, 1983: 22). Indeed, the decrease in oil revenue contributed to the slowdown in investment in all sectors of the economy as well as to a reconsideration of most investment proposals. In fact, this period was one of consolidation where firms overhauled their production processes in favour of higher efficiency, and the inefficient ones ceased production (EIB, February 1988: 91). The adverse impact of the Iran – Iraq war on investment climate may be considered as another factor that attributed to the slow down in the expansion of industry.

Geographically, there is an uneven distribution of industrial activities among the seven emirates. The oil-rich emirates have the largest shares in terms of number of establishments and size of investment and consequently in production value and employment. These emirates have greater ability to invest in capital-intensive industries due to the availability of the funds needed for such investment. Abu Dhabi and Dubai retain the largest shares in manufacturing investment, employment and value added (see Tables 4.4 and 4.5). Abu Dhabi is the main centre for the petroleum and natural gas based industries which dominate the industrial structure. It is also the major market for industrial goods and services (World Bank, 1983: 44). Excluding refineries, Dubai the first in terms of value added and employment, although it is second in terms of investment.

Table 4.4 Manufacturing value added and employment by emirate (%)

Emirate	1978 Value added including refineries	1978 Value added excluding refineries	1981 Value added including refineries	1981 Value added excluding refineries	1981 Employment	1984 Value added	1984 Employment
Abu Dhabi	29.2	21.9	39.2	20.8	21.2	17.3	17.3
Dubai	26.5	29.0	29.9	39.0	38.1	52.0	42.8
Sharjah	15.3	16.8	19.0	24.8	24.6	15.4	18.3
Ras Al-Khaimah	22.5	25.0	8.3	10.8	8.5	10.1	13.2
Others	6.5	7.3	3.6	4.6	7.6	5.2	8.4
Total	100.0	100.0	100.0	100.0	100.0	100.0	100.0

Sources: Atkins and Partners, *Industrial Planning for the Emirate of Abu Dhabi*, Abu Dhabi, 1983. Ministry of Finance and Industry, *Industrial Directory*, Abu Dhabi, 1988.

Almost all large-scale capital-intensive enterprises, including hydrocarbon-based industries, are located in Abu Dhabi and Dubai. The only large-scale projects in the remaining emirates are cement factories, in addition to the gas processing plant in Sharjah (the third emirate in terms of oil wealth). Ras Al-Khaimah occupies the fourth position and it is the premier location for the manufacture of cement. The remaining three emirates are relatively unimportant on all indicators and most of their investments are in small-scale industries, many duplicating plants in other emirates.

Structure of the UAE Manufacturing Sector at Industry Level

In our analysis, industrial activity in the UAE is grouped according to the United Nations International Standard Industrial Classification (ISIC). Table 4.6 is an aggregate survey of the UAE manufacturing subsectors. From the table, it is clear that the UAE's experience with industrialization started with emphasis on small-scale industrial activities. These mainly serve domestic markets. Thus, food and

Table 4.5 Distribution of invested funds in the manufacturing sector, by emirate (million Dh/1980 prices)

Emirate	1978 Fixed*	1978 Flow	1978 Total	1978 %	1981 Fixed	1981 Flow	1981 Total	1981 %	1984 Fixed	1984 Flow	1984 Total	1984 %
Abu Dhabi	12329.1	1092.3	13421.4	46.6	20048.5	1695.8	21744.3	60.1	18204.5	912.2	19116.7	56.3
Dubai	9329.2	336.9	9666.1	33.6	4698.3	1478.6	6176.9	17.1	4891.3	2168.2	7059.5	20.8
Sharjah	2600.4	291.6	2892.0	10.1	1889.2	1168.0	3057.2	8.5	3729.2	271.6	4000.8	11.8
Ajman	293.9	109.7	403.6	1.4	476.8	149.6	626.4	1.7	464.4	103.3	567.7	1.7
Amm Al-Quaiwain	221.5	0.5	222.0	0.8	498.5	7.7	506.2	1.4	168.8	90.0	276.8	0.8
Ras Al-Khaimah	1581.8	240.2	1822.0	6.3	1719.1	1267.7	2986.8	8.3	1433.8	748.9	2182.7	6.4
Fujairah	330.2	7.9	338.1	1.2	979.2	43.3	1022.5	2.8	557.3	177.9	735.2	2.2
Total	26686.1	2079.1	28765.2	100.0	30309.6	5810.7	36120.3	100	29449.3	4472.1	33939.4	100

* Fixed = Stock at beginning of year; flow = new investment in year.

Sources: UAE Ministry of Planning, National Accounts of the UAE 1975–1984, Abu Dhabi, 1985. UAE Ministry of Planning, Economic and Social Development of the UAE 1975–1985, Abu Dhabi, 1987. UAE Ministry of Finance and Industry, Industrial Directory, Abu Dhabi, 1988.

beverages, wood products, paper and printing and basic metals constitute the starting point of UAE industrial development. These were undertaken in response to the expanding demand for consumer goods during the boom period, and were pursued by the private sector. According to our data, these activities provided the highest contribution to value added in 1975. A structural change had taken place by the late 1970s, and it was at the beginning of the 1980s the government realized the need to organize and to regulate industrial development. Since then, both federal government and local governments have recognized the need for public capital to participate in manufacturing activities, and the need for government to direct investment to certain activities which are beyond the ability of the private sector. Government participation has changed the pattern of industrial growth, and public funds have been directed to large-scale capital-intensive industries. The key features of such industries are: high volume of invested capital, high technology in production, as well as a high level of administrative and marketing skills. There is also heavy emphasis on foreign capital and foreign expertise.

Investment in hydrocarbon-based industries has been noticeable since then, and the governments of Abu Dhabi and Dubai adopted independent strategies. Abu Dhabi embarked heavily on oil-related industries such as oil refining, gas liquefaction and petrochemicals. Dubai, on the other hand, favoured investment in basic metallic industries, particularly aluminium. The Dubai gas liquefaction plant was constructed mainly to serve the aluminium smelter. There are no available data regarding gross fixed capital formation for the Abu Dhabi gas liquefaction and petrochemical project. Gross fixed capital formation for the UAE basic metals industries in general has expanded substantially since 1980 and accounts for the largest share of the total, although its contribution to the value added has been of less significance. Medium- and small-scale investment in chemicals and plastic products was also pursued in the UAE as a response to the increasing demand for these products, and this sub sector's contribution to the value added outstripped the others in 1980 and 1985. Gross fixed capital formation in non-metallic minerals has also been substantial. This pertains to the heavy investment in cement and other industries related to the construction sector, such as the manufacture of tiles.

It is noticeable that a large proportion of employment is in subsectors that are dominated by small-scale establishments which require less technological expertise and knowledge and are characterized by labour-intensive processes. Two major kinds of industry are found under this type. The first is processing of domestic materials, such as food processing and building materials. The second is in conversion of imported semi- manufactured products into consumer goods by assembling, packing or bagging.

Performance and Efficiency of the Manufacturing Sector in the UAE

The descriptive discussion of the UAE's manufacturing sector has shown that the country's industrial development has been encouraged by many factors and obstructed by others. Availability of cheap energy and hydrocarbon feedstocks and abundance of financial resources that facilitate availability of foreign capital, technology and expertise are the most beneficial factors. At the same time many other factors work to obstruct manufacturing in the country. Lack of human resources, narrowness of local markets, dearth of local raw materials and weakness in planning and policy determination are among the important factors that have adverse effects on industrial development.

The structure of the UAE's manufacturing sector encompasses two types of industries. The first consists of industries that were established to serve the domestic market and which responded to the expanding demand for certain goods and services during the oil boom period of 1974–89. These industries are internationally uncompetitive because of their high construction costs, heavy dependence on foreign labour and expertise (especially in the management and international marketing fields), and dearth of local raw materials. Presently, with the exhaustion of relatively easy opportunities for most of these projects and the inability to ascend to a higher stage of processing, the majority of these projects are operating below capacity. Contraction in domestic demand resulted from the slowdown in construction activities. Government

Table 4.6 Value added, gross fixed capital formation and employment in the UAE by manufacturing sector (1980 prices)

Manufacturing sector	1975 Val.	1975 %	1980 Val.	1980 %	1980 GFC Format.	1980 %	1980 Employment	1980 %	1985 Value Added	1985 %	1985 GFC Format.	1985 %	1985 Employment	1985 %
Food & Beverage	75.5	16.0	241	5.8	517.1	5.2	5302	11.1	383.1	4.1	507.0	5.1	6619	11.1
Textile & Leather	–	–	210	5.0	10.1	0.1	8810	18.5	202.6	2.2	6.1	0.1	13481	22.6
Wood Product & Furniture	69.1	14.6	148	3.5	39.1	1.0	6077	12.8	322.6	3.5	33.7	0.3	5099	8.6
Paper Products & Printing	71.6	15.2	104	2.5	208.8	2.1	3880	8.2	228.8	2.5	164.2	1.7	3331	5.6
Chemicals & Plastic Products	38.4	8.1	2168	51.7	411.9	4.1	3618	7.6	6381.0	68.3	515.3	5.2	4547	7.6
Non-Metallic Minerals	49.9	10.6	831	19.8	1431.3	14.3	8340	17.5	807.5	8.7	2165.0	21.8	9282	15.6
Base Metals	69.1	14.6	263	6.3	6841.3	68.5	2058	4.3	565.5	6.0	5988.5	60.2	1893	3.2
Machinery & Equipment	43.5	9.2	166	4.0	311.2	3.1	8837	18.6	408.3	4.4	385.9	3.9	13878	23.3
Other	55.0	11.7	60	1.4	157.6	1.6	651	1.4	30.2	0.3	173.2	1.7	1401	2.4
Total	472.1	100	4191	100	9928.4	100	47573	100	9329.6	100	9938.9	100	59534	100

Sources: UAE Ministry of Planning, *National Accounts of the UAE 1975–1984*, Abu Dhabi, 1985. UAE Ministry of Planning, *Annual Statistical Abstract*, 1984. UAE Ministry of Finance and Industry, *Industrial Directory*, Abu Dhabi, 1988.

expenditure due to the fall in oil revenue and income had adversely affected this type of industry.

The second type of industry consists of large-scale hydrocarbon-based industries which were established to retain the country's comparative advantage. The pattern of growth in these industries has been unsteady, reflecting the flection in the government oil and expenditure policies. These industries are burdened with high conversion costs, require a long gestation period, and are performing poorly. This condition is explained by many factors. Since this type of industry is heavily dependent on the oil sector, it was affected adversely by the slump of the 1980s in the oil market. This can be perceived in the contraction of oil proceeds and the sharp reduction in the supply of associated gas due to the cut in oil production. Furthermore, the unfavourable effect resulting from the slump in the world petrochemical market (fertilizer in the case of the UAE) and the cut in international market prices for LNG and LPG, made it difficult to conceive optimal utilization of natural resources, given that most of these projects are operating below capacity.

It is still too early to judge the success or otherwise of the UAE's recent industrial experience. However, in light of the above discussion and under the prevailing conditions, the pattern and direction of this experience is not promising, and the long-term objectives may be hardly attainable. The role of the manufacturing sector in diversifying the country's economic structure away from oil has been insignificant. Although the manufacturing sector has increased its output in absolute terms, in relative terms its share of total GDP is still very low, while the oil sector maintains its dominance in terms of its contribution to GDP.

Enhancing forward and backward linkage with other sectors of the economy has not been encouraging so far, and in some cases it has been tenuous. As a matter of fact, most of the manufacturing plants have been foreign enclaves operated by foreign labour and expertise, in most cases using imported production factors; for some, their output is exported.

The role of the UAE's manufacturing sector as an engine to develop an indigenous technological base has turned out differently. Instead of training local unskilled labour to use and maintain imported equipment and machinery, reliance on foreign skills and technology has been persistent and dominant, and manufacturing that implies a change in behaviour has not been apparent.

With regard to the rule of industrialization as a way of securing private investment in manufacturing, experience has been precarious and unpromising. The private sector's preference to invest in commercial, real estate and banking dominates, and government attempts to attract private funds have had little success. Confusion and uncertainty among local investors undermine their desire to participate effectively in industrial activities. The rudimentary nature of authoritative bodies and institutions, the absence of industrial research, and inefficiency of data resources and statistical information, hinder their ability to grasp clearly the feasibility or not of investing in certain industrial activities.

THE OUTLOOK FOR INDUSTRIALIZATION DURING THE 1990s

It is not an easy task to measure the achievements of the manufacturing sector and project the future path of industrial development in the UAE. This is due to the fact that there is almost a lack of information and statistical data that permit such analysis. For example, information with regard to type and size of investment in manufacturing on both public and private levels is not available. The last industrial census carried out in the UAE was in 1980. Data on the sectoral division of GDP, the proportion of MVA to GDP, sectoral distribution of the labour force, and employment growth in manufacturing sector, mostly do not transcend 1985, and are incomplete and often unreliable.

However, if one depends on policy-makers' affirmation in the media and some partial information provided by official reports, it seems that government policy toward industrial strategy will remain similar to that already elaborated during the previous period. The government will continue to play a key role in the development of capital-intensive hydrocarbon-based manufacturing. Nevertheless, there has been a substantial slowing down of government investments; and reconsideration and postponement of most investment proposals identified during the 1980s. This is due to the continuing fluctuation in the oil market and the decline in oil export receipts. As a matter of fact there has been a transition from investment in new projects to operation and maintenance of the existing ones.

On the other hand, private investors are expected to remain responsible for small-scale industrial projects. However, the increased difficulties resulting from the Gulf War contributed to the slowdown and economic decline in all activities, and increased caution in the private sector, especially with regard to manufacturing activities characterized by relatively high investment cost. The fact that industrial finance has not received sufficient government attention, and with the continued cutbacks in government investment programmes and decline in public expenditure, the availability of cheap finance for new ventures will generally not be sufficient to off-set an infant industry cost and attract new participation by the private sector. Furthermore, in the absence of joint sponsoring projects between government and local investors and of govern ment- generated financing feasibility studies, the role of the private sector in industrial development will be limited.

CONCLUSIONS

The industrial exprience of the UAE is a recent phenomenon and only commenced with the emergence of the country as an oil-rich state. Thus, the pattern and direction of industrial growth have been mainly affected by development in the oil market.

As in other developing countries, industrialization in the UAE is expected to offer substantial dynamic benefits that are important for changing the traditional structure of its economy. Industrialization is visualized as creating a real yield, to contribute to diversification, promote employment and upgrade domestic labour and entrepreneurial skills. Significantly, industrialization would induce necessary and desirable changes in social and cultural attitudes and institutions through the modernizing impact of imported organizational methods and technologies.

However, manufacturing industry in the UAE appeared unable to attain rapid diversification of the economy; the oil sector continues to play a major in the economy of the UAE. The role of industrialization in upgrading local skills and developing an indigenous labour force and technological base has not been significant enough. The role of industrialization in changing the rest of the economy, its institutions and general social behaviour and attitudes has also been disappointing.

Learning by doing and mastering foreign technology have not been significant outcomes of the UAE's industrial experience.

Industrialization in this country has consisted of importing plant and industrial processes. The factories require imported labour, management skills, equipment and technology. The complexity of foreign technology dictated continued dependence on foreign labour and expertise. Hence, the local population has attained very little in terms of technology transfer.

Industrialization has not contributed to the development of entrepreneurship capabilities. Inconsistent economic policies and confusion and uncertainty hindered the development of indigenous entrepreneurship and undermined local investors' desire to participate effectively in the manufacturing sector.

The challenge and problems that face the UAE economy are great and complex, and difficult to remedy through the existing inefficient economic structure. In general, the absence of efficient economic strategy to channel funds into productive development projects, the prevalence of high consumption which is sustained without recourse to local production, and the existence of a high level of conspicuous investment, are the most obvious characteristics of the UAE economy. In fact, the prevailing industrial strategies lack any commitment to selecting objectives that should be given priority, elaborating and designing plans and programmes that guide and govern the fulfilment of these objectives, and providing means and procedures of implementation that evaluate projects on an economic basis.

In a situation where there is a lack of a coherent philosophy or strategy for industrial development, a dynamic approach to industrialization that is capable of dealing with the changing conditions and long-term circumstances is very important. A comprehensive industrial strategy that involves investment decisions, acquisition of technology, research and development plans and a manpower development policy, needs to be developed. This industrial strategy should be carried out in the context of a general development strategy. It has to be re-adjusted to become more applicable to the conditions and circumstances of society. Society's assimilation of new ideas and practices is very important. Hence, the industrial strategy has to be associated with the appropriate changes in attitudes, in government and management, and in labour structure.

The rapid emergence of political, social and administrative institutions which are capable of directing the expansion of economic activities and promoting industrialization is a very important prerequisite for growth and development. A clear policy for human resources development is needed. The importance of educational and training institutions in preparing a sufficient supply of local skills and a trained technical and professional workforce should be recognized. Research is important to the creation of knowledge and technical progress. Thus it is essential to invest in research and development centres.

Given the characteristics of the UAE and other Gulf state economies, the drive for industrial development will remain restricted unless it acquires a real regional dimension. A regional strategy for industrial investment may reduce some of the bottlenecks and obstacles that hinder such development. Adherence to a regional strategy may lead to more efficient resource allocation through reducing the cost of duplication and excess capacity of industrial projects. This strategy needs to be comprehensive and encompass policies related to all aspects of industrialization (such as regional incentive policy and regional policy for education and training, research and development, and human resources management).

Finally, it is essential to point out that industrialization is a multinational process: should any aspects of it lag behind, it hinders the whole process.

REFERENCES

Abdulla, A. (1985), *Political Dependency: The Case of the United Arab Emirates*, Ph.D. thesis, Georgetown University, Washington DC.

Al-Shamsi, F. (1990), *Industrial Development in the Arab Gulf: Policies and Experience In the United Arab Emirates*, Ph.D. thesis, University of ExeterUK.

Arab Monetary Fund (1990), *United Arab Economic Report* (Abu-Dhabi).

Devine, P., Hones, R., Lee, N. and Tyson, W. (1976), *An Introduction to Industrial Economics* (London: George Allen and Unwin).

Emirates Industrial Bank (EIB) (1988), *Journal of the EIB*.

International Monetary Fund (1988), *The United Arab Emirates: Recent Economic Development*, Unpublished study, June.

Mohyadden, B. (1992), 'Joint Projects and Regional Co-operation: A Study of the Experience and Future Opportunities in the Arab Gulf'. *Journal of Industrial Co-operation in the Arabian Gulf*, no. 16 (April).

Najjar, A. (1992), 'Economic Development and the Challenges of Nineties' (Arabic). *The First Conference of the Business and Economists Institute* (Abu-Dhabi: January 1992).

United Arab Emirates Ministry of Planning (1987), *The National Accounting of the UAE 1975–1984: Social and Economic Development in the UAE* (Abu-Dhabi).

World Bank (1983) *United Arab Emirates: Economic Development at a Crossroads*, Washington, DC, World Bank, Division II, Country Programs Dept II, Europe, Middle East, and North Africa Region.

5 Diversification through Industrialization: the Saudi Experience
Osama Saad Ahmed

Few countries in the world have experienced the accelerated economic development that has occurred in the Kingdom of Saudi Arabia. The economic situation of Saudi Arabia in the last quarter of the twentieth century is unprecedented in the history of the world. This is a country whose sparse population had, historically, been subjected to a harsh life and poverty, and came into riches beyond the range of a dream. It no longer requires what had become its traditional dependency, i.e. foreign aid. The high rate of socioeconomic change can be seen in the high per capita income, rapid expansion of education and health facilities, variety of development projects, huge industrialization programmes and well-established infrastructural base and communications networks. The Kingdom is indeed blessed with the largest oil reserves of any country in the world (26 per cent of world crude-oil reserves).

Only a couple of decades ago, Saudi Arabia seemed a most unlikely location for a major industrialization drive. There were limited resources, limited skills and relatively limited finances. The greater oil shock of 1973/4 opened up vast new opportunities for the Kingdom's planners to deploy the large influx of oil revenues for industrial and economic diversification to attain self-sustained growth before the oil resources got exhausted.

Industrialization, therefore, in the Kingdom remains at the heart of its development plans and strategies. It aims for economic diversification and the creation of alternative income resources besides oil. It is necessary to decrease the weakness that arises from an economy which is largely dependent upon the export of oil. This chapter discusses the growth of industrialization in Saudi Arabia and attempts to explore its different obstacles. The chapter starts by tracing back the genesis and follows the growth of industrialization. It also presents a brief view of the major industries which have been set up in the Kingdom. Although its pace of development was fast during the third Five Year-Plan period (1980–5), the Kingdom's industrial development has encountered a number of difficulties. For the purpose of analysing these obstacles, we divide them into internal and external factors.

THE NECESSITY OF INDUSTRIALIZATION FOR SAUDI ARABIA

The modern economy of Saudi Arabia which emerged after the 1962 reform programme is dominated by petroleum, of which the country is by far the largest producer within the Organization of Oil Exporting Countries (OPEC). The country owned 25.9 per cent of the world oil reserves and produced 13.4 per cent of the world total production in 1994 (Europa, 1996: 148–9).

Having achieved an annual gross rate of 10.6 per cent in the period 1968–80 due to the huge rise in crude oil prices, Saudi Arabia's gross domestic product (GDP) declined, in real terms, at an average rate of 1.8 per cent per year over the decade 1980–9, largely because petroleum output was reduced from a peak of almost 10m. barrels per day (b/d) in 1980 to 3.6m. b/d in 1985 (Europa, 1996: 835). Although production rose to more than 5m. b/d in 1988–9 and to 10m. b/d in mid-1994 (EIU, 1996: 36), depressed international prices resulted in substantially reduced revenues, with adverse consequences for the current account and national budget, both of which moved into deficit. At the same time, GDP showed a negative growth rate in 1994, after slumping from 10.7 per cent in 1990 and 9.8 per cent in 1991 to 5 per cent in 1992 and 1 per cent in 1993. And it has picked up slightly in 1995, when the economy grew by an estimated 1.5 per cent (AOGD, 1996: 392). Since the end of the Gulf War in 1991, petroleum has contributed an average of 40 per cent of nominal GDP, 75 per cent of government revenue and a little more than 90 per cent of export receipts (EIU, 1996: 12). The prices and production volume of Saudi Arabian oil are in part a consequence of the government's policies, but are also constrained by collective decisions taken within OPEC and underlying trends in the international oil market; as a result, the economy is highly vulnerable to shocks within the oil market. This was particularly evident in the wake of the Gulf conflict of 1990–1, when the Kingdom's average annual oil production increased by more than 60 per cent between 1989 and 1991 in order to compensate for the halt in Kuwaiti exports, and led to a rise of more than 9 per cent per year in GDP (EIU, 1996: 19). These fluctuations in the government revenue from oil exporting can be seen in Figure 5.1.

The Saudi government became aware of its precarious situation as a result of its dependence on a monoculture source of revenue – oil exports. Therefore, the massive revenues received from petroleum exports (particularly since the dramatic increase in international petroleum prices in 1973–4), have been diverted to finance ambitious programmes of infrastructural development and modernization, all of which are prerequisites of industrialization, as well as far-reaching programmes for health, social and educational purposes. Whereas in the 1970s and early 1980s Saudi

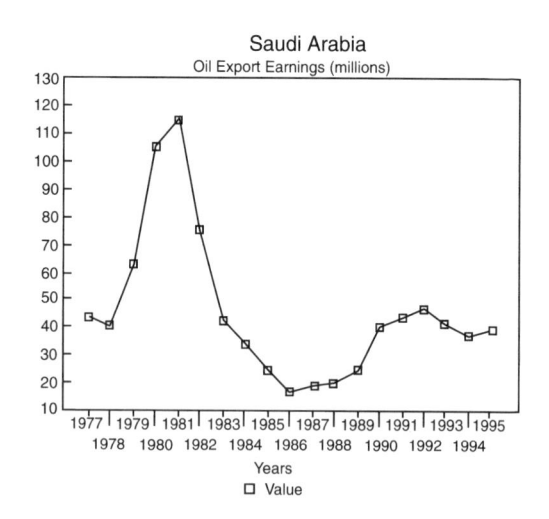

Figure 5.1
Note: The value of 1995 is an estimate.
Source: OPEC, Annual Statistical Bulletin, 1994.

Arabia's exports consisted almost entirely of petroleum, by the late 1980s non-oil exports stood around 10 per cent of total value due to huge investment in this sector. A similar pattern was apparent in the structure of GDP, enhanced by a sharp fall in petroleum production in the mid-1980s (UNIDO, 1986: 2). Thus, the positive growth of GDP during that period could be attributed to a slight increase in the share of the non-oil sector.

INDUSTRIALIZATION IN SAUDI ARABIA

The Genesis of Industrialization in Saudi Arabia

With the exception of traditional crafts and cottage industries, Saudi Arabia had no industry before the mid-1940s, when the first refinery became operative. In 1954 there were only five industrial companies with a total of invested capital of SR 42 million (Saudi Riyals; UNIDO, 1967: 112). The pace of industrial expansion was very slow, but began to accelerate during the 1960s after the implementation of the 1962 reform programme which allocated part of oil revenues to industrial development, the Promulgation of the Foreign Capital Investment Regulations in 1964, and the Company Law in 1965 (Al-Hajjar and Presley, 1993: 39). In 1964 the number of industrial companies rose to 67, with a total invested capital of SR 211 million (UNIDO, 1967: 112). By the 1970s, large-scale industries including five refineries and a fertilizer plant were established (Masood, 1988: 3). Recognizing that oil and natural gas reserves could be depleting and that future demand could diminish, the Saudi government embarked on a programme of industrial diversification, especially in the period 1975–84. The general objectives of the development programme have been to prepare the future growth and diversification of the country's economy.

Growth of Industrialization in Saudi Arabia

In Saudi Arabia, as in many other newly industrialized countries, a pronounced division has developed between import substitution industries and export-oriented industries.

Therefore, the industrial strategy has two directions: first, to implement manufacturing projects in which Saudi Arabia has a comparative advantage; second, to develop industries that offer import substitution. To achieve these objectives, the government has adopted two major strategies: first, it has established, in collaboration with foreign companies, basic industries utilizing crude oil and natural gas, and secondly, it has encouraged the private sector, through a wide range of incentives, to set up non-hydrocarbon related industries. Accordingly, the structure of industries consists of oil related industries (in which the Kingdom has comparative cost advantages resulting from reserves of crude and natural gas), and non-oil related industries. Like other Gulf countries, Saudi Arabia has been giving more importance to oil and gas related processing industries (such as oil refining, gas liquefaction, petrochemicals, chemicals and fertilizers), to stop the wastage of natural gas (associated with crude oil) which is produced in quite substantial quantities.

The industrial sector generally is strongly influenced by developments in the oil industry. Petroleum refineries accounted for some 50 per cent of total MVA in 1986 (UNIDO, 1986: 9), and accounted for 60 per cent of manufacturing GDP in 1994 (EIU, 1996: 12). Its share of GDP was only 5.6 per cent in 1995 (SCER, 1996: 15), and it has always employed a relatively tiny percentage of the work force (2 per cent) (EIU, 1985: 13). The share of non-oil industries to GDP is meagre, peaking at 2.1 per cent in 1978/9, and then declining, to stand at 1.7 per cent in 1981/2 (MERI, 1985: 85), and 1.1 per cent in 1990 (Looney, 1992: 214). Mining and quarrying of minerals has traditionally accounted for about one half of one per cent of GDP; its share in 1994 was the same, 0.5 per cent (EIU, 1996: 20), and has employed 0.3 per cent of the total labour force (MERI, 1985).

Since 1975, the overall structure of the non-oil manufacturing sector shows one essential change: the petrochemical industry has become increasingly important (Europa, 1996: 840–2).

Statistics (UNIDO, 1986) on the changing pattern of industrial development and the expansion of non-oil industrial activities between 1975 and 1982 show that the share of food products, beverages and tobacco in recorded

MVA increased from 10.3 per cent in 1975 to 12 per cent in 1982, and of petroleum refineries declined from 83.6 per cent to 73.9 per cent during the same period. Other non-metallic mineral products more than doubled their share of recorded MVA during 1975–82.

By the end of 1984 UNIDO, 1986 the number of industrial licences issued by the government jumped to 3,203, compared to 492 licences issued up to the end of 1975, an increase of 551 per cent. Of these, 1,785 factories were in operation in 1984 compared to 437 in 1975, an increase of 277 per cent. In terms of enterprise numbers, all manufacturing branches have grown significantly during a ten-year period since 1975. With 500 licensed factories in production in 1984, the metal industry ranks first, followed by the building materials industry (486), food, drinks and tobacco (287), chemical industries, including petrochemical, coal, rubber and plastics (256), paper and paper products (106), etc. Real MVA grew at an average annual rate of 8.2 per cent between 1973 and 1983.

INDUSTRIALIZATION RELATED TO OIL AND GAS

Oil Refining

Petroleum refining in 1994 accounted for 60 per cent of manufacturing GDP (EIU,1996: 12). The major projects are being undertaken as joint ventures between the state and foreign companies. Following its absorbtion of SAMAREC in mid-1993 and PETROMIN during the fifth plan period (1990–5), Saudi ARAMCO took charge of the management of the entire range of state petroleum refining and product-making interests. As well as handling the marketing of products from Saudi ARAMCO's Ras Tanura plant, SAMAREC had operated refineries at Jeddah, Riyadh and Yanbu and had been responsible for marketing the state share of output from export-oriented refineries at Jubail, Yanbu and Rabigh. Saudi Arabia's installed refinery capacity totalled 1,865,000 b/d in 1992, an increase of 1m. b/d of which about two-thirds was sold on the home market and the remainder exported (Europa, 1996: 840 and SCER, 1996: 20).

Gas Liquefaction

The expansion of the Kingdom's petrochemical industry depends mainly on the continued supply of natural gas. The construction of the master gas system in the 1980s to ease utilization of the Kingdom gas reserves by Saudi Basic Industries Corporation (SABIC) in Jubail and Yanbu was a natural decision to stop the wastage of gas and make its export possible. In 1994 Saudi Arabia's proven reserves of gas were estimated at 5,387m. cubic metres, or about 3.6 per cent of world reserves (EIU, 1996: 40). At present, Saudi Aramco operates the Master Gas System (MGS) which collects the gas produced in the Kingdom and either reinjects it for petrochemical sector use or processes and distributes it to the public and private sectors.

Petrochemical Industries

Since the size of the domestic market was not sufficient, petrochemical industry was to be established mainly to cater to the export market. It was expected that the export-oriented hydrocarbon-based petrochemical industry would diversify the economy and thereby reduce the exclusive dependency on oil exports. It was believed that the industrialization process would involve full utilization of indigenous productive resources and would generate forward and backward linkages, thereby producing the necessary spread effects that would ultimately lead to self-sustained growth. The availability of surplus associated gas has been one of the strongest arguments for developing a petrochemical industry which is used both as feedstock and fuel in the manufacture of petrochemicals.

During the fourth plan period (1985–90), SABIC (founded in 1976) invested more than $43 billion in plastic, fertilizers and other petrochemical industries in Jubail and Yanbu (AOGD, 1996: 379–80). In 1983 the Saudi Methanol Co. (Ar-Razi) plant at Jubail became the first venture to begin production. It was followed by four new projects that began operations in 1984: the National Methanol Co. (Ibn Sina) plant at Jubail; the Saudi Petrochemical Co. (Sadaf) plant at Jubail; the Al-Jubail Petrochemical Co. (Kemya) plant; and the Saudi Yanbu Petrochemical Co. (Yanpet) plant. In 1985 two new plants also came into operation at Jubail: the Arabian Petrochemical Co. (Petrokemya) plant, fully owned by SABIC; and the Eastern Petrochemical Co. (Sharq) plant, a joint venture between SABIC and a Japanese consortium led by Mitsubishi (AOGD, 1996: 380).

The target of Saudi Arabia, according to Looney and Winterford (1992: 583), in petrochemical industry is to attain only 5 per cent of the global basic petrochemical market. The total value of petrochemical production worldwide, according to Bhardwaj (1994: 553) in 1992 was $440bn. SABIC, with its total sales of nearly $2.7bn in each of 1992 and 1993, had a share of 0.6 per cent, 'a good result from a developing country representing only 0.3 per cent of the world population' (Bhardwaj, 1994: 553).

Aluminium

The most successful aluminium company in the Kingdom is the Aluminium Products Company of Dammam, which gained profits of US $35 million in 1985 (EIU, 1985: 19). The Saudi government is not only setting up industry but also buying shares in industries based in other Gulf countries – for example, the new Gulf Aluminium Rolling Mill (Garmco) with a capacity of 40,000 tons located in Bahrain, of which the Saudi government in 1988 was likely to take up a large portion of its eventual annual output of rolled aluminium sheet and coil. Saudi Arabia also offered the greatest potential for further downstream usage of aluminium products in general (Azzam, 1988: 155).

Fertilizers

In its drive for industrialization, Saudi Arabia has given priority to the fertilizer industry, taking advantage of the abundance of natural gas which is a basic intermediate for the production of nitrogenous fertilizers. According to Azzam (1988: 151), the relative importance of nitrogenous fertilizers in total world consumption of fertilizers has been on the rise. It went up from 30 per cent in 1950 to more than 59 per cent in 1984. The potential for this industry is, therefore, promising and the Kingdom is determined to capitalize on the comparative advantage it has and draw on its resource endowment to assume a key position in the world market for nitrogen. The most important fertilizer companies in Saudi Arabia are Al-Jubail Fertilizer Company (Samad), the Saudi Arabian Fertilizer Company (Safco) and the National Chemical Fertilizer Company (Ibn al-Baytar).

Industrial Minerals

In addition to oil and gas, Saudi Arabia possesses abundant mineral resources, including both precious and less precious metals and other industrial minerals. Exploitation of these minerals has been neglected in the past, in part because of the dominance of oil but also because the remote locations of many of the deposits make extraction and marketing both difficult and costly. Nevertheless, the government has shown renewed interest in working in conjunction with the private sector to develop other mineral resources as part of the strategy of diversifying the economy from oil. Gold is mined primarily at Mahd al-Dahab and Sukhaybarat. Gold from the Mahd al-Dahab mine amounted to 3.5 tons in 1991 (Europa, 1996: 842), up from 1.6 tons in 1988 (AOGD, 1996: 389). There are also schemes to mine copper, phosphate, bauxite, zinc and iron-ore deposits. One of the largest of these projects is the development of the Julamid phosphate deposits in the north of the Kingdom, which would include the construction of a major processing plant at Jubail.

NON-OIL AND GAS RELATED INDUSTRIES

Cement

Like petrochemicals, the cement industry has been stimulated by the huge infrastructure development programmes since the early 1970s. The abundant availability of raw materials in the different parts of the Kingdom has helped the dispersal of the location of the industry. The largest producer, the Saudi Cement Co. (Hofuf) accounted for 3.9m. tonnes of cement production in 1994. The Eastern Province Cement Co. came next with an output of 2.9m. tonnes (SCER, 1996: 7).

Due to high growth in the demand for cement, Saudi Arabia has undergone a fundamental change during the last three years. Cement production, currently covers 98 per cent of domestic demand (Europa, 1996: 842).

Iron and Steel Industry

The Saudi Arabian Petroleum and Mineral Organization (PETROMIN) introduced the first generation of steel plants in the Gulf by establishing a steel rolling plant in Jeddah in 1966 with an annual capacity of 45,000 tons, increasing to 140,000 tons in 1980 (Azzam, 1988: 150). In 1981, another SABIC-owned iron and steel plant, Hadeed in Jubail (the largest steel complex in the Gulf) had a production capacity of 850,000 tons annually (AOGD, 1996: 390). Due to presence of capital, new technology, cheap energy, raw materials and the high combined forward and backward linkages of the iron and steel industry, it has been argued that this industry, like petrochemicals, has a good comparative advantage in the Kingdom and a promising future.

Light Industries

During the 1970s much effort went into the construction materials sector to meet the apparently huge needs developed during the construction boom. With this sector now saturated, activities are being shifted towards production of consumers goods, chemicals, etc., in general import substituting industries. The Saudi Industrial Development Fund (SIDF) had up to 1985 provided finance for more than 1,000 projects at a total cost of over $10 billion. The total number of factories that were in operation by the end of 1985 was 2,700 and covering 15 per cent of local demand (Azzam, 1988: 155).

The Saudi government in its industrial development strategy had identified some 25 secondary industries and around 80 light industries and opened them for investment utilizing the Kingdom's hydrocarbon and mineral resources, together with attractive investment facilities by the various financial institutions. As a result private sector participation has increased sharply since the Gulf conflict, the total number of industrial licences have risen from 205 in 1989 to 625 in 1994. The applications for new licences in 1994 were mainly in chemicals, rubber and plastics (27.6 per cent), metal, machinery and equipment (24.2 per cent), and food and beverages (17.6 per cent) (EIU, 1996: 36).

INDUSTRIAL ZONES

The thrust of Saudi Arabia's industrialization effort has lain in the development of the twin industrial cities of Jubail and Yanbu, the former on the Gulf, the latter on the Red Sea. Development of the two cities was to take 10 years (started in the second plan, 1975–80) and cost around $70,000m. (Europa, 1996: 835). In their second-stage development Jubail and Yanbu are planned to contain major secondary industries, both stemming from the base chemical industries and other heavy industry (Montaque, 1985: 21). Currently, the number of factories at both cities has reached 21 for basic industries, 12 for secondary industries and 112 for light and supporting industries (SCER, 1996: 20).

Jubail was to have three petroleum refineries, six petrochemical plants, an aluminium smelter and a steel mill, as well as support industries, an industrial port and large-scale urban development. Yanbu was planned on a slightly smaller scale: two petroleum refineries, natural gas processing plant, a petrochemical complex, other lighter industries, an industrial port, and a new urban area. The Yanbu industries were to be supplied by an oil pipeline and a gas pipeline across the Arabian Peninsula from the eastern province (Europa, 1996: 835). The two cities, Jubail and Yanbu, are under the authority of the Royal Commission for Jubail and Yanbu (Montague, 1985: 22).

In addition to Jubail and Yanbu, the Saudi government established a number of other industrial zones during the third plan (1980–5), attached to the main population centres. The most important of these are Riyadh, Jeddah, Dammam, Dhahran and Al-Khobar.

OWNERSHIP AND INVESTMENT PATTERNS IN INDUSTRIES

Government Ownership

The government dominates the industrial sector by means of its ownership (wholly or partially) of the Kingdom's main refineries and its 70 per cent ownership of SABIC. The most important government institutions are as follows.

1) ARAMCO, a fully government owned enterprise. The company became a Saudi-registered, state owned concern in 1988, when its name was changed to the Saudi Arabian Oil Company (Saudi ARAMCO). Apart from producing 97 per cent of all crude oil, it is also responsible for the production of all liquid natural gas.

2) The General Petroleum and Minerals Organization (PETROMIN) was established by the government in 1962; its activities were confined to domestic marketing and distribution of refined products at the outset. But the organization progressively diversified into the fields of exploration, refining, transport and petrochemicals.

3) The Saudi Basic Industries Corporation (SABIC), was established in 1976 and is Saudi Arabia's main non-oil industrial enterprise, including among its holdings many major gas utilization projects. Chief among them are the petrochemical projects at Jubail, Jeddah and Yanbu. SABIC is a partner in a number of important joint ventures with overseas corporations.

Foreign Investment and Industrialization

The kingdom has encouraged foreign investment to help develop its industries and services. This has become increasingly important due to the need to raise investment in both infrastructure and industrial capacity over the next five years. According to the government industrial strategy, foreign investors are able to own 100 per cent of a local venture (EIU, 1996: 24). The share of foreign investment up to 1414 AH (corresponding to 1994), can be seen in Table 5.1, which shows that investment was concentrated in the chemical, metal, construction materials and food and beverage sectors.

Table 5.1 Production of factories under the foreign capital investment system by industrial activity, up to 1414 AH (corresponding to 1994)

Industrial sector	Total financing SR millions	No. of workers	No. of factories
Food and Beverages	8711.62	26610	346
Textiles, Wearing Apparel & Leather	1843.41	8607	81
Wood, Wood Products and Furnitures	1319.84	8009	100
Paper Products, Printing & Publishing	3812.94	10555	148
Chemicals, Petroleum, Coal, Rubber & Plastic	97227.02	46322	399
Construction Materials, Chinaware, Ceramics & Class	19788.29	37860	439
Basic Metals	4187.68	3304	10
Fabricated Metal Products, Machinery and Equipment	13142.00	48996	633
Other	766.60	3766	57
Transportation and Storage	420.66	1993	21
Total	151220.06	196022	2234

Source: Ministry of Industry and Electricity – Deputy Ministry for Industrial Affairs, *Statistical Indicators*, 1994.

Private Ownership and Industrialization

Traditionally, private ownership was concentrated in the trades and services. Major objectives of the third and fourth plans were to stimulate private entrepreneurship by providing a number of incentives to generate more job opportunities; and to reduce the role of the government as a means of rationalizing government expenditure. As a result, in 1984 20 per cent of SABIC was sold to the Saudi public (UNIDO, 1986: 27). Also, a total of eight industrial estates currently offer basic infrastructure and services at minimal charge, credit is available on favourable terms, and selected products are protected by duties on imports (Europa, 1996: 842). The

Diversification: the Saudi Experience 117

Table 5.2 Industrial licences issued in 1414 AH (1994)

Industrial sector	Total financing (Mill. SR)	No. of workers	No. of licences
Foodstuffs and Beverages	2263.75	5024	115
Textiles, Wearing Apparel, Leather Products	812.89	3461	59
Wood and Wood Products and Furniture	348.67	1428	36
Paper Products, Printing and Publishing	189.52	741	23
Chemicals, Petroleum, Coal and Rubber Products	4306.98	6242	180
Construction Materials, Chinaware, Ceramics & Class	990.88	2429	66
Basic Metals	745.60	513	9
Metal Products, Tools and Machines	3067.26	7304	149
Other	109.68	569	15
Transportation and Storage	0	0	0
Total	12835.23	27706	652

Source: Ministry of Industry and Electricity – Deputy Ministry for Industrial Affairs, *Statistical Indicators*, 1994.

Saudi Industrial Development Fund (SIDF), with an authorized capital of 18,738m. riyals in 1995, and the National Industrial Company (NIC), provide concessionary loans to private investors. Table 5.2 shows the industrial licences issued in 1414 AH (1994), by industrial sector. The number of licences increased from 389 in 1984 (UNIDO, 1986: 28) to 652 in 1994.

Industrialization and Joint Ventures

Joint ventures are regarded as a vehicle for industrialization in the country, so overseas partners are attracted by various generous government incentives. The general purpose of the incentives is to establish a sound industrialization through the transferring of technologies, experiences and skills, and to improve the skill structure of the national labour force.

Table 5.3 Foreign participation in joint ventures in Saudi Arabia by nationality and industrial sector, 1985

Sector	Licences	UK	Benelux	France	Germany	Ireland	Italy	Austria	Switzerland	Scandinavia	Other European Countries	USA	China	Korea	Japan	Taiwan	Other Asian Countries	Arab States	India & Pakistan	Not specified	Total foreign firms	Percentage of foreign investment
Foodstuffs, drinks and tobacco	540	4	–	3	4	3	3	1	–	9	–	3	–	1	–	–	–	21	–	1	54	1
Readymade clothes and textiles	83	1	1	–	–	2	–	2	–	–	–	1	–	–	–	–	–	9	–	1	16	
Manufactured Leatherproducts	33	1	–	–	–	–	–	–	–	–	–	–	–	–	–	–	–	1	1	1	4	
Manufactured wood products	114	1	1	–	–	–	–	–	–	–	1	–	–	3	1	–	–	10	–	–	17	
Manufactured paper, paper products, printing and publishing	152	1	–	1	1	–	–	–	1	–	–	–	–	–	–	–	1	20	–	–	25	
Chemical industries	395	5	3	1	5	–	2	–	15	9	–	24	–	1	2	–	1	21	4	3	96	
Manufactured china, pottery, glass, etc.	21	–	–	–	–	–	–	–	–	–	–	1	–	–	–	–	–	2	–	–	3	
Manufactured Building materials	662	6	5	5	12	–	7	2	6	10	–	8	–	1	–	1	2	34	2	9	11	
Metal indu.	571	9	1	1	10	–	5	1	6	5	2	11	–	1	3	1	3	52	4	7	11	–2
Manufactured other products	221	5	1	5	1	–	2	–	3	–	–	14	–	–	–	1	–	30	5	2	69	–2
Shipbuilding, automotive, railways, etc.	79	1	–	2	1	–	–	–	1	–	–	1	–	1	1	–	–	7	–	1	15	
Storage	58	–	–	–	–	–	–	–	–	–	–	–	–	–	–	–	–	–	–	–	–	

Source: Azzam, 1988: 139.

The government of Saudi Arabia opted for joint ventures with foreign companies on the basis of financial and managerial shares due to their marketing experience and capacities to market the country's products internationally (especially petrochemicals). The involvement of large foreign companies was expected to ensure proper execution and operation of the projects, the production of high quality industrial products, and their disposal in international marketing networks.

Apart from technology transfer, providing management, technical skills and capital, the foreign partner has to market most of a plant's output. 'Joint-venture partners, of course, are expected to market much of the oil products and petrochemical output.... in Saudi Arabia agreements require that not less than 65 per cent of output in petrochemical projects be marketed by their joint-venture partners' (McHale, 1983: 107). The clear importance of the joint venture system to industrial development in the Kingdom can be seen in Table 5.3. The table reflects foreign participation in joint ventures by nationality and industrial sector in 1985. It indicates the variety of technology and experiences from the whole globe that industrial sectors in the country can benefit from.

EXPORTS AND IMPORTS OF MANUFACTURED GOODS

Exports

Table 5.4 gives an overview of manufactured exports 1988–90, classified by industrial origin. Mining quarry (mainly crude oil) dominates the export structure (78.7 per cent in 1990). It reflects also the declining share of processed goods for final use from 33.2 per cent in 1988 to 20.7 per cent in 1990. Since 1991 the oil sector has also dominated the exports bill of Saudi Arabia.

The markets for Saudi petroleum and petroleum products (including crude oil, petroleum refining and gas) in 1992 were: US, 20 per cent; Japan, 18 per cent; Singapore, 5 per cent; France, 5 per cent; South Korea, 5 per cent (NTDB, 1996: 1). The main market for Saudi chemicals is the EC countries. India and China import 60 per cent of Saudi

Table 5.4 Exports by industrial origin 1988–90 (% of total value)

	1988	1989	1990
TOTAL EXPORTS	100	100	100
Agriculture	1.2	1.1	0.6
Mining Quarry	65.6	70.6	78.7
Manufacturing	33.2	28.2	20.7
Food Beverages, Tobacco	0.4	0.4	0.3
Textiles	0.4	0.3	0.2
Wood	0.0	0.0	0.0
Paper & Paper Products	0.3	0.3	0.2
Chemicals	29.0	24.2	17.6
Non-Metal minerals	0.1	0.2	0.2
Basic Metals	0.6	0.8	0.5
Metal Manufacturing	2.2	2.0	1.6
Other Manufacturing	0.1	0.1	0.2

Source: UN Dept. for Economic and Social Information and Policy Analysis, Statistical Office, 1994.

fertilizers. Building materials exports appear largely confined to the region, and are now experiencing a slump because of the fall in oil prices.

Imports

Table 5.5 indicates the high degree to which Saudi Arabia depended on manufactured imports in 1988–90. Import growth was a necessary factor for the development of the Saudi economy, since the endogenous supply was insufficient to meet the growing demand. In 1984, imports were 12.3 per cent lower than in 1983, and in 1985 were 37 per cent lower than in 1984 (UNIDO, 1986: 24). The decline in the value of imports of base metals and a few other products was attributed mainly to two factors: the drop in the prices of imported iron, metal products and wood products by 20 per cent; and the increase in the local production of certain items such as iron (UNIDO, 1986: 24). Machinery and transport equipment imports also decreased sharply in 1984.

The shift in commodities shares in imports was accompanied by a shift in the geographical origin of imports. Japan,

Table 5.5 Imports by broad economic category, 1988–90 (% of total value)

	1988	1989	1990
TOTAL IMPORTS	100	100	100
FOOD, BEVERAGES	13.4	14.5	13.0
Primary	8.3	8.9	6.9
For Industry	4.7	5.1	2.8
For Households	3.6	3.8	4.1
Processed	5.1	5.6	6.1
For Industry	0.5	0.5	0.3
For Households	4.6	5.1	5.7
INDUSTRIAL SUPPLIERS	23.7	22.9	25.4
Primary	1.1	1.4	1.3
Processed	22.7	21.5	24.2
FUELS	0.2	0.3	0.3
Primary	0.0	0.0	0.0
Processed	0.2	0.3	0.2
Motor Spirit	0.0	0.1	0.0
Other	0.2	0.2	0.2
MACHINERY, EQUIPMENT	15.1	16.1	15.0
Capital Equipment	10.3	11.9	10.5
Parts	4.8	4.2	4.6
TRANSPORT	17.1	22.1	24.2
Passenger Cars	–	–	6.4
Other	9.0	8.8	3.6
Industrial	8.9	8.7	3.5
Non-Industrial	0.1	0.1	0.1
Parts	8.1	13.3	14.2
CONSUMER GOODS	23.7	23.1	21.7
Durable	9.0	7.6	6.6
Semi-Durable	9.4	10.3	9.1
Non-Durable	5.4	5.1	6.1
	6.7	1.1	0.4

Source: UN; Dept. for Economic and Social Information and Policy Analysis; Statistical Division, 1994.

for instance, replaced the USA as the largest exporter to Saudi Arabia in 1984–5. The share of the Western European countries in Saudi imports was increased from 38.3 per cent in 1980–1 to 38.7 per cent. In the period 1992–3, the Saudi imports were machinery and equipment, chemicals, foodstuffs, motor vehicles and textiles, and the exporters by share were US, 21 per cent; Japan, 14 per cent; UK, 11 per cent; Germany, 8 per cent; Italy, 6 per cent; France, 5 per cent (NTDB, 1996: 1).

INDUSTRIAL LABOUR FORCE

In spite of the massive investment in industry, the industrial labour force remains a small proportion of the total force. The industrial sector accounted for 7 per cent of total Saudi employment in 1991 (Looney, 1992: 213). This was attributed mainly to the low participation of nationals in the industrial labour force and because of high capital-intensive ratios.

In the absence of official statistics about non-Saudis working in industry, it can still be said that the majority of the workers in Saudi industrial plants are foreigners. For example, 'for the Saudi Transformers Company, associated with the Belgium company Pauwels International, only the general manager is Saudi. The plant, the quality control engineer, and the head of maintenance and engineering are all Belgian. The production engineer is from the United Kingdom. The 120 technical staff are Philippians. Alupco, the Aluminum Products Company in Dammam, employs 800 to 1000 Indians and Pakistanis. Most of the production staff at Zamel Steel Building Company are Philippians' (Wells, 1986: 281).

The dominant presence of foreign workers in Saudi industrial labour force, combined with other factors, have led to slow industrial growth in addition to high industrial production costs. This fact has resulted in reducing their competitiveness in both domestic and international markets.

In summing up this part, it seems that, despite government's efforts to achieve the goal of diversification through industrialization, the kingdom has not reached its target. It still exhibits many of the characteristics of a single-commodity based economy. The country still largely relies on a single source of export earnings, i.e. oil, with petroleum products as the major export item. Data available show that since the end of 1991 petroleum and petroleum products have contributed an average of around 40 per cent of nominal GDP, 75 per cent of government revenue and more than 90 per cent of export receipts.

This also can be seen in the smallness of the size of the manufacturing sector and its share of GDP and employment. Its contribution to GDP in 1991 was less than 8 per cent (MEED, 1995: 75), 7 per cent of total Saudi employment in the same year (Looney, 1992: 213) and increased to only 8 per cent in 1994 (EIU, 1996: 20).

PROBLEMS OF INDUSTRIALIZATION IN SAUDI ARABIA

Due to a combination of different factors, industrial progress in Saudi Arabia has been slow and often extremely costly, relative to the gains achieved by other developing countries, especially those in East and South-east Asia. This section will examine some of the internal and external factors the Kingdom of Saudi Arabia is encountering in its attempts at further industrialization.

Internal Factors

Problems related to Planning and Feasibility Studies
Although this section will undertake an evaluation of the nature of the process (problems) of industrialization in Saudi Arabia, it is important to recognize that the process has taken place over a very short period of time, and thus the effect of industrial development on the economic and social growth in the country is not easy to quantify. In fact, industrialization in Saudi Arabia has not been a long historical process but took off as a result of a sudden inflow of cash into the economy which can be attributed to the immense rise in oil prices during the 1960s, and to a great extent in the early 1970s. Consequently, the process of industrialization has depended on external rather than internal dynamics. According to Al-Maojil (1986: 11–12),

> The fact that industrialization has been an external rather than internal process for the societies of the Gulf resulted

in a false understanding of the true meaning of industrialization based on a confusion between the theory of industrialization in its broad sense and the practical process of installing industrial plants through turnkey contracts with foreign construction and engineering companies. Factories set up in the Gulf on this turnkey basis belong to the region in a geographical sense, but the existence and continued functioning of the factories is dependent on external factors. In other words, the process of industrialization in the Gulf has tended to be a geographical rather than an historical phenomenon.

This trend, together with several recent assessments of Saudi industrialization, according to Looney (1988: 485 and 1994: 213), suggest that:

1. Investments have been largely in projects seeking to utilize locally available raw materials. Basic industries have been created in isolation without the vital intermediate transsectoral industries which in time might allow the growth of a self-perpetuating industrial base.
2. Industrial development began as a function of factors unrelated to the socioeconomic reality of the Kingdom. It depended mainly on the need to use the flared associated gas and accumulating capital. As a result, the pace of the process of industrialization was dictated by external conditions and not by the needs and capabilities of domestic society. This led to heavy dependence on foreign manpower, expertise, management and technology.
3. Sudden, easy access to wealth created a consumer-oriented society in which the relationship between productivity and reward largely disappeared. Many investment decisions were based on overly optimistic economic assumptions. The decisions were often speculative rather than based on long-term economic viability. The post-1982 oil revenue decline significantly changed the relative factor proportions from those in existence after 1973–4.

Cost of Production and Size of Domestic Market
The high cost of imported intermediate material and equipment as well as the dependence on expensive expatriates, increase further the average cost of production and render

locally-produced import substitution commodities less competitive. The small size of the domestic market and the low forward and backward linkages of industries have worked as obstacle for industrial development.

The low price of competitive imports, the consumer's preferences, and the dumping policies followed by certain countries exporting to the Kingdom have worked as obstacles in the context of the development of industrialization in the country. Several exporters have adopted cut-price policies to preserve their market in the Kingdom, even if their profit margins would be drastically reduced.

In the case of the private sector, the (mostly light) industries are sensitive to a level of government spending which depends highly on fluctuating oil revenues, since government funded or supported projects provide the basis for demand for many light industrial products. By the end of 1983, for instance, and due to huge reduction in oil prices and government expenditure, ten private sector factories had closed, and some forty enterprises were reporting serious problems in meeting financial obligations or launching marketing campaigns (MERI, 1985: 87).

Natural Resources
Oil and gas have been the two most predominant resources in the country for the last two decades, and are likely to remain so in the foreseeable future.

Agricultural production in the country is restricted by a number of limitations such as official negligence, nature of land tenure, availability of fertile land and shortage of water and labour. Only 2 per cent of the total land area (800,000 square miles) is arable, where there is sufficient rainfall. In addition to the high cost of desalination of salt water for irrigation, there is the cost to construct dams to create more controlled watering conditions. There is over-consumption of underground aquifers (85–90 per cent of the Kingdom's water consumption is by agriculture alone), creating the danger of fast depletion of the source. The environmentalists estimate the lifespan of these aquifers to be 15–30 years at current rates of consumption (EIU,1996: 41). Saudi Arabia thus does not have an agricultural sector that could complement the development of the industrial sector.

The Manpower Shortage

The absence of an adequate skilled local labour force (both men and women), represents a critical challenge with regard to industrial development. The composition of the Saudi labour force is highly dominated by foreigners. The industrial labour force will remain a small percentage of the total labour force because of its high capital–labour ratio on one hand, and on the other, the disinclination to very formal or structured work, high rate of illiteracy, inability of the education system to provide adequate technical skills, and low participation of women in the labour force. The negative domestic social attitude towards manual and technical jobs has led to total dependency on the migrant labour which dominates the industrial sector. The cost of expatriates combined with other factors have led to high industrial production costs, 'the cost of engineers, technicians and workers required... is significantly high as compared to that in the US. The medium annual salary for scientists and engineers in the US is about $30,000 while the same US professionals in Saudi Arabia cost about $60,000' (Masood, 1988: 58).

Technology

Since capital intensive industrial projects usually involve a high level of technology and require a skilled labour force, the execution of projects in the Gulf countries has been based on joint ventures or turnkey agreements, in which the foreign partner is usually for providing the feasibility study, technical design, importation of machinery and equipment. After the execution of the projects the foreign partner is normally responsible for its operation, management, marketing of the products, and also responsible for training of the indigenous.

Karam (in Ghanem, 1992) criticizes this type of agreement in that they do not permit the local partner to be involved in the various stages of the establishment of the project and to benefit from the transfer of technology in the process. 'Whether a project is a joint-venture or of the turn-key type, the foreign side of the contract controls all technology matters. What is transferred is technology outputs in the form of imported equipments and foreign experts. Actual technology, that is information, is not transferred except on the narrowest scale possible, and even then it is usually passed by the foreign company to its foreign employees working on the project' (Ghanem, 1992: 104).

In fact, transfer of technology, through a joint ventures system or turnkey contracts, and by a cluster of diversified migrant groups, is highly handicapped by the weakness and inefficiency of universities and higher education institutions in Saudi Arabia, and other Gulf countries which emphasize quantity rather than quality.

External Factors: Problems related to Marketing Overseas

High Competition
Saudi Arabia is trying to industrialize itself at a time when there are many well-established industrialized countries marketing their products in international markets – for example, the NICs (newly industrialized countries), North American, the EC, India, etc. This fact leaves very limited opportunities for Saudi Arabia to direct the orientation of its industrialization towards export. If Saudi Arabia wishes to expand export, it should be ready to achieve high efficiency in terms of the cost and quality of its industrial goods.

Protectionism
Saudi industrial products (export-oriented industries) have been facing serious marketing problems as a result of protectionist measures adopted by the European Community, the USA and Japan, which in turn hinder the development of industrialization in the Kingdom. The reasons behind the protectionist measures can be grouped as follows.

1) The impact of new petrochemical products in the mid-1980s from the Gulf in the world market has been overdramatized. Several European countries and the United States called for tariff shelters. They argued that petrochemical exports from the Gulf are the result of subsidized capital and feedstock prices (MERI, 1985: 87). Prices competition was interpreted as 'dumping' and the EC commission was asked to set quotas and impose tariffs on petrochemicals imported from the Middle East. As a result, in 1985, the European Economic Community (EC) imposed 13.4 per cent customs duties on polyethylene from Saudi Arabia,

claiming that the Saudi exports of this product exceeded 15 per cent of annual EC consumption in the first half of 1985 (Azzam, 1988: 143–5).

2) In terms of other export markets, the US legislature has several forms of protectionist tariff at its disposal, some of which are mandatory and some of which can only be imposed following complaints by US manufacturers of unfair competition likely to endanger their livelihood. According to Looney and Winterford (1992: 587), Saudi Arabian heavy industries have run into opposition from their American counterparts on just such grounds based on the allegation that the 60 per cent of capital costs provided in the form of a soft-term loans by Riyadh's Public Investment Fund represents an 'unfair' subsidy.

High Costs of Export-oriented Industrial Goods
The low cost of natural gas used as a feedstock in the petrochemical industry is offset by several burdens on Saudi industries, including the cost of transport to the petrochemical importing countries, the high capital cost of the industries, the high cost of managing the projects, the rapid rate of depreciation, and high expatriate wages. In addition, Saudi petrochemical products, produced mainly from natural gas, are largely basic products. Intermediate petrochemicals require many other components which are not currently manufactured in the Kingdom and are therefore imported from abroad. The basic petrochemicals which are exported are themselves feedstock for final petrochemicals which are in turn exported back in large quantities from the EC to Saudi Arabia.

Inefficiency of the Marketing System
Saudis believe that foreign equity participation (in the form of joint ventures) in their industrialization would assure market access to the products. Unfortunately, this has been found to be partly true only in the cases of Japanese and Taiwanese companies. Thus, for example, when the Taiwanese government issued a decree banning imports of urea, it exempted the Al-Jubail Fertilizer Company (SAMAD), in which the Taiwan Fertilizer Company is the joint venture partner (Looney and Winterford, 1992: 586–587).

From the foregoing discussion it becomes evident that the challenge facing industrial development in Saudi Arabia is developing the ability to produce and sell competitively, despite the limited raw material base, manpower shortage, high labour and management costs, a restricted home and overseas markets, and the limited tariff protection offered by the tariff system which leads to the dumping of foreign products in the Saudi market. Beside that, the Kingdom needs to come up with a coherent industrial strategy if it wants to emerge as one of the top industrialized countries.

But the industrialization strategy, to be sustainable, needs to help in the growth of internal dynamics. Therefore Saudi Arabia requires industrialization to develop its human resources for the post-oil era. Hence, the training of the people is the most important long-term consideration in the industrialization strategy of the Kingdom, since the non-renewable oil wealth should be utilized to create a productive nation that can support itself without oil in the distant future.

REFERENCES

Al-Hajjar, B. and Presley, J., 1993. Managerial Inefficiency in Small Manufacturing Business in Saudi Arabia: A Constraint upon Economic Development. *Industry and Development* No. 23. UN Industrial Development Organization, Vienna; a UNIDO Publication.

Al-Moajil, H. Abdulla, 1986. Industrialization in the Arab States. *Arab Gulf Industry, 1986.*

AOGD (Arab Oil and Gas Directory), 1996. *Saudi Arabia: Industry and Development.* Arab Petroleum Research Centre.

Azzam, T. Henry, 1988. *The Gulf Economies in Transition.* Macmillan Press, London.

Bhardwaj, J. S., 1994. Technical Report: *National Strategy for the Development of Down-Stream Petrochemical Industries in the Developing Countries.* UNIDO, Vienna.

EIU, 1985 *Saudi Arabia: Country Report. The Economist* Intelligence Unit Ltd.

EIU, 1995 and 1996. *Saudi Arabia: Country Profile. The Economist* Intelligence Unit Ltd., London.

Europa, 1995. *The Europa World Year Book 1995.* Europa Publications Ltd., London.

Europa, 1996. *The Middle East and North Africa 1996.* Europa Publications Ltd., London.

Ghanem, M. A. Shihab, 1992. *Industrialization in the United Arab Emirates.* Ashgate Publishing, Avebury, UK.

Kirkpatrick, C. H., et al., 1984. *Industrial Structure and Policy in Less Developed Countries.* George Allen and Unwin, London.

Looney, E. Robert, 1988. The Impact of Technology Transfer on the Structure of the Saudi Arabian Labour Force. *Journal of Economic Issues,* vol. 22, no. 2 (June).

Looney, E. Robert, 1994. *Manpower Policies and Development in the Persian Gulf Region.* Prueger, Westport, Conn.

Looney, E. Robert and Winterford, D., 1992. Patterns of Arab Gulf Exports: Implications for Industrial Diversification of Increased Inter-Arab Trade. *German Journal for Politics and Economics of the Middle East,* vol. 33, no. 4, 579–97.

Masood, R., 1988. *Economic Diversification and Development in Saudi Arabia.* National Institute of Science, Technology and Development Studies (CSIR), New Delhi.

McHale, T. R., 1983. The Hydrocarbon Processing Industry in the GCC – Its Economic and Political Future in a Changing World Marketplace. *The Journal of Energy and Development,* vol. 8, (1982–3), 99–108.

MEED (Middle East Economic Digest), 1995. *Saudi Arabia: Towards an Industrial Society.* Middle East Economic Digest (MEED), Profile no. 5.

MEED (Middle East Economic Digest), 1996. Saudi Arabia – Practical Guide. London.

MERI (Middle East Research Institute), 1985. MERI Report: *Saudi Arabia.* Middle East Research Institute, University of Pennsylvania. Croom Helm Ltd.

Montague, C., 1985. *Industrial Development in Saudi Arabia: Opportunities for Joint Ventures.* Special Report, Committee for Middle East Trade (COMET), Geneva, February.

NTDB, 1996. *National Trade Data Bank: The Export Connection.* World Fact Book, 1996.

Saudi Commerce and Economic Review, 1996. No. 22 (Feb.).

UNIDO (United Nations Industrial Development Organization), 1986. *Industrial Development in the Arab Countries.* United Nations Industrial Development Organization. Selected Documents Presented to the Symposium on Industrial Development in the Arab Countries, Kuwait, 1–10 March 1966.

Wells, A. Donald, 1986. The Effects of Saudi Industrialization on Employment. *Journal of Energy and Development,* vol. 11, no. 2.

Part II
Human Resources and Gender Relations

6 Population Policies in the Countries of the Gulf Cooperation Council
Baquer Salman Al-Najjar

INTRODUCTION

The main objective of this study is to identify the measures, regulations and laws which form the population policies of the countries which belong to the the Gulf Cooperation Council. Also, it will look for factors behind these measures and regulations and their implications for the size and the structure of local as well as expatriate communities. However, a study of regional population policies relates more to the foreign population, since most of the measures and regulations adopted have been prompted by the Gulf governments to limit its size and influence. This was deemed necessary to consolidate power, to preserve identity and to 'protect' so-called interests and rights of the indigenous population.[1] To assure the latter objectives, the Gulf countries adopted various discriminatory policies against their foreign communities. In 1982, the population problem was considered by the General Secretary of GCC to be 'the greatest problem facing the council'.[2] Policies declared and undeclared, as well as information and experience were generally shared by all members. Such cooperation was considered important to 'protect the rights of the migrants and their dependents as well as the interests and security of the host countries'.[3]

These policies were not restricted to maintaining an optimal ratio of expatriates to the local population or to increasing the fertility rate among locals, but were enacted in order to strengthen either the coalition between various religious, tribal and ethnic groups, or to favour one particular group against others, depending, of course, on internal socio-political factors. Concern over the size of the native population in spite of economic implications has become an important statement of military and political power. In Oman as well as other Gulf states, the size of the villages were seen by the local population until recently in terms of 'numbers of guns'.[4] In other words, the number of inhabitants meant the number of active supporters. The larger the tribe, the more powerful it became. This explains in part why family planning was forbidden in Saudi Arabia and why Saudi Arabia has suppressed the publication of correct census figures, which are guarded as zealously as military secrets.

POPULATION INCREASE OR CONTROL?: POLICIES AND ATTITUDES TOWARDS THE EXPATRIATE POPULATION

The wide importation of Bedouins from Jordan, Iraq and Syria to Kuwait and also from Jordan and Syria to Bahrain, and Yemenis to Abu Dhabi, were prompted by concern over the small size of the local population *vis-à-vis* non-local population, or the small size of the ruling family *vis-à-vis* non- tribal groups. Moreover, the importation of Yemenis to Abu Dhabi in addition to its oil wealth, has enhanced its political weight with respect to other emirates of the Trucial Coast. Because the native Gulf population has had its fragile existence continually threatened by powerful neighbouring countries, i.e., Iraq and Iran, the Gulf countries have tended to seek support from Pakistan with its large population, post-Shah Iran (under the umbrella of an 'Islamic Coalition'), and more recently Egypt under the pretext of protecting 'Arab Sovereignty' and maintaining 'a moderate political stance'. When Saddam Hussein invaded Kuwait in August 1990 they again turned to the USA and Europe for protection.

Another factor which played an effective role in promoting a drive to increase the number of nationals was the large presence of foreigners which in some cases, such as Abu Dhabi, exceeded 80 per cent of total population. This presence has been viewed as a potential element of political destabilization, especially with regard to some Arab communities, and recently the Shia community. This is most obvious in the case of Kuwait, which hosts a large Palestinian community estimated at 400,000 and quite a large Shia community originating from Iraq and Iran. Relations between each of these communities and local governments have passed through periods of strain, because they have been blamed for internal political troubles. A recent report described the situation in Kuwait and elsewhere in the Gulf region as follows: 'The role of Kuwait security organizations increased substantially in 1984, particularly with regard to the non-citizen community. Conscious of being a minority in their own country, the Kuwaitis' sense of vulnerability has been heightened by increased political turbulence in the region... Increased attention to law and order is viewed by some Kuwaitis as a means to protect their society against the threat they perceive to Kuwait's moral and social values from a large foreign population'.[5]

This situation pushed the governments of the Gulf towards a policy of population balance between the two segments of this society. A fifty-fifty formula of locals to expatriates was one of the main slogans in the Kuwait national assembly election in 1985; it was also one of the central issues in the country's 1985–90 plan. The demand to balance the Kuwaiti population was only made possible after the liberation of Kuwait in February 1991. The number of Palestinians was reduced to 30,000 and Iraqis to 1,000. The government crackdown in May 1992 on illegal immigrants was initially directed towards the remainder of "unliked" foreign communities: Palestinians, Iraqis, Yemenis and Sudanese. It was expected that these communities would lessen by 40 per cent.[6] In other Gulf states, calls were made for a reduction in the number of foreigners. Asians were the particular subject of these slogans in the UAE, Qatar and to some extent Bahrain.[7]

A third factor played an important role in the pressure for measures which will control the growth of the foreign population, and emphasize the need for an increase in the number of locals in the unsettled political atmosphere in the area since the overthrow of the Shah's regime in Iran. By the end of the 1970s regional political events produced new expressions of unrest and insecurity, which the entire region had not as yet experienced before or even during the Nasse era. Between February 1979 and the end of that year, the Shah was overthrown and the clergymen seized power. A few months later mass rallies and demonstrations took place in various Gulf centres to support the Islamic republic in Iran and calling for the return of democracy in Kuwait and Bahrain and some kind of political participation elsewhere in the Gulf. From 1979 to 1981 there was unrest among the Shia peoples but this was not the case in all Gulf countries, varying according to the size and position of the respective communities. In November 1979 the region was rocked by the attack and the occupation of the Mosque in Mecca by the Juhayman group, which included some Gulf nationals.[8] Other internal security incidents added to the sense of siege: in Kuwait, government and large company offices were either bombed or attacked. Assaults were also made on offices and companies belonging to Iran and Iraq. The offices, companies and embassies of France and the United States also came under attack. In July 1984 traditional Kuwaiti coffee shops were bombed and a number of Kuwaiti citizens died, and an assassination attempt was made on the Amir of Kuwait in May 1985. Also in more recent times planes owned by Kuwaiti Airlines have been hijacked during 1986 and again in May 1988. In the latter hijacking incident, which lasted for two weeks, the Shia 'Islamic Jehad' group turned out to be responsible. During the end of 1981 a plot was discovered to destabilize the political structure in Bahrain. Rumours continued about the discovery of weapons and an Iranian inspired underground group. The blame for all these events lay with the Shia fundamentalists, and arrests among locals and deportation of expatriate Shias were frequent. Restrictions concerning the entry of Iranians, Iraqis and Lebanese was adopted by all the Gulf states. Talks took place to minimize the role and number of these nationalities, and newspaper articles appeared calling on the Gulf governments to "get rid off the traitors and those who have no sense of gratitude and loyalty". *Al-Azminah Al-Arabia* (the *Arabian Times*) and the *Al-Khaleiji* were the leading local magazines adopting this stance. These events no doubt contributed effectively to limiting the number of new entrants from these communities and restricted their employment. It also meant that some locals of Persian origin or Arab immigrants in key positions were given early retirement. Also, some members of the Iranian, Iraqi and Lebanese communities were deported due to their actual or perceived violation of internal security. Occasionally members of the Pakistani community or citizens of the other Gulf states were deported on the same grounds.[9])

As a result of the Iraqi invasion of Kuwait attention was once again focused on the presence of Iraqi, Palestinian and Yemeni communities. Restrictions were placed on Palestinians, Iraqis, Sudanese and the Yemenis who were now practically non-existent in Kuwait. These restrictions were also imposed on their presences and entry to other Gulf states. Around 800,000 Yemenis who had been long-term residents in Saudi Arabia were then expelled. 200 Palestinian families were asked to leave Qatar. Other Gulf countries followed suit by either asking the Palestinians and Iraqis to leave or denying them work and residence permits. The Gulf crisis seems to have brought a solution to the problem of Arab migrants in the Gulf, but on the other hand increased the presence of Asian labour, especially in Kuwait, which traditionally used to be, before the Iraqi invasion, the major recipient of Arab labour. James Akins, a former US Ambassador to Saudi Arabia, commented as follows: 'The problem of foreign workers in Saudi Arabia seems to have been solved already: the Palestinians, Yemenis and Jordanians will rapidly be phased out. They will be replaced by Asians, preferably non-Muslim, of course some Egyptian and Syrian workers will be hired but not many and not on a long term basis'.[10]

The relations between labour exporting and labour importing countries, and especially the dispute over common borders, have been affected by inter-Arab politics which directly or indirectly influences the size and treatment of migrant communities in the area. For example, during the Qassim era in Iraq from 1958 to 1963 and more recently in 1973, border disputes between Kuwait and Iraq led the Kuwaiti authorities to seal off a whole Kuwaiti village, Al-Doha, due to the large presence of Iraqi families. Kuwait also adopted some tough measures to restrict the entry and employment of Iraqis in Kuwait.[11] Furthermore, in April 1986 when conflict over islands of Huwar erupted between Bahrain and Qatar, Qatar adopted tough measures on Bahrainis living in there. Bahraini newspapers wrote about the fact that there had been 200 or more Bahrainis working and studying in Qatar who were now deported. Others who were working in the public sector were asked not turn up for work for some time.[12]

The fourth factor which pushed the governments towards adopting a policy of substitution of nationals and a corresponding reduction in number of migrants was the pressure of strong public opinion. Public opinion often constituted the prime moving factor behind governments which relaxed or restricted the stay and employment of immigrant groups and pressed for more privileges for the locals almost by virtue of their citizenship. For example, the increase in the demand for housemaids by Kuwaiti families has pressured the Kuwaiti government to allow the entry of 200,000 Asian migrant workers between May to December 1991, constituting almost 40 per cent of the total foreign community in Kuwait.[13]

In general the relationship between the local population and migrant groups was somewhat strained with mutual resentment stemming from both residential segregation and discriminatory policies in terms of employment and social privileges. Local newspapers have always described the migrants as 'money grabbers who take away our money and leave' or as 'violators of internal security'.[14]

A Kuwaiti newspaper said the following: 'We have to stop naturalising more foreign workers, they have no love for Kuwait and their main objective is to gain as much as they can from our country's wealth. Thus they acquire [Gulf] nationality towards enjoying more social and economic rights like their [native] counterparts with whom they compete'.[15]

One would assume that this resentful attitude towards migrant communities would apply only to non-Arab groups, whereas an examination of the actual situation reveals that what applies to non-Arab migrants also applies in differing degrees to Arab migrant groups. Birks and Sinclair talk about the case of Saudi Arabia as follows:

> Migrant workers are ever more necessary to the economy but the contemporaneously fear grows that the immigrant communities will increase and eventually outnumber the Saudi Arabians themselves. Concern is only expressed over the number of Indians and Pakistanis present but despite a veneer of Arab solidarity, Saudi Arabian nationals feel a detachment from Palestinians, a lack of respect for Yemenis

and mistrust and dislike of Egyptians, all of whom, they feel, are benefiting inordinately from Saudi Arabian development.[16]

Gulf governments responded to widespread public opinion concerning migrant workers by adopting tough measures which favoured the native population over immigrants and inevitably slowed down the process of naturalization.

In spite of the reasons mentioned above, it was the economic factor which was the most effective deterrent to growth of the expatriate population. Over-expansion of economic activities in the late 1970s accelerated the demand for foreign labour while, conversely, economic recession during the second half of the eighties slowed down the demand for foreign workers. Calls were made by the local newspapers and officials to expel the surplus foreign labour as fears of unemployment problems started to emerge among locals. In Saudi Arabia, for example, the Five Year Plan for 1983–8 suggested that some 600,000 foreign workers should leave the country during the life of the plan. The UAE announced that by the end of 1987 it would have already rid itself of some 20,000 of the foreign workforce. Other countries from the Gulf also witnessed some reduction in the employment of foreign labour, especially in the construction and services sectors, which were badly affected by the 'Second Oil Shock' in 1983.[17] A recent official study concerning the UAE has suggested that the continuing economic welfare of the native population would depend on a major reduction in the size of the migrant population: '... the UAE can usually restructure its growth model by reducing the number of immigrants and therefore, of its total population – thus reducing the exploitation rate of its oil revenues and ensuring a much longer period of wealth to its future generations of citizens without any appreciable loss of benefits occruing to them'.[18]

Others have cited the process of replacement and an increase in the participation of women in the labour force as factors contributing to reshaping the structure of the labour force, and hence the population as a whole. In other words, a greater degree of local participation in the labour force would be mirrored by a greater reduction in non-nationals' share in the total population.

Naturalization was another effective way of increasing the local population, particularly in the case of Kuwait, which granted citizenship in the 1960s to some Persians and Bedouins brought from Iraq and Saudi Arabia. The motive behind this was to increase the political support for the ruling family via those naturalized, against opposition groups and the competing merchant class. Abu Dhabi adopted the same method when it naturalized a large group of North Yemenis but with the aim of strengthening its power *vis-à-vis* other emirates in the Trucial Coast. Recent political events in the region contributed effectively in reducing the rate of naturalization among expatriate groups, particularly the Arabs of the Levant and those of the Persian region. Nevertheless, natural expansion remains the most effective method for the governments of the Gulf to increase their respective populations. This policy is being given a boost by Islamic revivalism, which encourages the new generation to practice polygamy and emphasizes the benefit of a large family.[19]

An important demographic feature which can be drawn from Table 6.1 is the sharp contrast in terms of sex composition between nationals and the foreign community. The sex ratio among immigrants is generally disproportionate (particularly among certain ethnic groups). This disproportionate sex ratio varies from country to country. In 1994 it was highest in Oman where the ratio is 4 males to 1 female. Kuwait

Table 6.1 National and non-national population in the Gulf by gender (1994)

	Nationals			Non-nationals			Total		
	Female	Male	Total	Female	Male	Total	Female	Male	Total
Bahrain	171	175	346	61	143	204	232	318	550
Kuwait	332	339	671	294	655	949	626	994	1,620
Oman	742	769	1,511	112	426	538	854	1,195	2,049
Qatar	64	65	129	122	281	403	186	346	532
S. Arabia	6,463	6,590	13,053	1,564	3,563	5,127	8,027	10,153	18,180
UAE	307	321	628	560	962	1,522	867	1,283	2,150

Source: UN – Economic and Social Commission for Western Asia (1995), Demographic and Related Socio-economic Data Sheets, No. 8.

before the war was the main recipient of Arab migrants who were usually accompanied by their dependants – which explains why the natural increase among Arab communities in Kuwait was the highest in the Gulf region.[20]

However, one may argue that the expulsion of Palestinians and also Iraqis along with some other Arab nationalities, who have a tendency to familial migration, may serve the final Kuwaitis goal of balancing their population. A goal of 40 per cent to 60 per cent of the entire population has been set. Nevertheless, one should note that their goal will be obstructed by the fact that Kuwait alongside other Gulf states cannot avoid depending on their 'guest workers'. In fact Kuwait after its liberation faced a large shortage of labour in all categories (skilled and non-skilled). A call to import Arab and Asian labour has once again brought the figure to over 50 per cent of the total population of Kuwait. Furthermore, it is very important to state that any substantial reduction in foreign workers means a serious blow to private housing and the commercial sector, which are largely owned by the Kuwaiti ruling commercial tribal coalition. Given all of these factors Kuwait and most other Gulf states have a very long way to go before they can make a 'substantial reduction' to their expatriate community. Their economic as well as political survival is based solely on the presence of foreign labour.

The highly disproportionate gender ratio among migrant communities may be attributed to the following:

1. Most of the recruited foreign labour for the last ten years were semi- and non-skilled workers receiving very low wages, sometimes not exceeding $100 per month, who could not afford to bring their dependants with them. Due to financial difficulties some migrants found it impossible to be recruited with their families.
2. The introduction of strict immigration laws made it impossible to bring their families.

While it is a side-effect of the authorities' deliberate policy, the large presence of male migrants, unaccompanied by families, is a subject of public concern, and particularly for those living in the old parts of the city, because it is there that most of the single males usually live. Articles appeared in the newspapers accusing single immigrants, Asians in particular, of introducing new types of crime which had been previously unknown in the area.[21] Migrant labour in general has always been seen by a large proportion of the local population as being a carrier of diseases such as T.B., and Aids, and also as precipitating an element of destruction of the local heritage and traditional values. An article appeared in a Kuwaiti newspaper accusing these immigrants of disrupting the social life of natives in the old parts of the Kuwait City: 'the existence of large numbers of single immigrants in neighbouring houses is causing tremendous disturbances due to noise caused by them and the social restrictions they impose on the movement of our families' female members'.[22]

POPULATION POLICIES: POLITICS AND SOCIETY

Two different sets of population policies can be identified in most of the Gulf countries:

1. The policy of encouraging (albeit not necessarily publicly) the national population to maintain a high birth rate.
2. Measures and regulations which aim at controlling 'foreign settlements' in the area and hence reducing the number of particular foreign groups if possible.

Policies toward the National Population

It can be said that none of the GCC countries has, as such, a declared population policy with regard to their nationals. Nevertheless, there are a number of measures that promote an increase of fertility rate among the national population. One such measure is the provision of free and comprehensive health services. The high quality of health services in the area as a whole has led to a substantial decline in the rate of mortality. For example, the mortality rate Bahrain decreased among children aged five and under, from 25 per cent in the 1950s to 13.5 per cent in the 1960s, followed by 5.3 per cent in the 1970.[23] However, with more couples being educated there is a relative decrease in the fertility rate, especially among educated couples in Bahrain and Kuwait.

Another government policy that aims at increasing fertility among locals is a social allowance to encourage early marriages in Kuwait, Saudi Arabia and the UAE. For example, the Kuwaiti government grants 2,000 Kuwaiti dinars ($6,480) as a marriage allowance to a national marrying for the first time. Others, with the exception of Kuwait, Bahrain and the UAE, have introduced legislation which prevents male and female natives from marrying outsiders (unless they get permission). This stand may have a two-fold objective: first, to protect what is called 'the purity of Gulf heritage'; and secondly, to slow the losses among natives by reviving the idea of endogamy. This attitude has been strengthened over the last ten years or so and tends to hinder even intermarriage between different ethnic groups of the local population: Shia versus Sunni and tribal elements of the local population versus non-tribal.

It has also been suggested that the government housing programme aims at raising the birth rate among natives. In all the Gulf countries, with some differences, the governments sell houses at cost price or grant a plot of land on which to build. They also give long-term loans with low interest rates, which in the case of Bahrain is paid over 25 years, or without a cumulative interest rate in the case of Kuwait. In other countries, the national is obliged to pay only half or three-quarters of the cost. These facilities obviously are granted only to nationals and are denied to foreign labour.

Another government policy seen as encouraging large families among nationals has been the granting of social allowance to each child of any male head of household working in the public sector. While this system has been adopted by most of the Gulf countries, this privilege is restricted in these states to the natives. The social allowance granted for each child applies up to a maximum of three children in the case of Kuwait, Saudi Arabia, Qatar and the UAE. In general these measures have proved to be effective among certain strata and ethnic groups, and a tremendous increase has taken place in the size of the national population over the years. However, these measures contradict the views of newly emerging educated couples who prefer to have small families. Therefore, these measures seem to have gained most among the rural and Bedouin population rather than urban settlers and the educated. Social norms and customs appear to be the most influential factors among the former, while educational and economic factors are more important among the urban settlers.[24]

As has been mentioned before, naturalization has until recently been one of the most effective methods of increasing the local population. The process of granting local citizenship is sometimes influenced by internal events. The naturalization of Bedouins or others in Kuwait and elsewhere in the Gulf is sometimes aimed at balancing the distribution of power among different ethnic and religious groups. It further aims to enable the ruling 'institution' to administer and regulate any internal social conflict. By increasing the number of certain groups in relation to others, the intention is to weaken the bargaining position of some groups *vis-à-vis* the ruling institution and/or to expand the membership of certain groups at election times, as was the case in Kuwait during 1960s. The recent expulsion of over 100,000 unproven Kuwaitis (*Bedoon*) as a result of the Gulf crisis was also seen as a precautionary measure taken by the Kuwaiti regime to avoid any local pressure to naturalize the majority of a group who played a major role in the resistance during Iraqi occupation (August 1990 to February 1991). This group was seen as a potential supporter of Kuwaiti opposition groups, and it may have tipped the internal balance of power in favour of the opposition, especially during the time of the election for the Kuwait parliament in October 1992. Some of the Bedoon groups because they originally came from the southern parts of Iraq and Jordan, were accused of being collaborators with the Iraqi regime – particularly those who used to work in the lower strata jobs in the military and police forces (they constituted 75 per cent of the total).[25] Unfortunately their expulsion made the Kuwait military and police an institution of generals without an army. A Kuwaiti writer described this problem as follows: 'The problem that the Kuwaiti government will face after the expulsion of all its badoon police and military personnel is how to rebuild these security sectors with Kuwaiti officers only'.[26]

Finally, it can be concluded that none of the Gulf countries has formulated a comprehensive and explicit population policy. With the exception of Kuwait, which due to its internal problems raises the issue of population balance from time to time, this stance seems to be general and non-committal. Most Gulf countries' attitude to the population problem seems temporal and occasional, and influenced by internal and regional political events. None of them has taken seriously such important issues as the potential increase of unemployment among the national population, which was estimated at over 30,000 in 1991 in the case of Bahrain,[27] and the question of job opportunities for coming generations.

Policies toward Migrant Labour

Local legislation concerning the presence and employment of foreign labour has passed through different stages. Three types of legislation can be identified which have different roles and functions, and each of them is implemented or run by a different government body. However, the role of the Ministry of Labour is most prominent as it implements labour legislation which hands over control to the local market. Strict implementation of these laws and regulations differs from one ethnic group to another and from one strata to another. The legislation usually controls the movement of foreign workers within the local market. One of the most unfortunate types of legislation, which has often been misused, is the sponsorship system which can turn foreign labour, especially those working at lower strata jobs, into 'wage slaves': the migrant labourer has no freedom of movement within the local market. His freedom begins only when he steps out of the country. The sponsorship system has become a source of income for a number of influential people. The nationals are allowed to 'import' up to three people; sometimes the number can rise according to the influence and power of the local sponsor. Many of the Asian and Arab labourers were left to seek employment in the local market in return for a monthly payment to the sponsor which can reach $250.

To control the increase of foreign labour there are laws which give locals priority over non-natives in the field of employment. However, this section of the labour law has never been strictly implemented because merchants and contractors, gaining more influence over the labour market, obviously prefer for cost reasons to use foreign labour. But the proper implementation of this legislation may help to move the nationals from marginal jobs to more productive ones. This would correct the over-dependence on foreign labour and consequently alter the imbalance in the population. Fear of growing unemployment among nationals and its socio-political implications may force the Gulf governments, especially in the case of Bahrain, to press for more indigenization of work.

Another policy which aims at controlling the growth of the non-national population was the one adopted by all Gulf countries in 1982/3. It requires a non-national applying for entry visas for his/her family to have in addition to decent accommodation previously arranged, a minimum income of approximately $1,500 per month. However, many migrant labourers have managed to overcome these stipulations by presenting false information through the help of influential locals, or by seeking marriage with migrants of the same ethnic group working in the host country.

The decision of Saudi Arabia to adopt a quota system following the 1988 season of pilgrimage is another indication of the growing concern of local regimes over the politicization of foreign communities. Saudi Arabia was worried over the continuous attempts of pilgrims to stay in the country and acted upon this after the Iranian attempt to politicize the pilgrimage in 1986 and 1987. Because of this concern, the quota system was adopted in May 1988 by the Islamic Conference Organization and enacted by the Saudis during the 1988 pilgrimage. However, the Iranians were allowed to send more than their quota as soon as their relation with Saudi Arabia improved. This once again substantiated what has already been discussed, that politics play an effective role in formulating the Gulf governments' behaviour with regard to the presence of expatriate communities.

A further policy aimed at the containment of the foreign population is the prevention of foreign communities from having free social services such as health and education, or the imposition of high fees in return for their enjoyment of these facilities. For example, articles appeared in Kuwaiti newspapers asking the government to restrict admission to the school of medicine and engineering to national students only. In July 1991 the Minister of Education in Kuwait banned the admission of non-Kuwaiti students to government schools. This decision has put tremendous pressure on the parents of more than 15,000 Palestinian, Iraqi, Egyptian and Sudanese students, who have as a result had to leave school.[28] Saudi Arabia, due to economic difficulties, decided to impose a 30 per cent tax on the income of migrant labour in 1987. This decision prompted great discontent in the migrant communities and many planned to leave the country. The fear of losing foreign labour from key jobs drove Saudi Arabia to halt the implementation of its decision. From this one example, it is clear that the Gulf Countries cannot afford to get rid of foreign labour since national labour can neither quantitatively nor qualitatively run the affairs of their countries.

Thus one may question the validity and applicability of the recent call made by the Kuwaiti and other Gulf officials to reduce the presence of foreign labour in their countries. As I have already mentioned, the economic and social welfare of the area depends solely on the presence of migrant labour. The expulsion of Palestinians and Iraqis from Kuwait is now posing a major challenge for the government and the private sector. Their survival depends to a large extent on the presence of both Iraqis and Palestinians. A prominent figure from the Kuwait Chamber of Commerce commented as follows: 'One should start to question in a more rational way, who will replace the Palestinians in Kuwait and what kind of people they are. Would Asian labour play their economic, social and intellectual roles?'[29]

Kuwait has already started to complain about the performance of Egyptian and Asian labour. Egyptians and Philippinos were the first to complain about Kuwaiti maltreatment. The expulsion of the Palestinians and Iraqis in particular, who constituted the largest migrant group in Kuwait (400,000 and 200,000 respectively), will influence the future life of Kuwait for some time to come.

CONCLUSION

Clearly there is a lack of an explicit policy concerning population on both the local and regional levels in the Gulf area. There do exist a few regulations and rules which usually are only short-lived responses to present problems rather than studied, long-range policies. For example, when the UAE was badly affected by the sudden decline in oil prices in 1983–6, it started shipping 'un-needed' foreign labour back home in the hope that such a measure would alleviate domestic economic problems. More recently, when it started to gain back some of its economic strength, the UAE started recalling foreign labour. However, most importantly, political issues and concerns have been the determining factors underlying the changing attitudes of the Gulf governments towards the presence and employment of foreign labour. This was clear in their attitude towards Egyptians during the Nasser era, towards Palestinians in the late 1960s, and towards Shia of Iran, Iraq, Lebanon and elsewhere during the first years of the Iranian revolution in 1979. This was also clear during the Iran–Iraq war from 1980 to 1988 and more recently in the case of the Palestinians, Jordanians, Iraqis, Sudanese and Yemenis since the Iraqi occupation of Kuwait. In other words, politics and security rather than economics were and still are the main determinants of attitudes to the presence and employment of foreign labour. This political factor also applies to the manipulation of the national population, where the decision to increase the number or power of specific groups is a response to the internal power struggle between various ethnic and tribal factions or to external threat.

It is important to state that despite the continuous call for a significant reduction in the foreign communities, and the recent expulsion of Palestinians, Iraqis and Yemenis from Kuwait, Saudi Arabia and elsewhere in the Gulf, the need for them will continue for some years to come. The interest of powerful merchants, property owners and labour recruiters in addition to the economic and social welfare of the region depend on the presence of foreign communities. Surely they are to stay for an unforeseeable time to come.

NOTES

1. For more details on the historical development of the foreign community in the Gulf region see B. S. Al-Najjar, 'Employment

Policy in the Oil Companies of the Arabian Gulf Countries', *Arab Gulf Journal*, vol. XI, no. 48, October 1986.
2. Sharon Stanton Russel, *Uneasy Welcome: The Polictical Economy of Migration Policy in Kuwait*. Ph.D. dissertation, Massachussetts Institute of Technology, 1987, p. 224.
3. Ibid.
4. J. S. Birks, 'The Demographic Pattern in the Gulf', Paper presented at the Symposium on 'The Gulf and the Arab World', Centre for Gulf Studies, Exeter, July 1986, p. 6.
5. Russel, p. 222.
6. *Al-Hayat*, newspaper, 2 June 1992.
7. *Arab Times*, 19 January 1989 (Kuwait English newspaper).
8. Valerie York, 'The Gulf in 1980s' (Chatham House Paper no.6). The Royal Institute for International Affairs, London, 1980. See also Avi Plascov, *Security in the Persian Gulf 3: Modernization, Political Development and Stability* (London, Gower, 1982), p. 70.
9. Russel, op. cit., and see also Mardechai Abir, *Saudi Arabia in the Oil Era* (London, Croom Helm, 1988), pp. 152–8 and Shahram-Chubin et al., *Security in the Gulf* (London, Grower, 1982).
10. James E. Atkin, 'The New Arabia'. *Foreign Affairs*, Summer 1991, p. 213.
11. Abdullatif H. Al-Rumaihi, *The Dynamics of Kuwaiti Foreign Policy*. Ph.D. dissertation, University of Exeter, 1983, p. 301.
12. See, for example, anthony H. Codesman, *Western Strategic Interests in Saudi Arabia* (London, Croom Helm, 1987).
13. B.S. Al-Najjar, *Population in the Gulf* (Cairo Population Council, February 1992).
14. B. S. Al-Najjar, *Aspects of Labour Market Behaviour in an Oil Economy: A Study of Underdevelopment and Immigrant Labour in Kuwait*. Ph.D. dissertation, University of Durham, 1983, p. 254.
15. Ibid.
16. J. S. Birks and C. A. Sinclair, *Arab Manpower* (London, Croom helm, 1980), p. 116. See also Christine S. McNulty, 'An Evaluation of Saudi Arabia's Policies for Economic Diversification'. MA thesis, University of Durham, 1984.
17. B. S. Al-Najjar, 'Arab Return Migration in the Gulf Area', *Al-Mustqbal Al-Arabi*, no. 105, November 1987, p. 57. See also Russel, op. cit., and Nader Farjani, *Impact of Oil Prices Change on Employment in Oil Producing Countries* (Tanjah, Arab Employment Institute, 1986).
18. World Bank, *United Arab Emirates: Economic Development at a Crossroads* (Washington, DC, World Bank, 1983) p. 33.

19. There are continuing calls by Islamic groups to encourage polygamy and thereby increase the number of births in each family. See for example *Al-Watan* (Kuwaiti newspaper), 21 January 1984, and also *Al-Ayam* (Bahraini newspaper), 25 April 1989.
20. See for example United Nations, *Kuwait* (New York, 1988), pp. 23–4. This will mean that the Kuwaiti people will once again be a minority in their own country.
21. Abul Basit A. Mucti, "The Social Cost of Asian Labour in the Gulf", *Al-Mustaqbal Al-Arabi*, no. 37 (March, 1982), p. 49.
22. Al-Najjar, *Aspects of Labour Market Behaviour*, p. 238.
23. Yasser Al-Naser, 'Infant and Childhood Mortality in Relation to Socio-Economic, Health and Environment Aspects in Bahrain'. Ph.D. dissertation, School of Tropical Medicine, University of London, 1991.
24. United Nations, *Kuwait*.
25. Bedoons are estimated at 225,000. They are a very diverse group who moved to Kuwait at different stages from southern parts of Iraq and Jordan, northern parts of Saudi Arabia, Iran, Eastern Africa and India. Some of them moved to Kuwait as early as the 1920s and 1930s. A large proportion of them are of tribal origin from Iraq and Saudi Arabia. Most of them work in the lower strata jobs in the government or private sectors. The Kuwaiti authorities treat these people as non-Kuwaitis; they receive low salaries and are denied privileges that Kuwaitis enjoy with respect to housing, education and health. Many of them were left behind during the Iraqi occupation as they had no travel documents and none of the neighbouring countries would receive them.
26. Shamlan Al-Essa, 'Policy of Naturalization in Kuwait', paper presented at a conference entitled 'Kuwait and the Challenge of Reconstruction', Cairo University, 6–11 May 1991.
27. *Al-Hayat*, newspaper, 12 July 1991.
28. Department of Economic Studies, *The Study of the Labour Market: 1988* (Bahrain, Ministry of Finance, 1988), p. 2.
29. *Al-Hayat*, 21 August 1991.

7 Overview of Major issues in the Development of National Human Resources in the Gulf
Adil Osman Gebriel

INTRODUCTION AND OVERVIEW

The reliance of the Gulf Cooperation Council (GCC) economies on foreign labour is well-established and apparently enduring. Three-quarters of the Gulf labour force or 5.1 million people are foreigners (Looney, 1991: 121). The average percentages of migrant labour in the total labour force in all GCC economies during the past two decades were estimated at: 46.5, 65.2, 70.0 and 67.7, in 1975, 1980, 1985 and 1990 respectively (ESCWA, 1992). There are several factors which contribute to the high dependency of the GCC economies on migrant labour:

1. The relatively young structure of the population of the GCC countries (48.7 per cent of the total national population was under 15 years of age in 1994–ESCWA, 1995) and the smallness of the population base in the region (in 1994 the total number of the national population of all GCC countries was 16,338,639 and the total population of the region, nationals and non-nationals, was 25,082,798 (ibid.). In addition to manpower shortages, Looney (1993: 37) argues that GCC countries suffer from manpower under-utilization and structural imbalances in the labour force.
2. The relatively high rate of illiteracy.
3. The low participation rate of women in the labour force.
4. The rapid economic growth and ambitious development programmes during the two previous decades.
5. Social attitudes towards work, especially towards technical and manual jobs.

6. Political instability in the region which stimulates the building of armies and security forces.

The purpose of this small chapter is to investigate how some of these factors either singly or collectively act as obstacles to the creation of a sound national labour force in the GCC countries, and to increase their dependency on migrant workers. To achieve this goal, the chapter is organized into five sections. In section one, reasons behind lower female participation are discussed. Section two analyses social values and attitudes to work. From this analysis emerge such issues as government policies on employment, education, training and technology, which transcend all sections but are further discussed in sections three and four. Finally, suggestions on future areas for consideration are summarized in section five.

1. WOMEN'S PARTICIPATION IN THE LABOUR FORCE

Female participation in the labour force (as percentage of the total labour force) in the GCC countries is very low compared to other developing countries. This was estimated in 1990 as follows: 14 per cent for Kuwait, 7 per cent for Qatar, 10 per cent for Bahrain, 6 per cent for the UAE, 7 per cent for Saudi Arabia and 8 per cent for Oman (UNDP, 1993: 144).

Lower female participation is attributed to the sociocultural and religious systems and values prevailing. (However, the impact of these factors varies from one country to another.) Lack of financial motives is also a strong reason for women's low rate of participation. Webster (1986: 199) argues that 'Development for many ordinary women in the Gulf has meant the loss of their former economic roles and stricter confinement within the stereotype of respectable seclusion. In the past, seclusion was an ideal that acquired Kudos because it was unattainable except by the very wealthy. Now that it is available to all it must lose its allure. There is nothing attractive about enforced boredom'.

In Saudi Arabia, for example, men and women are totally segregated at the workplace. According to Serageldin et al. (1983: 36), for Saudi Arabia, 'there is a clear implication for Saudi Arabian planners: dependency on migrant labour can be reduced significantly if women are utilized in the labour force [because there is] a growing body of educated women...the crude participation of Saudi Arabian females, even of higher education attainment, tends to be lower than elsewhere'.

In a country like the UAE, where the population base is small and the participation of the nationals in the labour force is less than 10 per cent, the real and wider participation of females in the labour force becomes crucial in the country because they represent more than one-third of the total population.

Bahrain and Kuwait are different from the rest of the GCC countries. In Bahrain women represent 20 per cent of all government employees. They are also a significant presence in education, nursing and banking. Bahrain's Ministry of Education in the early 1970s adopted an employment policy that permitted the female-national teachers to dominate primary education. The percentage of females to total national labour force increased from 3.1 per cent in 1971 to 8.8 per cent in 1991. This successful innovation, which has been tried in Kuwait and Qatar, is regarded as a good example of increasing female participation and creating a suitable environment for female-national employment in the modern sector. While the sociocultural and religious inhibitions hindering the horizontal expansion of female participation in the labour force have somehow been overcome, sex discrimination seems to be hindering women's vertical expansion into leading positions. The percentages of females in administrative and managerial jobs during 1980–9 were 4 per cent for Kuwait, 4 per cent for Bahrain and 1 per cent for the UAE (UNDP, 1993: 50).

Seikaly (1994: 421) argues that 'There is also a conviction among professional women that the general employment policy of the government is to block the promotion of women even when they are better qualified and have had longer training and experience than men.' The relatively high participation rate of Bahraini women in the labour force could have been even higher had all of the educated women participated. It was estimated that in 1984, 32 per cent of women with doctoral and master's degrees, 22 per cent of bachelor's degree holders, 17 per cent of diploma holders and 65 per cent of secondary school graduates were not engaged in any employment (Ghanem, 1992).

In Kuwait, the female labour force participation rate increased from 2 per cent in 1970 to 10 per cent in 1980 and 14 per cent in 1990. About 52 per cent of the working women were concentrated in educational and health services (Shah, 1986). Clerical and related work is the second important job category for females. While Kuwaiti women are relatively very well educated, their percentage in administrative and managerial jobs was 4 per cent in the period 1980–8 (UNDP, 1993: 150–2).

The promotion and encouragement of female participation in productive work in the region has to be planned in accordance with the sociocultural structure. Ghanem (1992: 42) cites the idea which has been expressed in more than one Gulf Conference, that is, that there is 'the need for laws and regulations to enable Gulf women to work part-time so as to be able to participate in the labour force without unduly affecting their domestic duties'. Another idea by Roukis and Montana (1986: 171) suggests: 'segmentating work into modules and assigning such work on a cottage-like basis to womensize could resolve the cultural antipathy against employing women'.

2. SOCIAL VALUES AND ATTITUDES TOWARDS WORK

The abundance of huge financial resources generated by oil wealth in the region has created low morale and a negative attitude towards work. The nationals have little inclination and desire to work in arduous occupations and production work. Even Kuwait, which has relatively higher participation of both male and female nationals in the labour force, faces declining participation rates of both in production and related work categories. The participation rates of Kuwaiti males and females in production and manual jobs decrease from 23.1 per cent and 2.7 per cent in 1970 to 15.6 per cent and 0.6 per cent in 1980 for both sexes respectively. As well, there was a higher concentration of Kuwaiti males in non-productive service and administrative jobs (Shah, 1986: 827). These figures are supported by a follow-up study of graduates from the vocational training centres in Kuwait. This study shows that 49.2 per cent of the total number of graduates neither accepted nor performed any kind of manual work (Al-Misnad, 1985: 131). Similarly, another survey conducted in the UAE in 1985 indicated that only 4.9 per cent of the national labour force were technicians and only 0.4 per cent of them were regarded as skilled labour. The percentages of the total labour force in industry and services respectively during 1989–91 in the region were as follows: 28 per cent and 69 per cent for Qatar, 35 per cent and 62 per cent for Bahrain, 38 per cent and 57 per cent for the UAE, 14 per cent and 37 per cent for Saudi Arabia and 22 per cent and 29 per cent for Oman (UNDP, 1993: 168). Apart from socio-cultural systems, government policies on employment and human resource development have contributed to the low motivation and poor attitudes towards work in this region.

First, the government employment policies which secure jobs for nationals regardless of their qualifications have led to over-concentration in public services and administrative jobs, the tendency to move away from production or 'blue-collar' work. This in turn has increased the dependency on foreign imported labour and consequently changed the social value of manual work – as less desirable.

Second, the government work guarantee for nationals has created luxury employment where the nationals 'have never really been required to compete in the modern labour market on economic terms. They have effectively gained a "rent" from being nationals ... their remuneration being quite divorced from marginal productivity' (Serageldin et al., 1983: 27). Shah (1986: 823) also argues that 'the easy availability of jobs, the lack of competition, and the lack of an objective system of rewards and punishment are all likely to result in a low level of job commitment, and as such low productivity, among the indigenous labour force.' In Kuwait, labour market segmentation and employment discrimination policies enable the Kuwaitis to earn on the average about 49 per cent more than migrant non-Kuwaitis. This is in spite of the similar qualifications of the two categories and indications of lower productivity and efficiency among nationals (Al-Qudsi, 1985).

Third, GCC countries, according to a certain school of thought, are regarded as 'rentier' states in which the entire economic structure is based on external rent generated from oil mines. The function of the state in this respect entails distribution of the country's wealth. The majority of its citizens are involved in distribution and utilization of that wealth, and few actually participate in this generation (rent). This socioeconomic structure creates the 'rentier mentality' because, according to Beblawi (cited in Looney, 1994: 30–1), 'for the national worker, the work–reward causation has no meaning. Reward is a matter of chance, a windfall, an isolated fact, and is not considered to be the end result of a long, systemic and organized process of work.' The direct result of this structure is the lower productivity rates of nationals and the domination of migrant labour in the labour market.

In addition to the above there are other factors which affect negatively the stability of the labour force and decrease both worker's commitment and morale. These include: the temporary nature of migration, low degree of interaction between local and migrant labour, presence of various competing nationalities, and the social disparity between different sections of society. These factors increase labour alienation. As well, 'the impact of such an environment on the indigenous labour force is bound to be negative since the social relations within the work situation are likely to be based on mutual hostility and mistrust rather than on cooperation and trust' (Shah, 1986: 830).

In retrospect, without changing social attitudes towards work and increasing the real participation of nationals of GCC countries, the future of these economies is bleak. A pessimistic picture of the future is seized in the novel *Mudun al-Milh* (Cities of Salt; 1986) of Abdel-Rahman Munif. Munif portrays oil-based societies as ones built of salt, and with the end of oil resources these societies would crumble or melt away because they have 'the ability to buy everything without being able to produce any thing, scorning work and dependence on others for securing the simplest needs of life...[a condition which may] end in tragedy' (Munif cited in Richard, 1986: 220). He further concludes that 'in twenty or thirty years' time ... these giant cities built in the desert will find no one to live in them ... [because] natural and continuous process from nomadic life to civilization has not actually happened' (ibid.).

As such, the sudden, unexpected wealth of the GCC region, which has changed their Bedouin life into highly modern one, is not followed by a parallel sociocultural change. There is need for sound human resource development policies to improve and upgrade the qualifications and skills of nationals, and change the social attitudes towards blue-collar jobs and production work. This is essential in increasing the value added participation of nationals in the labour force and decreasing the total dependency on migrant labour. An efficient educational system and appropriate financial incentives and employment policies will, in harmonious sociocultural change, encourage the participation of nationals in technical occupations and increase their work morale and job commitment.

However, the long-term strategy entails changes in the education system. The education system, especially at the elementary level, can play a crucial role in reshaping and stressing the importance of manual work. Education also has wider implications in shaping the sociocultural and religious institutions of the societies and the media in those countries. This small contribution will not enter into issues of content of education in this way. Below, some issues related to the relevance of (higher) education will be discussed.

3. EDUCATION AND TRAINING

The availability of huge financial resources in the region has made it possible for GCC countries to build large educational infrastructures within a short time. As a result, the literacy rates and enrolment ratios at all levels have been going up (see Chapter 1 in this book).

The problem, however, seems to be not in the quantitative expansion but in the orientation of the educational system. A major problem with this system is that it gives high social prestige to university education and underestimates the significance of technological education and technical training: it is believed that only school drop-outs and academically poor students enter the latter. This belief is further strengthened by employment policies in all GCC countries which encourage this education structure by offering priority employment opportunities in the public service to university graduates, thus making technical and vocational education even less attractive and socially more undesirable. Al-Misnad (1985: 130–1) observes that 'technical education has been the less popular among Gulf Youth ... and has been declining steadily'. For instance, Kuwait University data in the 1980s shows that about 40 per cent of Kuwaiti males and 53 per cent of females studied arts, in contrast to 12 per cent and 33 per cent of non-Kuwaiti male and female students respectively. Only 8 per cent of Kuwaiti males compare to 29 per cent of their non-Kuwaiti counterparts enrolled in engineering or petroleum studies. A survey in 1985 in Kuwait shows that 78 per cent of the secondary school students favoured non-technical studies and only 17 per cent favoured technical subjects (Al-Misnad, 1985).

Similar patterns emerge across the education systems in other GCC countries. According to ESCWA (1993) data, the number of students in academic secondary schools of Qatar in 1991–2 was 9,869 compared to 546 students in the vocational secondary schools. Furthermore, out of 6,546 Qatari students in universities, only 1,094 were in applied science specializations. Although Saudi Arabia in 1991–2, had 21,533 teaching staff in academic secondary education, only 2,573 teaching staff were in the vocational and technical education during the same period.

The science university graduates (as a percentage of the total graduates) between 1988 and 1990 in the GCC countries were estimated as follows: 18 per cent for Kuwait, 13 per cent for Qatar, 52 per cent for Bahrain, 12 per cent for the UAE, 14 per cent for Saudi Arabia and 24 per cent for Oman (UNDP, 1993: 144).

The GCC countries, according to Scrageldin et al. (1983: 39–41), 'are most unlikely to spend and improve the external and internal efficiencies of their education and training systems to an extent sufficient to prevent increasing reliance on expatriate manpower in all but the least skilled of occupational levels ... very huge proportions of labour force entrants will continue to have little if any education. The skill mix of labour market entrants continues to fall short of meeting the progressively higher occupational requirements of their economies.'

It is imperative that in order to reverse these trends and generate a more productive national labour force capable of changing the structure of their economies (by diversifying away from dependence on oil), and meeting the increasingly technical occupational requirements of their labour market, the GCC countries must put emphasis upon technical and industrial education which allows easier transfer and adaptation of the experience and technology that now come to the region from all over the globe. While measures to reform the educational and training system will be needed, these alone will not be enough. These measures have to be adopted in harmony with reoriented employment policies and efficient monitoring and management of the labour market.

Since all the GCC countries face the same challenges – the need to reduce dependency on foreign labour and diversify their income sources through industrialization – they should coordinate and link their human resource planning policies and strategies. The smallness of the national population base and of the labour force are on extra reason for the need to coordinate by creating where possible regional rather than national education, training and research institutions. As well, GCC countries ought to benefit from opportunities offered to them by a cluster of various experiences and skills in the form of joint ventures and partnerships with foreign companies.

4. TECHNOLOGY AND HRD

For sound industrialization, technology acquisition has been regarded as the key factor. According to Muntarbhorn (1993: 102), 'technology is not merely hardware in the form of machinery and tangible materials. It also incorporates "knowledge", embodied in the term "software". Hence the close linkage with education and socialization.' This 'software' technology refers to the ability and capacity to devise, adapt and produce at lower cost. In developing countries this is regarded as the most important condition for technology transfer and can be achieved only through appropriate education, training, and research and development systems and institutions.

Table 5.3 in this book, which presents foreign participation in joint ventures in Saudi Arabia in 1985, provides a good example of the importance of the joint venture system in industrial development and technology transfer to the region. It portrays diversified technology and technical experience coming from a variety of countries and employed at a variety of industrial branches. Unfortunately, the foundation of huge industrial projects in the region has not developed into a strong technological base. Zahlan (1981) establishes that despite 584 oil related and petrochemical projects built in the Arab region (most of which are in GCC countries), the region has not developed and promoted indigenous (software and hardware) technologies to build such projects independently of foreigners. Zahlan findings are confirmed by Turnma (1987), who shows that the Arab region established 567 new petrochemical industries but virtually none of them achieved any real technological transfer that can enable the region to build similar projects. Looney (1993: 264) also has reached the same conclusions: 'The absence of technological capacity accounts for the Arab states' inability to create a real partnership with the multinationals which execute 95 per cent of the petrol and petrochemical projects in the Arab world.'

The problem seems to lie in lack of technology transfer and HRD policy in the region. Joint venture firms are not encouraged (or compelled) to establish links with local universities, research institutions and training centres to increase applied research activities and develop relevant technology curricula. The 'turnkey' contracts should be modified to allow the internal local institutions to participate in planning, designing and constructing the projects. GCC countries should and must insist that foreign enterprises sub-contract to local companies an increasingly complex segment of their tasks; and adopt efficient and extensive on-the-job training for the national labour force and allow them to participate at various levels in the project. This is of course to be matched with other training and employment policies which will encourage the nationals to join these modern industries. So far the small rates of technology transfer have been passed to other migrant labour rather than to the local labour force.

The scope of technological development in each of the GCC countries might be limited by the small size of most of them. Ghanem (1992) argues for the establishment of a central body, at the GCC level, responsible for technology and research. Such a body could advise and guide GCC countries and foreign countries on agreements regarding transfer of technology (i.e. licences, patents and trademarks), and strengthen the cooperation of GCC countries in the field of technology, technology transfer, technical and vocational training programmes to economize on financial and manpower resources. As well, this body could be responsible for other activities, including: advising industries on technology matters, patents, and establishment of technology centres; sponsoring research projects related to diffusion of adaptive technologies; and encouraging coordination and cooperation between various technological institutions and groups in the region.

5. SUMMARY AND CONCLUSIONS

The economies of the GCC will continue to depend on migrant labour due to the following factors: (a) demographic factors, populations characterized by smallness in size and youthfulness in structure; (b) the low level of female participation in the labour force and social disapproval of manual and technical jobs; and (c), inadequacy of the education and training system in creating sufficiently skilled manpower and in the right mix required by new industry characterized by high capital intensiveness.

In GCC countries, unlike other developing countries, where financial constraints represent the major obstacle for development, the human resource factor is regarded as the critical challenge for future development. The availability of financial resources and the presence of a joint venture system represent a unique opportunity for GCC countries to improve the education and skills profile of the national labour force, as well as to develop sound technological capability. These opportunities are still to be realized.

The promotion and encouragement of female participation in the labour force is crucial for reducing dependency on migrant labour. Measures have to be taken to create a suitable sociocultural environment for their productive participation in the work force.

There is a growing necessity in the region to reform and re-evaluate employment policies for nationals in order to encourage efficient and productive participation. The structure of education has not been in harmony with the economic development of the region. Efficient and well-constructed human resource development planning is required at the national and regional levels to economize on resources and to build strong HRD links both within and between GCC countries, and between them and the rest of the world.

REFERENCES

Al-Misnad, Sheikha (1985), *The Development of Modern Education in the Gulf*. London, Ithaca Press.

Al-Qudsi, Sulayman S. (1985), Earning Differences in the Labour Market of the Arab Gulf States. *Journal of Development Economics*, 18 (1985), 119–32.

ESCWA 1983–92 *Statistical Abstract of the ESCWA region*, 1983–92. Amman, Jordan: UN Economical Social Commission for Western Asia.

Ghanem, Shihab M. A. (1992), *Industrialization in the United Arab Emirates*. England, Avebury Ashgate Publishing Limited.

Looney, Robert E. (1991), Factors Affecting Employment in the Arabian Gulf Region, 1975–1985. In *Population Bulletin of ESCWA 1991*. Amman, Jordan: UN Economic and Social Commission for Western Asia.

Looney, Robert E. (1993), *Industrial Development and Diversification of the Arabian Gulf Economies*. London, JAI Press.

Looney, Robert E. (1994) *Manpower Policies and Development in the Persian Gulf Region*. Westport, Conn.: Praeger.

Ministry of Planning, UAE (1981), *First Five Year Economic and Social Development Plan Project, 1981–85*. Abu Dhabi.

Muntarbhorn, V. (1993), Technology and Human Rights: Critical Implications for Thailand. In Weeramantry, G. G. (ed.), *The Impact of Technology on Human Rights: Global Case Studies*. Tokyo, United Nations University Press.

Netton, I.R., Ian N. (1986), *Arabia and the Gulf: from Traditional Society to Modern States*. Lanham, Md.: Barnes and Noble.

Roukis, S. G. and Montana, P. J. (1986), Development and Human Resource Management in the Arab Oil Rich Gulf States. In Roukis and Montana (eds), *Workforce Management in the Arabian Peninsula*. Conn.: Greenwood Press.

Seikaly, May (1994), Women and Social Change in Bahrain. *International Journal of Middle East Studies*, 26 (1994), 415–16.

Serageldin, I., et al. (1983), *Manpower and International Labour Migration in the Middle East and North Africa*. Washington, DC: Oxford University Press for the World Bank.

Shah, Nasra M. (1986), Foreign Workers in Kuwait: Implication for the Kuwaiti Labour Force. *International Migration Review*, vol. 20, no. 4.

Tumma, Elias H. (1987), Technology Transfer and Economic Development: Lessons of History. *The Journal of Developing Areas*, 21 July 1987, 403–28

UNDP (1993–5), *Human Development Report*, 1993, 1994 and 1995. Oxford, Oxford University Press for the United Nations Development Programme.

Webster, R. (1986), Human Resources in the Gulf. In Netton, I. R. (ed.), *Arabia and the Gulf: from Traditional Society to Modern States*. Lanham, Md.: Barnes and Noble.

Zahlan, A. B. (1981), *The Technological Depth of Arab Unity*. Beirut, Arab Unity Studies Centre.

8 Women, Income Generation and Gender Relations in Rural Oman
Charlotte Heath

INTRODUCTION

This chapter will be looking at some aspects of development and gender relations by focusing on the ways in which two different groups of rural women, one *badu* (lowland pastoral people) and the other *hadhar* (sedentary communities), have responded to a government implemented weaving project; a project aimed at helping rural women by providing them with a means of earning some income.

The intention is to throw some light on how rural Omani women, who might be considered submissive and downtrodden, respond to and use a state intervention such as the weaving project to their own ends. In a country where absolute poverty is not really an issue and project earnings were very irregular and, it appeared, relatively insignificant, the question of why they wove at all became central. This brief comparison of the responses of the two different groups of women involved, aims to initiate an enquiry into how, and why, the semi-secluded and semi-masked Bedouin women appeared to be able to take greater advantage of the project than the unsecluded and unmasked village women.

GENDER ISSUES AND RURAL ARAB WOMEN

This section provides a brief introduction to some of the gender issues affecting the lives of rural Arab women generally, and how this might relate to the context of Oman and the issues which this paper is attempting to address.

In rural Oman *sexual segregation* can be more a matter of 'tact and mutual co-operation' (Eikleman, 1984), with the division of space being as much a social as physical construction, and relatively informal. It can depend on the nature of the relationship between husband and wife, and if good, the interaction of kinsmen and male neighbours with women within the home boundary may be more informal. Amongst the Bedouin (in this area) the nature of space, and the women's behaviour in it, was defined more by the status of the people present i.e. there were categories of deference, thus the status of the space may change accordingly (Ardener, 1981; Abu Lughod, 1985); the critical factor being the 'absence or presence of strangers' (Chatty, 1986). Space can change from being private to public by the presence of strangers. The women's behaviour will change accordingly, and they will, for example, withdraw to a more private place.

In the project area *masks* are worn by most of the older Bedouin women and some of the younger ones, outside the 'private' sphere, and ensure that when they move out of the home they remain hidden from strange men. The mask forms a sort of mobile seclusion zone. It is also a statement of modesty, and symbolizes a woman's committment to her married status (only married Bedouin women mask in this area of Oman). Amongst these Bedouin both men and women preferred to see the use of it as the woman's choice, but if a husband disagreed (which was rare) with his wifes's decision she would defer to his wishes. At other times women seemed to make their own decisions, even at the risk of knowing that their husbands might disapprove. In these cases the security was in numbers, and what might be seen as part of womens 'cooperative strategies' (Kabeer, 1991).

The *seclusion of women*, or control of women's mobility, varied between households and according to age. Amongst the Bedouin those most constrained were the younger unmarried women, followed by those newly married (the constraints might last from six months to two years). The women in well-established marriages potentially had more freedom but were constrained by their children, and older, post-menopausal women were the most free. It is suggested that where women are not automatically constrained by children (and pressured by older women and peers to be 'good' mothers), the men are more likely to assert their authority through seclusion practices. Much depended on the relationship between a couple, and the attitude of the senior man. There were only two cases in the project area where women were constrained un-negotiably within the 'private sphere': one was a young wife with children, and the other a childless older woman (40 years old).

The *hadhar* have always lived much closer together and always in solid permanent dwellings, which probably explains why space is less of a social construction and more or a physical one, and why the 'women's secrets' world is more active. Their close living arrangements therefore, might explain why their 'separate' world seems, in some ways but not in others, more separate to the men's, than that of the Bedouin women.

The nature of space in the house and village area changed less than amongst the Bedouin community, and areas that were private or public remained so. The house was predominantly female space, to the extent of male exclusion, and areas in the village such as the mosque and attached reception room were exclusively male space. As a result, the whereabouts of men and women was far more predictable. When passing each other between these areas, i.e. in the village generally, there was mutual avoidance from both men and women, eyes would be averted, and the manner would be deferential. Young unmarried women would not be expected to stop and talk, but once married it was acceptable to pause and exchange a few words with a man, but only for a minute or two, whilst older post-menopausal women were free to talk, and even to go down to the men's areas if necessary. Seclusion is not practised, and there is no masking or veiling.

There are questions posed by observing the women's involvement in the weaving project. For instance, is it true that women will favour an income generating activity because it does not challenge cultural norms such as sexual segregation, seclusion and male authority, as suggested by Kabeer (1991), or is it because it is a legitimate activity that they have autonomy over and so can stretch these boundaries, enabling empowerment?

Women's subordination has been subject to a number of interpretations, but frequently comes in the same breath as Arab or Muslim. In the context of Arab Muslim society it has been blamed on Islam (Ghoussab, 1988), or patriarchy (Mernissi,

1975, 1988; El Sadaawi, 1982), or with women's links with nature and their lack of independence from, or control over, the natural aspects of reproduction, interpreted as moral rather than sexual inferiority (Ortner, 1974. Abu Lughod, 1986). The wearing of a veil or mask, seclusion, or a deferential manner are often misinterpreted by Western observers as indications of submissiveness and subordination. There is also confusion around women's status as believers and as citizens (El Sadaawi, 1988; Mernissi, 1988; Tabari, 1980); meaning that women are subject to two authorities, one inside the household and one outside,where civil rights can be denied them by virtue of 'Islamic' tradition. As citizens they may have to contend with the social or political construction of women, the 'ideal' woman. This can be restricting, as in the case of Saudi Arabia, where enforcing the ideal of the 'Islamic' woman is bound up with political stability and used to prove the power of the monarch (Doumato, 1992). Ironically this denies women their rights as believers or as citizens.

The nature of women's subordination, however, has to be considered in the context of a society's ideologies and social construction of women, and the self-perceptions and subjective interpretations of the women concerned. For instance, neither the Bedouin women nor the *hadhar* women in Oman expressed any feelings of being subordinate to men; they felt equal. They do not compare themselves to men but draw their strength from the society of women (Abu Lughod, 1985) which runs parallel to the society of men. Other groups of rural Arab women in Oman have expressed similar views (Wikan, 1982; Eikleman, 1984; Chatty 1986).

Women have various strategies for lessening any direct experience of subordination. Earlier in this paper some of the strategies for dealing with this have been mentioned in connection with women's separate world and 'secrets'. The Arabic saying that 'camouflage is the best form of shelter' is appropriate because behind this 'camouflage' of compliance and deference, which ensures continuing support from kinsmen, women do have room to manoeuvre to their own advantage. In both the Omani communities the women had different manoevring and coping strategies to deal with subordination, and this affected the ways in which they were able to make use of the project.

THE WEAVING PROJECT

The Weaving Project was started in Khabura, in 1977, with the aim of helping rural women to earn some income, and reviving spinning and weaving skills which were in decline. Initially it came under the Ministry of Agriculture and Fisheries, and in 1983 moved to the Ministry of Social Affairs and Labour where it was integrated into Phase II and III (1982-6, 1987-1) of the National Community Development Programme, as part of the National Five Year Plan (1986-90).

The philosophy of the Programme was 'to promote local development through self-help and people's participation' (UNDP DP/UN/OMA-81–003/1 1987). Its objectives were 'to introduce grass-roots development in the overall development plan, achieve self-help amd community participation through socio/economic development of the rural population, and stabilise migration from rural areas by improving productive capacity with a view to enabling the rural population to effectively contribute to the national economy'.

Women's integration into the development process was to be achieved through the 52 Women's Development Centres, whose curricula included primary healthcare, home economics, nutrition, maternity and childcare, and income generating projects. Five of these Women's Development Centres are Weaving Project Centres. Products are bought from the weavers by two women who had been weavers but are now employed as social workers, by the Directorate of Community Development, to coordinate the weaving project in the Ministry of Social Affairs and Labour. The products are marketed on a rather *ad hoc* basis through their shop in Muscat, and public exhibitions. In theory the weavers can earn around 80–100 OR (£50–70) per month, but the purchase of weaving and payments are extremely irregular, which means that there is little incentive to weave more because it does not necessarily mean more income.

The weavers in the mountain villages buy all their raw materials from the local Community Development office, and the Bedouin weavers are self-sufficient in spun yarn and fleece, so only buy dyes. All the weavers do their own dyeing. The bedouin weavers produce more traditional rugs, cushions and wall hangings on ground looms, and the *hadhar* women produce tapestries depicting their environment and activities.

The Project currently covers four Bedouin communities along the northern coast near Khabura, and three villages in the mountains of the interior near Rustaq. The Bedouin women had been weavers, but the *hadhar* (village) women had never woven. In 1989 about 217 settled Bedouin women were spinning and weaving, and about 92 *hadhar* women (the weavers) and shepherds (the spinners) were participating.

RESPONSES TO THE PROJECT

This section will be looking first at the initial responses of the two groups of women, the *hadhar* and the Bedouin, to the project, and will then focus on the weaving centres, looking at the different ways in which the women used them.

Attitudes

When the Project was suggested to the Bedouin community in 1977 there was initial suspicion from the community generally; but some of the women obviously saw an opportunity here, and one woman tried to explain it by saying 'we knew that if we went on producing weaving the government would have to put someone here to collect it'. It could have been perceived, therefore, as a sort of reciprocity between them and the government (Lancaster, 1988), with the production of weaving in return for government presence in their community, or merely a strategic move.

In 1983 the project expanded to the *hadhar* community. Here there were no objections from the men to women participating in an income generating activity, or doing an activity that is actually a male one in their area. In fact the women saw themselves as carrying on the tradition in the men's absence (the *shiwawi* or shepherd men were the traditional weavers of the area, but many were now old, and their sons sought alternative employment rather than carrying on the tradition), and felt that if the initiative came from the government 'it must be good'. As the men of the village were the first to be approached by male social workers regarding the possibility of the project, and had agreed, it would have been unlikely that the women would do other than also agree; any negative comments might be construed as criticism of the men's decision. It might also have been a tacit acknowledgement of the benign nature of the government, in an area that had protested against it as late as the late 1970s.

In 1988, in conjunction with the 'Year of the Craftsmen/ women', the Sultan issued a directive (in the face of potentially serious unemployment problems, but not aimed specifically at the Project), telling the people to value their traditions and to apply their education to improving the traditional occupations of their fathers. When asked about the weaving project one male informant from the *hadhar* considered that 'government policy is to encourage a return to tradition, so people are doing this and returning to things like weaving. We did not ask for help from the government, but they asked us to go back to our traditions, so we did.' He is probably recollecting that directive, along with all the media coverage since then, and his opinions reflect his wish to present the community as good citizens. He specifically wanted to make it clear that they never 'asked' for help or in any way promoted themselves, but responded to a request. In the same vein, an educated female informant (a 20-year-old non-weaver) says 'they do it [weave] because the Sultan says they should, because it is tradition, and because visitors can see what they are doing in their village'. Putting the onus onto the Sultan is a way of disguising or camouflaging any elements of self- or village promotion, aptly demonstrating the importance attached to the maintenance of the status quo mentioned earlier.

These comments highlight the different attitudes of the two groups. In the case of the Bedouin the Sultan's directive seemed to give them the confidence to be seen to be actively promoting themselves as part of the Bedouin tradition, thereby helping him to improve and develop the country, a two-way deal; whereas the *hadhar* were responding to a request.

The intense competition for resources amongst Bedouin families was something acknowledged equally by men and women, and both acknowledged a work ethic over and above the financial returns. In their words the challenge for them is to make the best products so that more people buy them and greater benefits accrue all round – an interesting example perhaps of the perceived suppression of individual goals for the sake of the whole. They assert themselves as individuals and weave a good product, and when that is bought before those of their colleagues, will deny that it had anything to do with their efforts, but was because the purchaser liked it. Although her intention was to sell and benefit, the weaver is more likely to side-step any allusions to personal ambition by saying, as one did, 'What can I do – it is not my fault that they bought mine and not yours.'

Amongst the *hadhar* any competition, or jealousy, that might exist between weaving families or individuals is verbally denied by all parties. The women in the project would go to some lengths to uphold the group solidarity or cooperation on which their strength depended. If visitors came into the village and met up with one of the weavers, she would not show them her products until at least one other weaver was present, and word had been sent out to the others, via the children. Until recently the weavers would not sell their products to passing visitors unless the price had been set by the person in charge, thus avoiding any individual decision on the price, and the risk of getting it wrong and being criticised of the others. This is very different from the assertive action of individuals in the Bedouin community, and implies that group solidarity meant more to them than cooperating to ensure the survival of the project. It was observed, however, that particularly good weavers were tacitly acknowledged and as a result gained muted respect.

The Weaving Centres as a 'Place of Work'

Gender relations seem to operate in a different way in the weaving centres, so the question is, how do the women And men perceive the weaving centres? Are they an extension of the home and if so how are they excused from the normal workings of gender relations? And if not, what were the centres modelled on? Both groups of women made a distinction between the weaving centre and the home, but for slightly different reasons.

The Bedouin women clearly stated that the centre was for 'work', therefore things could be different. For instance, they do not offer coffee to any of the visitors who come to the centre and expressed this with relief, saying 'we can only do this because it is a work place'. This would be impossible in the house.

The concept of 'work', in terms of a remunerative activity, was not new to the Bedouin women. Before the mid-1970s they used to go out to work in the coastal settlements, selling dairy products for cash to both men and women of the Luwatiya coastal communities. The Bedouin informants made a direct connection here between the 'work' that they used to do, and going to the centre to 'work', and the distinction between behaviour dictated by 'work', and that resulting from social interactions.

The weaving centre was placed within the settlement area and was the focus for weaving activities. The local male social workers could come and go freely from it, although they would always wait a few minutes before entering, to give the women time to rearrange themselves. None of the younger married women would mask, the middle aged women might not bother to put it on, and the older ones would have them on anyway. In some respects it is like an extension of the home, where women can be unmasked, although masking in front of non-kin males inside or outside the house would normally have been obligatory. All the older married women, and most of the younger ones, would have worn a mask if going to the local Community Development office to meet the same social workers, or to the hospital, or another village.

The Director of the local Community Development office sometimes visited the women in the weaving centre, out of office hours, to see how they were getting on, and men were rarely present. However, even if invited, neither he nor the male social workers would have gone into a weaver's house unless they were sure a man was present. Other government officials, including the Under Secretary and Director General, would occasionally visit, as would UN and other development consultants; but because of the official nature of the visits and the pre-arranged time, at least two of the older men were likely to be present outside the centre. Groups of foreign residents (men and women), from Muscat, occasionally come to see the weaving at weekends; these do not require the presence of any men, partly because the visits are not of an official nature, and partly because of the 'neutrality' of male foreigners.

Is it because the women are seeing the centre as an extension to, or revival of, their previous income generating dairying activities, that they are able to invoke a different set of rules governing social behaviour in 'work' circumstances? The women seem to relish the opportunity to re-establish some lost autonomy and women's solidarity, as well as primary access to resources. The main centre was built on government land, and in so much as it was not a home or the property of any individual, was relatively neutral and a space where the women's behaviour was only marginally affected by the status of the men who entered it. Men were not excluded, but their inclusion did not change the nature of the space. In some cases kinsmen came into the centre to have a look at the weaving and offer good-humoured advice. This either implies that the women were not afraid of a male takeover, or that the legitimacy of spinning and weaving as a basically female activity prevented it. The suggestion that the centre was 'foreign space' (Doumato, 1992) and therefore invited foreign behaviour is insufficient. The centres were built by them in local materials within the 'private sphere' or settlement areas, and the group activity that took place within them in many ways mirrored the group activity that had been involved in making and selling dairy products.

The events mentioned in the weaving centre could not have happened in the houses with the same degree of control by the women. During group discussions they stated that they were responsible for the weaving centre, and the men were responsible for the house, so their autonomy in the weaving centre and the strength gained from women's solidarity is clearly very important to them. Government officials seemed able to 'sanction' events such as bringing official visitors or taking the women to Muscat, and in some respects became surrogate male 'kin' via the weaving project.

The village women were less sure about any distinction between home and the centre. They said they used the centre because it was provided for them by the government, not that it was a better place to work, as the Bedouin women expressed. They did not feel it was theirs, or that they were in charge,and found it difficult to explain why things were different there from what they were accustomed to in their houses. They agreed that if the Director of Community Development visited the centre on his own or with guests no other man needed to be there, but if he visited them in the village a man would have to be there. Where, however, they differed from the Bedouin women was in the change in their behaviour when strange men entered the centre, at which they assumed the deferential demeanour expected of them. Their own kin never came into the centre, which supports the importance of the spatial element of sexual segregation in the *hadhar* community, as opposed to the nature of space being dependent on the status of persons present, as is prevalent amongst the Bedouin community. In the centre coffee sessions amongst the women were numerous, and often produced for the social workers, male or female. Again they differ from the Bedouin, whose attitude was one of relief at not having to bother about producing coffee because this is 'a place of work'.

The *hadhar* women have never gone out to work for money, and there is no expressed work ethic, unlike the Bedouin women, who said 'if we want good money we must do good work', and where losses and gains in respect were so closely linked to a person's ability to contribute to the household. This perhaps explains why the *hadhar* women have nothing on which to model the centre, and expressed it as being all right and acceptable for things to be different in the centre because it 'comes from the government', whereas the Bedouin clearly state that their behaviour is different in the centre primarily because it is a place of work.

The Weaving Centre as 'Space'

Another factor to be considered is the way in which space is used in this context. In both cases the centres were situated within the 'private sphere'. In the Bedouin community the centre was not subject to changes of status due to the presence or absence of strangers or men generally. Amongst the *hadhar*, however, strange men could make the step over the boundary (of sexual segregation) into the centre, but in so doing changed the nature of the space which in turn resulted in changes in the women's behaviour.

'Space' and the Bedouin
In the Bedouin houses space can either be male or female, or both. There is no exclusively female space, the nearest being a couple's bedroom, or exclusively male space the nearest being the *meglis* (reception room for guests). The status of space is defined more by the people in it. For instance, common household space can be occupied by men or women, but if there is a seated majority of men or women, the incoming minority, whether men or women, will often go elsewhere. When there is no alternative place to sit outside, either because it is wet/cold or dark, the men of the household will occupy the *meglis*, leaving the common space in the house for the women and children. Although kinsmen and kinswomen are able to socialize together, they tend to spend most of their time apart. Modern incursions such as the television, which is usually in the common area of the house, act as a focus, and both men and women (from the same family) sit and watch it together.

The Bedouin households have always lived much further apart from each other than those of the *hadhar*. Sexual segregation was practised using mobile boundaries such as the mask, or social boundaries such as seclusion, rather than the static physical boundaries relied on more by the *hadhar*. Now, of course, things have changed, and to the regret of the older women physical boundaries such as enclosing walls are the norm, curtailing their ability to see what is going on. The effect this has had on gender relations is considerable. It is possible that the Bedouin women feel a need for their own defined space outside the compound walls – they no longer have the legitimate 'space' that going out to work selling dairy produce or minding the goats gave them – so the weaving centre provided them with that opportunity, legitimized and neutralized by the State. This implies that they prefer sexual segregation, which suggests that rather than being an agent of disempowerment, they consider increased female solidarity a means of regaining or retaining power (Abu Lughod, 1986).

The centre or Project provides the women with their own space, thereby giving them primary access to state machinery, a sort of mediatory zone for interaction between the women and the wider world and state. The most dramatic manifestation of this was when the bedouin women stirred things up by talking to all visiting officials about the fact that they never got paid. This caused the State Consultative Council (the highest appointed body in the land) to respond by holding a meeting locally, which the women attended and spoke at.

'Space' and the Hadhar

The use of space in village houses is different. The space in the house is more exclusively female, and men can be actively excluded and do not go into their own house if they know that their wife has women friends there. Time is an important factor; for instance, the women know that the men may be in their houses at lunch time, and so will not visit then. The men spend most of their free time in the village *meglis*/mosque sitting area, but in some of the households, in the evening, men and women from that household may sit in the same room, but apart, and watch television.

In the villages sexual segregation is more formalized in some respects, probably because living conditions are more crowded and seclusion and masking not practised. The village women have a more defined female space at home so perhaps do not have the same need for extra space. This might explain why they feel less strongly about the weaving centre, do not feel that it belongs to them. A more fundamental reason could be that their lives have changed less dramatically than those of the Bedouin women, because of their isolated location. If this is the case then perhaps they feel less of a need to regain lost ground, or are 'muted' (Ardener, 1975) and therefore less able to assert themselves.

SOME OF THE ISSUES

Patriarchy and the Relationship of the Communities and Women to the State

Many of the Bedouin women said their relationship with unrelated male social workers is different because they are government employees and therefore 'like a brother': the implication being that the Sultan at the head of the government is like a father. Indeed many of them stated that 'he is like a big father to everyone' and that 'children know Qaboos before they know their father'. These words are quoted here as they were spoken, they are not literal but more an expression of the impression they wish to present. (The effects of the political climate are difficult to judge.) In return, the women expect payment for their weaving, and the continued presence of the project in their area. There are obviously pay-offs between the men and the community, and the government. If the men allow the women to cooperate with the Ministry, through the project, the success of the project is increased, and government presence in the area is ensured, along with any beneficial spin-offs (such as increased access to social workers, therefore an increased chance of getting any benefits they might qualify for). The profile of the community is raised within the government (through the project as a national institution), and it is the women's belief that there is a direct link here to the Sultan, and that this will have pay-offs such as the large orders they received last year from the Diwan of Royal Court Affairs. On the basis of this it seems that both groups are extending kin relations to the male social workers, and that patriarchal dominance is being shared by the father or husband, and state. This shift of balance implies that the state is in a position to sanction situations that might be difficult for a husband, such as their wife visiting Muscat.

In the case of Oman, the government is able to act as 'guardian' to the women through the project, enabling them to participate in public activities that would otherwise have been impossible for them. The negative side to this is a lack of belief that the women can organize themselves, which may have something to do with the urban/rural divide and the lack of knowledge that urban dwellers, the majority of policy-makers and officials, have about rural communities, as well as a general disregard for the Bedouin. It is also consistent with the patriarchal, or in this sense, the Muslim, male 'right' of 'looking after' women. In 1990 (Oman *Observer*) Dr M. S. Elbualy (a highly respected Health Ministry official), referring to the quality of life of Omani women and the need to reduce infant mortality, said: 'A woman is not just a machine to produce babies cheaply. She has her own rights as a person, her own rights as a wife, and her own rights as a mother.' He goes on to say that the Koran clearly states that men should be responsible for looking after women, and that 'we are not doing it, not in the comprehensive way we should. In fact we are doing exactly the opposite.'

The *hadhar* community is much more reticent, and talks in terms of the government, rather than the Sultan. They are aware that through the continuation of the project within their village there may well be benefits, so ensure minimal cooperation with the social workers. One of the village men said 'because the government wants Aisha to go [to Muscat] I cannot be angry, she is going to get new experience not income'. There was more emphasis from male informants in this community, on gaining 'experience', and less admittance to the importance of the financial gains, when in fact the 'actual' (as opposed to the 'perceived') financial benefits of the project are probably more important to them than to the Bedouin. The idea of reciprocity and assertive action is less prevalent in this group, and the differences in attitude can be clearly illustrated through their different reactions to the fact that the Ministry is in debt to both groups of weavers by about seven months. In a discussion with three *hadhar* women about the Ministry, one of them said, 'we don't trust them any longer because they don't do what they say they are going to do, they take our weaving and don't pay us for it'. She went on to say that she was going to withhold some of her products, and try and sell them herself in the nearest town. A Bedouin woman of a similar age said on the same subject: 'the money isn't the important thing, there is trust between the women and the Ministry so it isn't an issue'. She continued by saying that it was more important to keep good relations with the Ministry; 'after all we are working towards the same thing, they are trying to help us'.

Whilst denying any lack of trust between themselves and the Ministry, resistance by the Bedouin women to non-payments and non-activity by the Ministry was more assertive, and took the form of letters, phone calls or verbal complaints to relevant Ministry officials. The *hadhar* women, on the other hand, although more willing to admit to a loss of trust, took up the more passive forms of resistance that rarely brought about face to face confrontations, and engaged in little assertive action.

Certainly the use of the Project by the Bedouin women is far more socially and politically manipulative than that of the village women, and presumably the way in which they respond must mirror the sort of patriarchal bargains being worked out in their homes.

Patriarchy and Subordination

Male attitudes amongst the weaver's husbands towards women generally or their wives never appeared to be arrogant or unthinking, although this did not always tally with the women's accounts. Their attitude to the Project was usually positive, with a few reservations about the fact that it was often difficult for women to go to Muscat on Project business because of the children. One of the Bedouin husbands said, 'if you are called to serve the country there are limits, so that the house doesn't collapse, work and the house must be balanced'. His wife is now employed by the Ministry and working at village level as the project trainer, and employs a live-in Sri Lankan housemaid to look after their ten children.

The feedback from men in both communities was that they recognize that the women have been left behind in terms of development and are therefore becoming less effective partners. The past seemed to indicate that unless a woman was strong in her own right the survival of the family was at risk. The men emphasized that one of the main benefits of the project to the women was 'experience'. This clearly indicates that the men have identified 'experience' as having been the way forward for them, and want the women to benefit in this way and be better able to cope with changing circumstances. Alternatively some men did mention the financial benefits, but to dwell on it might have been to admit to their own shortcomings. The women talked about both sorts of benefits.

If being subordinate conjures up images of passive, submissive and downtrodden women then neither of these groups conform, because they are not powerless. However, we have to look at concepts and levels of 'subordination', and more importantly women's perceptions of themselves. Is a woman 'subordinate' if she clearly feels she is not? How do you distinguish between what she feels and what she is able to express? (Ardener, 1975), or ways in which she might avoid the direct experience of 'subordination'? (Abu Lughod, 1986); and is a woman 'subordinate' if her society does not attach any value to a comparative judgement between men and women?

In Oman the state as senior patriarch plays a dominant role. Therefore it might make sense for the state to superimpose its authority, and create a space, as in the weaving project, that allows women to respond to a new patriarchal relationship that offers legitimate possibilities for self-determination. What might be the implications for gender relations and how does one reconcile this to patriarchy as being a system that reinforces women's subordination? Alternatively, could it mean that this extra household 'space' also allows the men to retain their dominant position *vis-à-vis* the household, whilst gender relations are re-negotiated and legitimzed in a 'safe' setting that does not compromise either party? Is it significant that several of the women (and men) have mentioned that Oman is now a much 'safer' place?; and hence, according to them, the constraints on their mobility and with whom they consort is becoming less strict.

CONCLUSIONS

Initial conclusions indicate that these rural Arab women have been able to use the Project to move boundaries and pursue autonomy. The Bedouin women who operate within the apparently more constrained set of social boundaries were the most able to respond to any opportunities that led to changes in these boundaries, and pursue their goals through the Project. Not only that, but it further blurs the distinction between the 'public' and 'private' spheres, and the ease with which the Bedouin women operate the link between the two, suggests that it is not as alien to them as is generally supposed, and much more importantly, is on their agenda.

It is particularly interesting that the weaving centre, especially in the Bedouin community, provides permanently 'female' space, and unlike the more 'private' situation at home, actually provides space that can legitimately become public and remain female. This allows the women legitimate interaction with, and primary access to, the formal/wider world that might otherwise be very difficult. For this to happen the neutrality of the centre is vitally important. In both cases the two more successful centres are those on land donated by the owners to the government for use by the people, hence no one stands to benefit (apart from the benefits expected by the owner from the government for his generosity – a form of reciprocity).

Furthermore, through the project, the state appears to be providing the women with a new, more abstract, extra-household, patriarchal relationship, which may offer the women potential for greater self-determination (or is it merely shifting the 'right of control' to all men?). A potential that not surprisingly seems to be understood more quickly by the older women, who have experienced losses in autonomy and bargaining tools, than the younger ones. Does this apparently new patriarchal relationship put the women at the centre of a new set of dependency links, and if so what is the quality of this relationship? And what is the new patriarchal bargain?

Further efforts to understand the ways in which these women used the project to re-empower themselves, and the meaning of that empowerment, are continuing, in support of the belief that women 'can do it'. The workings of gender relations, in conflict or cooperation, and the fact that so-called 'subordinate' women have their own agenda, are capable, and know best the 'tools' they require to further their goals, are still largely ignored by development agencies (non-governmental organizations or governments). For the women these goals have to be achieved in the context of their lives, which when dependent perhaps on 'patriarchal bargains' (Kandiyoti, 1989) and the acceptance of male dominance, can be misunderstood, or difficult for the 'listeners', and ultimately the development agencies, to accept as real expressions of their best interests.

SELECTED BIBLIOGRAPHY

Abu Lughod, L. *Veiled Sentiments. Honour and Poetry in a Bedouin Society.* University of California Press, 1986.

A Community of Secrets: The Separate World of Bedouin Women. *Signs: Journal of Women in Culture & Society*, 1985, vol. 10, no. 4, 1985.

Agarwal, B. Patriarchy and the Modernising State. In Agarwal (ed.), *Structures of Patriarchy*. Zed, 1989.

Ardener, E. Belief and the Problem of Women. In Ardener, S. (ed.), *Perceiving Women*. Wiley, 1975.

Ardener, S. Women and Space. In Ardener, S. (ed.), *Women and Space*. Croom Helm, 1981.

Bruce, J. Homes Divided. *World Development*, vol. 17, no. 7, 1989.

Chatty, D. *From Camel to Truck: The Bedouin and the Modern World*. Vantage, 1986.

Doumato, E. A. Gender, Monarchy, and National Identity in Saudi Arabia. *British Journal of Middle Eastern Studies*, vol. 19, no. 1, 1992.

Eikleman, C. *Women and Communities in Oman*. New York University Press, 1984.

Eickleman, D. Kings and People: Oman's State Consultative Council. *The Middle East Journal*, vol. 38, no. 1, Winter 1984.

El Sadaawi, N. Women and Islam. In Al Hibri, A. (ed.), *Women and Islam*. Pergamon, 1982.

El Sadaawi, N. The Political Challenges Facing Arab Women at the End of the 20th Century. In Toubia, N. (ed.), *Women of the Arab World*. Zed, 1988.

Ghoussab, M. Feminism – Or the Eternal Masculine in the Arab World. *New Left Review*, no. 161, Jan./Feb. 1988.

Harris, O. Households as Natural Units. In Young, K. et al. (eds.), *Of Marriage and the Market*. CSE Books, 1981.

Kabeer, N. *Gender, Production and Well-being: Rethinking the Household Economy*. Institute of Development Studies, Discussion Paper no. 288, Brighton, IDS.

Kandiyoti, D. Bargaining with Patriarchy. *Gender & Society*, vol. 2, no. 3, 1989.

Lancaster, W. Fishing and Coastal Communities Indigenous Economies, Decline or Renewal? In Dutton, R. (ed.), *Journal of Oman Studies, Special Report no. 3*. Diwan of Royal Court, 1988.

Mernissi, F. *Behind the Veil*. Wiley, 1975.

Mernissi, F. Moral Intervention. In Toubia, N. (ed.), *Women of the Arab World*. Zed, 1988.

Moors, A. Gender Hierarchy in a Palestinian Village. In Glavanis, K. & P. (eds.), *The Rural Middle East*. Zed, 1990.

Ortner, S. Is Female to Male as Nature is to Culture? In Rosaldo, M. & Lamphere, R. (eds.), *Women, Culture and Society*. Stanford University Press, 1974.

Sen, A. Gender and Co-operative Conflict. In Tinker, I. (ed.), *Persistent Inequalities*. Oxford University Press, 1990.

Tabari, A. The Enigma of Veiled Iranian Women. *Feminist Review*, 5, 1980.
Webster, R. The Al Wahiba: Bedouin Values in an Oil Economy. *Nomadic Peoples*, 28, 1991.
Wilkinson, J. C. *Water and Tribal Settlement in SE Arabia*. Clarendon Press, 1977.
UNDP, *Human Development Report*. Oxford University Press, 1990.
Wikan, U. *Behind the Veil in Arabia*. Johns Hopkins University Press, 1982.

9 The Saudis and the Gulf War: Gender, Power and the Revival of the Religious Right
Eleanor A. Doumato

The heading on a broadsheet posted in public places in Riyadh read, 'here are the names sluts who advocate vice and corruption on the earth'. The broadsheet had been circulated by the *Mutawwa'in*, the morals policemen of Saudi Arabia, in the wake of the women's driving demonstration of 6 November 1990. Listed under the heading were the names and ages of 49 women from well-known families, and prominently displayed at the top were the names of five women with the title 'doctor'.[1]

It was an inauspicious end to a demonstration which had begun at a time of optimism among Westward-looking circles in Saudi Arabia. In August, King Fahd had invited American forces to defend the kingdom after Saddam Hussein's invasion of Kuwait, and American women military personnel were becoming a highly visible – though controversial – presence in the Kingdom. In September, the King had issued an edict calling for government agencies to train women volunteers to work in civil defence and medical services. The response was one of elation by women who hoped it would be the beginning of a much larger role for women in the work force. Those who participated included not only the Western-educated, but also women of the royal family, who organized and attended training sessions at Riyadh hospitals. By early October, hundreds of women in every section of the country were volunteering for these sessions, even in the arch-conservative town of Buraidah, the site of rioting 30 years ago when the first elementary school for girls opened.

The King's alignment with the United States and his bold initiative for women's civil defence work appeared to hold out the possibility of a decline in religious-conservative influence and the further opening of Saudi society to the West. Nowhere was this optimism more acutely felt than among the Kingdom's Western-educated women. The driving demonstration's organizers were in fact encouraged by the king's apparent commitment to increasing women's participation in public life. A letter requesting permission for women to drive, reportedly sent to the mayor of Riyadh, Prince Salman, on the day the driving demonstration took place, began by praising the King's edict: 'Opening the door to the Saudi woman to volunteer to serve her country was an act of great generosity by the servant of the Two Holy Shrines, and demonstrates his deep belief that women are an important asset to the country.' The letter appealed to the Prince 'in the name of every ambitious Saudi woman eager to serve her country under the leadership of the Servant of the Two Holy Shrines and his wise government to open your paternal heart to us and to look sympathetically on our humane demand which is to drive in Riyadh.'[2]

A sympathetic hearing is not what the women received. The demonstration was stopped by *Mutawwa'in*, who were angered that the women refused to acknowledge their jurisdiction and insisted on being taken to police headquarters instead.[3] The Interior Ministry, headed by Prince Naif, came down firmly on the side of the religious police, and made the previously unofficial ban on women's driving official. The Ministry also issued a ban on all political activity by women in the future. The state-funded Directorate of Islamic Research, Ruling, Call and Guidance, headed by Shaikh Abdullah bin Abd al-Aziz bin Baz, sanctioned the Ministry's ruling by issuing a fatwa which stated that 'women should not be allowed to drive motor vehicles, as the Shariah instructs that the things that degrade or harm the dignity of women must be prevented'.[4]

Those who participated in the demonstration, and the husbands of those who participated, were punished by having their passports confiscated for a year so that they could not travel abroad. Those who were employed as teachers were suspended from their jobs for a year. Some of the women were subsequently harassed by phone-callers accusing them of sexual immorality and of being agents for Western vices.

Moreover, the demonstration became an occasion to inject fresh vigour into the image of ideal Islamic womanhood as secluded wife and mother projected in the public media: in December, while the American military build-up was at its height, the state-funded media turned the demonstration into a moral object lesson for children, when a television programme featured a group of little girls singing a song with the words, 'I am a Saudi women and I do not drive a car'.

The question of women's right to drive was not a new issue, but one which had been publicly addressed many times in the past, through newspaper articles, meetings at women's clubs, and private overtures to government officials. With the preparations for war consuming public attention, the King committed to participation by women in the war effort, and sympathetic listeners within the royal family, the participants had reason to feel that the time was at hand to press for the right to drive.

Why then was the government's response so focused on reaffirming traditional attitudes about women's roles? Why did the government respond to a convoy of women drivers as if the act was revolutionary? The reason is that the demonstration brought to the surface the underlying tension in Saudi Arabia between those who want a more liberal, evolutionary Islam and those who want to retain the literal Islam of the country's Wahhabi heritage. Traditional roles for women have become a symbol of that heritage, and have been co-opted by the monarchy as an emblem of its own Islamic character. The demonstration, in making a public appeal to alter Saudi Arabia's unique Islamic character, in effect represented a challenge to the stability of the monarchy.

This paper discusses the construction of gender ideology in the political culture of Saudi Arabia. It looks at the way gender constructions become a useful instrument of state policy and of state security.

GENDER IDEOLOGY: THE IDEAL ISLAMIC WOMAN

Gender ideology promoted within the political culture of Saudi Arabia constructs an ideal type, one which may be called 'ideal Islamic woman'. It is an ideology that has been expressed in official government statements, state policy decisions, and religious opinions issued by the state-supported ulama since the late 1950s, when women's role first became a focus of contention over the question of public education for girls. The idealized women is a wife and mother. Her place is within the family, 'the basic unit of society', and men are her protectors. Women who remain at home are the educators of children and the producers of traditional values. As the mother of future generations, the idealized woman is in effect the partner of the Saudi state, which is dedicated to protecting the family and guarding 'traditional values' and 'Islamic morality'.

The official version of the ideal woman tends to elevate the public separation of women from men as the hallmark of Islamic society. It defines the particular Muslim society of Saudi Arabia as something distinct from and morally superior to the West, as well as being superior to other Muslim countries where women are less rigidly separated.[5] The ideal woman, therefore, stands among other symbols which define a national identity that is uniquely Saudi Arabian.

Within the Kingdom, this ideology emanates not only from religious scholars and conservative writers, but is nurtured within state agencies and incorporated into public policy, sometimes with the explicit objective of correlating Saudi rule with the preservation of Islamic morality. For example, when a newspaper article published in *Ukaz* criticized men in general for considering themselves the guardians of women, the state-funded Department of Religious Guidance responded by issuing a fatwa citing the Koranic verse, 'Men are guardians of women by what God has favored some over the other and by what they spend of their money', and stated that the author of the letter and the publisher of the newspaper should be punished for suggesting otherwise. The fatwa also explicitly credited the Saudi rulers for upholding what it viewed as the Islamic moral value of protecting women within the family under the guardianship of men:

> Our government,thank God, is known for its deference to the Shariah law and its enforcement of it on its subjects and this is part of God's favor on it and the reason for its survival,

glory, and God's siding with it. May God keep it on the right path, and help it to protect His religion, His Book and the Sunnah of His prophet from the mockery of the mockers, the atheism of the atheists and the scorning of criminals.[6]

The language used to construct the 'ideal Islamic woman' is very similar to the 'fundamentalist' or 'Islamist' perspective expressed by the Muslim Brotherhood[7] and others in Egypt,[8] Hamas in Gaza,[9] the Islamic Salvation Front in Algeria,[10] and also that of the ideologues of the Islamic revolution in Iran.[11] In Saudi Arabia, however, the relationship between the ideology of the ideal woman and the reality of women's lives is closer than in most other places where Islamist opinion attracts a following . In fact, in Saudi Arabia, values of sex-segregation outside the private home remain in practice to a degree that is unknown in most of the Muslim world.

The reason is two-fold: first, Saudi Arabia's social fabric was not disturbed by a colonial experience, and Western influence is of a very recent date and has arrived, to some degree selectively, by the Saudi's own choosing; second, social conventions and religiously based attitudes supporting sex-segregation, female domesticity and dependence on men have been incorporated into public policy.

These policies are well known, and thus only a few examples are cited here. Shariah laws of personal status remain unmodified and are enforced through the courts: Men retain prerogatives in marriage, divorce and child custody, and also in the practice of polygyny, which has been modified in some Muslim countries and outlawed in at least one.[12] Women are not allowed to travel without the permission of a Mahram, a male guardian,[13] a policy which is enforced by the state at airline check-in counters, railroad stations, and hotels, where women travelling alone may not register for a room. Further, women may not receive a commercial licence unless a male manager has been hired, and certain courses, such as engineering, are not open to female university students because employment in engineering is viewed as incompatible with sex-segregation practices.

The ideology of the ideal Islamic woman is reiterated in royal edicts, policy statements and official regulations. In Saudi labour law, for example, the state recognizes its responsibility to protect the family according to Islamic values, and women and children are cited together as individuals in special need of government protection. Sex-segregation ('in no case may men and women co-mingle in the place of work') is stated as the fundamental requirement of women's being allowed to work.[14] Consequently, women are excluded from working in shops or in offices where men are present, including most of the Ministries, the very place where women in neighbouring countries, such as Kuwait, have most readily found employment. The ideology of the ideal women is also inscribed on the cornerstone of the official girls' education policy of the kingdom: 'The purpose of educating a girl is to bring her up in a proper Islamic way so as to perform her duty in life, be an ideal and successful housewife and a good mother, prepared to do things which suit her nature like teaching, nursing and giving medical treatment.'[15] The same policy, which prescribes sex-segregation at all levels of education, also justifies the closing of certain university courses to women, such as engineering, geology and meteorology, which might lead to employment in male-dominated fields.

However pervasive this ideology, it does not define policy. It is rather the idiom through which policies regarding women's issues are articulated, and sometimes the idiom is used to initiate what are for Saudi Arabia quite liberal policies. For example, the leaders of the women's driving demonstration employed the Islamist idiom in their petition for the right to drive: 'Since we have noted your highness' spirit of understanding of the demands of this age, and of the working women's creative efforts which are undertaken in the light of the teachings of our Islamic religion, we appeal to you...'[16]

King Fahd's September 1990 edict on women's volunteer work is another case in point. The language of the edict promised that the volunteer programme would be carried out 'within the context of fully preserving Islamic and social values,'[17] even though the rigid sex-segregation practised in Saudi Arabia is incompatible with women's work for civil defence. Incorporating Islamist language into the edict, however, cushioned its impact sufficiently to prevent criticism of the sort that would have nullified the edict's intent. Had the edict been implemented at a less politically stressful time, it might have become the cornerstone of a new area of employment for women.

In effect, the volunteer edict might have brought about radical change for women in the same way that instituting women's education did thirty years ago. The official girls' education policy cited above clearly limits education to what is compatible with marriage and motherhood, but even so, this policy, regularly reiterated,[18] has been the means by which secular education for girls has been able to grow into a nation-wide system of secondary schools, eleven women's colleges, and five universities which accept female students. When it was written in 1968, secular education for girls was still a revolutionary idea, one which had met in the early 1960s with considerable hostility from those who saw secular education as incompatible with traditional Islamic morality. It was the Islamist idiom, the assurance that education for girls would be carried out in a sex-separated environment and only for the purpose of making girls into better wives and mothers, which opened the door for education to go forward.

By the same token, the Saudi labour law limits the kinds of places where women may work by mandating sex-segregation, but at the same time these labour restrictions open up a legitimate space for women in the workplace. For example, women were not supposed to work in the banks, and out of propriety, could not comfortably patronize one, but the rubric of Islamic morality justified the opening of banks operated by and for women, which have come into being under government auspices without significant opposition. Similarly, the separation and 'protection' of women clauses in the labour law have provided the rationale for securing very progressive policies for the benefit of women who do work. Women employees, for example, are entitled to ten weeks' maternity leave, in some cases with full pay, and daily time off for nursing an infant when they return to work. Women employees are also entitled to employer-paid medical coverage and cannot be fired during illness or pregnancy leave. Official assurances of sex-segregation in the workplace furthermore make it possible for many women professionals to work unfettered by moral police in journalism, computing utility companies, some ministries and especially in healthcare, where contact with men is unavoidable.

The idiom of the ideal woman is deployed not only for issues relating to women. In order to defuse concerns about the harm imported Western culture may bring to Saudi society, nearly all development projects which require the importation of foreign labour have been prefaced by the Saudi's promise that such projects will be carried out within margins of Islamic values, values which are symbolized most commonly by the separation of women.

The ideology of the ideal Islamic woman has thus been a useful instrument in securing both progressive and restrictive policies. The idealization of women's domesticity and the elevation of female separation to an Islamic imperative has remained consistent on the level of official policy in Saudi Arabia because idealized definitions of gender are intimately connected to the ideologies which legitimate the monarchy.

THE LEGITIMATION OF THE SAUDI MONARCHY: RELIGION AND TRIBAL AUTHORITY

As a political entity, the Kingdom of Saudi Arabia is a collection of families and diversed ethnic and religious groups which were united through conquest by Abd al-Aziz ibn Sa'ud during the first quarter of the century. In order to establish the legitimacy of the Saudi monarchy among its newly incorporated constituencies, the ruling family did not attempt to undo these identities, but tried to create overarching loyalties based on a common social and religious community in which membership has its privileges, placing themselves as the locus of these loyalties.

These loyalties are grounded in myths of identity which translate, with varying degrees of success, into perceptions of Al Sa'ud leadership as legitimate leadership to the present day. The first myth is that the Kingdom is a cohesive national entity fused by a common loyalty to Islam as shaped by the Wahhabi tradition, and that the Al Sa'ud family are qualified – and uniquely so – to defend Islam and to ensure the moral well-being of the Muslim community; the second is that the Saudi Arabian state is an extension of the tribal family.

Islam and Al Sa'ud Leadership

The father of King Fahd, Abd al-Aziz ibn Sa'ud, inherited from his eighteenth-century forebears a political and religious ideology which he used to legitimate his own rule and the expansion of his rule across the peninsula. This ideology grew out of the teaching of the eighteenth-century scholar Muhammad ibn Abd al-Wahhab, whose philosophy effectually converted political loyalty into a religious obligation. According to ibn Abd al-Wahhab's teachings, a Muslim must have presented a bay'ah, or oath of allegiance, to a Muslim ruler during his lifetime in order to be redeemed after his death,[19] while the ruler is owed unquestioned allegiance so long as he leads the community according to the laws of God.[20] According to his teachings, the whole purpose of the Muslim community is to become the living embodiment of God's law: the responsibility of the legitimate ruler is to ensure that the people know what are God's laws, and live and conformity with them.

To the Wahhabis of Najd, living according to God's law means following the Koran and Sunna of the prophet in all one's daily affairs, adhering only to the interpretations of the early jurists of the first three centuries of Islam and avoiding later interpretative readings. This has affected the Wahhabi attitudes about women's roles in two ways. First, the Wahhabi Ulama reject the kind of reformist interpretations of Koran and Hadith which have been essential to bringing about changes in dress, education and Islamic personal status laws in other places such as Egypt and Syria. Second, sex-segregation and face-covering, which are substantiated not so much in the literal word of Koran and Hadith as in local interpretations of religious doctrine and local established practices, are continuously being reinscribed back into society through religious decree and state policy as an essential component of leadership in the community which wishes to live in conformity with God's laws.

Wahhabi attitudes that affect women's roles have been promoted along with the promotion of Wahhabi religious doctrines by Abd al-Aziz. Employing religion as the glue that would hold his kingdom together Abd al-Aziz subsidized

Koran memorization classes and Hadith studies and sent missionaries to all the villages and towns. The Koran was to be the constitution of the Kingdom. Universal male participation in public prayer five times a day in the mosque was enforced, with women allowed to participate on holidays, and in some areas, on Fridays. When public education for boys was instituted in 1953, and for girls in 1960, religious education became mandatory, constituting to this day the largest block of school hours in the curriculum, as much as 12 hours a week. Mosques continue to be built in every neighbourhood, and two Islamic universities sponsor 47 secondary-level religious institutes across the Kingdom and have produced thousands of religious studies graduates.[21]

Ibn Sa'ud's campaign to evangelize the Bedouin as a means of encouraging them to settle on the land also became a medium for reinscribing Wahhabi attitudes about women's roles. Beginning in 1912, Ibn Sa'ud subsidized agricultural communities known as *hijra*, meaning 'the move from the land of polytheism to the land of Islam',[22] where newly settled Bedouin would apply Islamic law and Sunna to daily life. In these settlements some of the most rigid sex-separation practices were instituted in the name of religion, practices which have been observed among descendants of *hijra* settlers to the present day, such as forbidding women to enter the public marketplace, or to speak when attempting to get a merchant's attention.[23]

During his lifetime, Ibn Sa'ud also created religious institutions which would symbolize the continuing partnership of his regime with the scholars of religion: These were a select body of state-funded ulama, and the committee for the promotion of virtue and prevention of vice, whose task is to enforce compliance with Islamic law and practice as interpreted by the ulama.[24] These institutions had an interest in maintaining Wahhabi interpretations of Islamic rulings about women, and they have been in fact on the front-line of shaping the ideology of the ideal Islamic woman. As civil-service employees, the ulama are employed in religious education, in the Ministry of Justice, and in Islamic missionary preaching. They are also employed as the supervisors of mosques and *awqaf*, and as notaries public, as well as in the World Muslim League and the World Assembly of Muslim Youth, created by the Saudi government to propagate Wahhabi principles internationally and enhance the prestige of the Saudi monarchy abroad.[25] Most important, civil-service ulama are the designated overseers of girls' education.

The Directorate of Religious Research produces and distributes literature explaining Wahhabism, but its main purpose is to recommend policies on religious matters and to express opinions (fatwas) based on the Shariah regarding matters submitted to them by the King:[26] in effect, to provide Islamic sanction for policy decisions taken by the government. For this reason, when the Directorate issues a fatwa forbidding women to drive on religious grounds, it is nearly certain that the position taken by the ulama in the fatwa is one that is acceptable to the Saudi rulers, if not one actually requested by them.

The function of the *Mutawwa'in*, patrolmen of the Morality Committees, is to demonstrate the government's readiness to enforce standards of behavior approved by the ulama. In the past, the *Mutawwa'in* have been responsible for supervising the closing of shops at prayer time and the attendance of men in the mosque for prayers, and for preventing infractions of public morality such as playing music, smoking, drinking alcohol, men and women mingling in public places, and immodest dress for both men and women. In the 1920s, these morality police obtained extraordinary powers of enforcement ranging from personal embarrassment to trial, imprisonment and corporal punishment. In 1930, Ibn Sa'ud incorporated the Morality Committees into the Directorate General of the Police Force.[27] In 1976, the director of the committees was assigned ministerial status, and the society now exists as one of a number of independent departments in the state administration which report directly to the King.[28]

The jurisdiction of the *Mutawwa'in* is usually limited to overseeing the closing of shops at prayer time, public decorum, and proper dress, especially for women. The *Mutawwa'in* have often worked alone on their patrols, and have been drawn from the among the least educated. Without the capacity to enforce infractions, they sometimes have tended to be ignored and ignorable. At other times, especially during times of political instability, the *Mutawwa'in* jurisdiction has been broadened to include an arbitrary range of moral infractions, including the presence of women in hotel swimming pools, women employed in shops serving customers, or women in cars with an unrelated man, and morals policemen may be accompanied in their duties by police and charged with the capacity to make arrest. With the increase in sensitivity to Western penetration during the Gulf War, the morality committees have received substantial government funding to upgrade the educational level of their patrolmen and increase their patrols.[29] At all times, whatever their capacity for coercion, the *Mutawwa'in* have been a powerful instrument of social control through intimidation.

All of the civil-service religious departments, including the morality committee and the scholars of the Department of Religious Guidance, serve at the pleasure of the monarchy. These institutions are regulated to a symbolic position when not needed or when religious attitudes are incompatible with government policy.[30] Whenever deference to religious opinion can cover political benefit, however, these religious institutions become a useful instrument for promoting popular support for the monarchy.[31]

The Tribal Family

The second myth of identity undergirding the monarchy is that the Saudi Arabian state is an extension of the family, with the monarchy fulfilling the patriarchal obligations of the tribal shaikh: mediating disputes, defending his people, conducting warfare, dispensing largesse, guarding the gates of admission to the tribal family and securing the honour of all its members. When Ibn Sa'ud rose to power, he broke up tribal alliances by undercutting the obligations of weak tribal groups toward stronger ones,[32] and assumed for himself, both symbolically and concretely, the functions of tribal leadership over a multitude of tribal affiliations.

The most important function was economic: the tribal shaikh is expected to assure the welfare of his group by such means as receiving tribute and dispensing largesse, and his position of respect is secured by his willingness and his capacity to do favours for those who come and ask. While consolidating his conquests, Ibn Sa'ud subsidized the settlements of the

Ikhwan Bedouin. When the camel economy went into decline at the end of the First World War, he became the source for the most basic necessities of life, dispensing food, clothing and cash to males who came to ask.[33]

The sons of Abd al-Aziz carry on the same tradition, only the source of largesse is the material resources of the country, which is operated as a family-owned business, and the recipients are those who are privileged to be citizens of the Kingdom of Saudi Arabia. Whereas Ibn Sa'ud actually handed out rations through his personal staff, the sons offer free medical care, welfare payments for women who have no male to support them, subsidies for agriculture and industry, grants for housing and land, jobs in ministries, forgiveness of personal debt, contracts for government projects, and rules requiring majority ownership for Saudi citizens in joint-venture companies operating in the kingdom. Nomads receive livestock subsidies, veterinary services, and mechanized water supplies, as well as land, equipment and training for those who wish to settle.[34] Financial incentives for marriage through a fund to provide the *Mehr* (bride price) are offered to men who are citizens and can demonstrate that they are practising Muslims.[35]

The economic benefits from the monarch's largesse do not flow to women in the same way that they flow to men: through their male relatives, women, for example, are not entitled to separate citizenship cards, but are included as dependants on their father's or husband's card.[36] For women in rural areas particularly, this means that they are unable to obtain certain forms of government assistance, such as livestock subsidies, or to apply for loans to purchase land or housing.[37] Whatever the intended purpose of eliminating identity cards for women, the effect was to bolster women's economic dependence on men, and to re-inscribe in society the the values patriarchal privilege within the family.

On a symbolic level, the functions of the tribal shaikh as one who determines marriage alliances and keeps the bloodlines pure have also been assumed by the monarchy. Citizens who wish to marry foreigners are supposed to obtain special permission to do so: for male citizens wishing to marry a foreign woman, permission is possible but not easily forthcoming; a Saudi woman wishing to marry a non-Saudi man

Gender, Power and the Saudi Right

does not ask. In this way, the ruling family symbolically acts as if it were sustaining the integrity of the tribal family, which favours marriage back into the paternal line and rejects marriages outside the extended tribal network. Guarding the gates of admission to the patriarchal tribal family – if only on a symbolic level – contributes toward the shaping of the myth of the whole country under Saudi dominion as one vast, exclusive tribal family patronized by the Al Sa'ud. Since admission to the tribal family confers entitlement to the largesse of the shaikh, the Saudis have created powerful incentives for their citizens to buy into the myth of Saudi national identity, an identity fused by religion, in which membership is in fact a coveted privilege bestowed by birthright.

THE 'IDEAL ISLAMIC WOMAN' IN ACTION: HOW IDEOLOGY PROMOTES STABILITY

Over the past thirty years, the ideology of the 'ideal Islamic woman' has proven to be a dependable vehicle for the Saudi monarchy to play out the myths of national identity which undergird its legitimacy. By promoting the imagery of the ideal Islamic woman, by controlling women's mobility and independent access to the resources of the state, and by enforcing women's public separation from men, the heterogeneous people of Arabia become a homogeneous Islamic community, the patriarchal family is sustained, and the Al Sa'ud gain the appearance of the nation's guardian. The political utility of the ideal Islamic woman is most vividly highlighted during times of political instability: the state's responses to the mosque seizure of 1979 and to the women's driving demonstration of 1990 are two cases in point.

In November 1979, Juhaiman ibn Muhammad ibn Saif Al Utaiba, a former seminary student and protégé of Saudi Arabia's most influential religious scholar, bin Baz, drove a Toyota pick-up truck laden with food, water, guns and ammunition into the grand mosque at Mecca. Convinced that the advent of the fifteenth century of Islam signalled the arrival of a Messiah (Juhaiman's brother-in-law) who would bring about the Kingdom of God in the Kingdom of Saudi

Arabia, he and his followers began shooting at worshippers and custodians in the mosque precincts.

In a series of pamphlets distributed the previous year, Juhaiman had called for an end to Western influences stemming from the Kingdom's development projects, to television, gambling, Western-style universities, conspicuous and extravagant spending on the part of the Saudi princes, and the presence of all foreigners. He was also opposed to the liberalism of the civil-service ulama who are called on to interpret Islamic law on behalf of the government. He and his followers called themselves Ikhwan, considering themselves the spiritual inheritors of the Wahhabi movement's most militant proponents under Ibn Sa'ud.

Juhaiman's insurrection presented no small challenge to the Saudis. It took the lives of 127 Saudi soldiers, as well as help from foreign forces, to extricate him and his followers from the mosque precincts. Juhaiman's movement was effectively ended when he and 62 of his followers were beheaded, but the yearning to set boundaries around Western influence, as the movement advocated, had struck a deep chord of sympathy across the society.

The Saudis' immediate response was to mollify those sympathies by putting renewed energy into the campaign to limit Western influences which had begun the year before with the publication of Juhaiman's pamphlets. The society for the promotion of virtue and prevention of vice issued 'Guidelines to our Brothers in Humanity about proper Dress and Behavior in Saudi Arabia', and a similar circular in all the major cities, which asked foreign women to wear clothing that covered their hair, legs and arms.[38] The *Mutawwa'in* rigorously sought to discipline female secretaries working in offices, unmarried couples eating in restaurants or riding in cars, and improperly dressed women. The French Cultural Institute was compelled to exclude all women from language classes, the British School was given the ultimatum of separating men and women in its evening classes or facing closure, and church services held in foreign housing compounds came under scrutiny. The Interior Ministry issued new rules instituting sex-segregation in recreation areas of foreign housing compounds and set penalties for foreigners who obtained work permits illegally.[39] Scholarships for Saudi women to study abroad were curtailed, along with commercial licences for women who had failed to provide a male manager to run their business, and a fatwa was issued saying that a woman must be physically accompanied by a male guardian in order to travel.[40] The *Mutawwa'in* removed mannequins, stuffed animals and dolls from shops, ordered changing rooms in clothing stores closed, and arrested unmarried couples discovered eating in restaurants. The Ministry of Education took steps to remove Muslim school children from foreign schools.

At the same time, other 'Ikhwan' established their own vigilante police in the Eastern Province, and their activities were backed up by government police. Their aim, like those of Juhaiman, was to remove what they perceived as corrupt Western influences, and these influences centred on things that women do: these Ikhwan, for example, closed down an ARAMCO clerical training programme for young women, because, in their view, the women were being trained to work as secretaries where they could be exploited by male employers.[41] Also closed were beauty salons in the Dhahran area on the grounds that such places offer no legitimate service that women cannot do for themselves and, like any place that offers body services, act as covers for prostitution. A Dhahran hotel was also compelled to cease offering musical entertainment in its dining room, and the hotel subsequently published an apology in the press, first, for having offered entertainment before a mixed audience of men and women, and second, for having advertised Christmas festivities.

During this 1979–80 year of political turmoil, whether the decrees, fatwas and police actions were addressed to foreigners or to Saudi citizens, the main thrust of them all was women's behaviour and the public separation of women from men. The purpose behind the articulation and zealous enforcement of these rules was to undermine and appease the broad coalition of sentiment which resented Western influence, of which Juhaiman and his group represented only the most extreme fringe. The strategy was to do so in ways which were politically safe, which would not alienate other significant constituencies. The Saudis were not prepared to step down from power, nor to halt economic development programmes or curb the nascent industrial sector in order to stem the flow of Western influences; nor were they prepared to close the universities or lower their personal standard of living. However, by focusing on women's role and defining this as Islamic, the monarchy could demonstrate its readiness to act with vigour to uphold Islamic morality against the West, without actually having to make any personal sacrifices or alienate other significant constituencies.

When the Saudi monarchy responded to the women's driving demonstration, their responses and the reasons for them were very similar to those that pertained in the period of the mosque siege. In November 1990 the monarchy was facing serious challenges. The Iraqis had invaded Kuwait, and King Fahd's request for protection from Saddam Hussein raised questions about the wisdom of aligning with the United States. People were questioning American motives, expressing concern that going to war could benefit no country in the region except Israel, and wondering aloud why a negotiated settlement was not being pursued. Questions were also raised about the competence of the Saudi military. Why should it be necessary to invite the Americans, people were asking, when vast sums had been spent on arms from the West, even as the price of oil had declined and spending programmes for social services were being curtailed? Some also felt that Saddam Hussein was an Arab problem that should be solved within the Arab region, without outside interference. A major emotionally-laden issue also raised concerned whether or not it was legitimate in terms of religion to invite unbelievers to defend the birthplace of Islam.

In addition to these challenges, both conservative and less conservative groups were asking for some recognized form of participation in government decision-making. When the Muslim World League was convened in Mecca at the behest of King Fahd to lend Islamic legitimacy to his invitation to American forces to defend the Kingdom, the League sanctioned the call for help as expected, but also called on Muslims to return to the Islamic system of Shura (Consultation): criticism of the Saudi monarchy's failure to institute a consultative assembly, which has been perpetually 'under consideration' for decades, was implicit, and three weeks later the king offered a fresh pledge to review plans for a consultative assembly.

As the build-up for war progressed and American troops poured into the country, the King's edict authorizing women to train for civil defence and medical service was receiving a positive response in many quarters, but still fed into concerns about the moral implications of American dominance – enough so that Iraqi propagandists identified the edict as a potential spur to opponents of the monarchy. In one of a series of clandestine broadcasts, 'Holy Mecca Radio' equated the edict with a violation of Islamic decency, and claimed that the Americans were importing 'immorality and evil into Dhahran, in a way that threatens all values and norms with which the Muslim Arab woman has been raised...it is amazing that someone should accept that the honorable and pure Arab woman in the Arabian peninsula has become a target for the evils of the infidel American and Zionist, his arrogance, his drunkenness, and profanity of all values and norms.'[42]

The driving demonstration occurred at an opportune time for the monarchy. It provided a ready-made platform to diffuse whatever resentment the volunteer work edict may have provoked, and to deflect attention away from its inability to defend the holy places of Islam, not to mention the Saudi oil fields. As with the response to the mosque siege, raising the flag of Islamic womanhood was an opportunity to garner support without alienating any powerful constituencies. Punishing the demonstrators was a chance to deflect attention away from the war and to tap the widespread emotional undercurrent which resents Western influences, which wants to feel that God's laws are being fulfilled in daily living, and which views the traditional roles of women as emblematic of those moral values.

WHY WOMEN, AND NOT MEN, SYMBOLIZE ISLAMIC TRADITION

All across the Arab Muslim world, modest clothing and the public separation of women has become the predominant political symbol of Islamic tradition. Historically, however, the piety of the Muslim community has been publicly measured by things that men do. This was especially so in Saudi Arabia. During the era of Abd al-Aziz, indeed throughout the entire history of the Wahhabi movement in Najd, the actions of men represented the community living according to God's laws: it was men who went to the mosque, and it was men, not women, whose attendance was enforced. Boys' successful completion of Koran memorization classes received a public celebration, and men assumed the highest positions of authority in religion. Conformity in the length of a man's *aba'a*, the presence or absence of an *aghal*, the trimming of the hair and beard in a certain way, not smoking, and not wearing gold or silk, were outward symbols of communal piety.

Theoretically, therefore, the Saudi rulers of the post-development twentieth century could demonstrate their willingness to uphold Islamic tradition by focusing on things that affect men's actions, such as enforcing male attendance at the mosque, the wearing of a beard, ensuring that brothers pay to sisters their Koranic share of inheritance (as ibn Abd al-Wahhab himself attempted to do), and closing up interest-bearing accounts in banks. Such regulations are in fact not without supporters: for example, a petition addressed to King Fahd and signed by scores of Islamic scholars, judges and university professors asked that banks be cleansed of interest payments, and among other things, that piety and observance of prayer be a consideration in making appointments to government posts.[43]

The reason why the monarchy, when pressured politically to reaffirm its commitment to Islam, does not press for conformity in the religious behaviour of men is that it cannot do so without courting resistance. Saudi Arabia is a different place than it was even thirty years ago, and attempts to regulate male behaviour to a uniform standard would invite opposition of a sort from all quarters, including Wahhabi fundamentalists, as well as those who are Western-educated, have travelled abroad, are secularists, or Shiites, or those who desire greater participation in decision-making, more independence for women, or greater allowance for the individual in determining what constitutes Islamic behaviour. Attempts to control the behaviour of men, in effect, would shatter the illusion of nationhood fused by a common vision of Islamic community.

Today the Saudi rulers enforce Islamic tradition selectively, in ways which demonstrate their commitment to public piety without burdening their male constituents with having to demonstrate their own: shops are closed at prayer time, for example, and mosques are built in every neighbourhood and shopping mall, but men are not forced to enter. *Zakat*, a Muslim tax, is deducted from the wages of salaried employees, but only in place of income taxes.

Women separation, by contrast, is enforced because it can be. The veiled separation and dependency of women emerges from a long historical trajectory and represents values which are continuously reproduced at home and in the political culture of the Kingdom. In spite of the aspirations of many Westernized, liberal Saudis, women's modesty and separation continue to appeal to much of the population, cutting across the interests of diverse ethnic, religious and economic groups in the Kingdom. Over the past ten years that appeal has been growing,[44] as the symbols of the Islamic community living according to God's laws have been gradually evolving from being represented mainly by things that men do to things that women do not do.

Elevating the separation of women to an essential Islamic imperative fills a symbolic void: like praying in the mosque or fasting during Ramadan, the separation and non-public presence of women are a way of making Islam visible. The public invisibility of women has become a way to display one's faith, to make of religion something tangible that can be measured by others. When adopted as a moral cause by the monarchy, as shown in this paper, the public invisibility of women becomes a visible sign of the monarch's piety.

THE CONTINUING UTILITY OF THE 'IDEAL WOMAN'

Gender ideology works as an instrument of legitimation because it appeals directly to the myths of nationhood which undergird the monarchy: the nation as Islamic community, the nation as patriarchal tribal family, and the Al Sa'ud as guardian of both. Co-opted by the monarchy, ideal Islamic woman became a symbol of national identity.

Ideal Islamic womanhood works as an instrument of legitimation because it has intrinsic appeal. Women's modesty, family values, and women's dependency on men represent support for the integrity of the patriarchal family. In a time of rapid change, the monarchy must provide stability, and support for the patriarchal family and 'traditional values' is support for stability. When the monarchy, either directly or by non-interference with the religious organizations, promotes the values of family and Islam, it is offering people a refuge. Measures such as limiting the sale of contraceptive devices, sustaining the Shariah as the only basis for marriage, divorce and child custody, requiring official permission for a Saudi man to marry a foreign woman, issuing identity cards to males only, and limiting the types of employment to which women are entitled are ways of ensuring continuity in religious values and family traditions, even as the physical and social environment is being unrecognizably transformed.

The promotion of Ideal Islamic Womanhood has an unquestioned appeal to the mass of people of Saudi Arabia. Such government policies speak to the empowerment of men: they work to shore up the patriarchal family at a time in which male authority is being challenged by the centralizing state. The combination of women's education, of population mobility, and of young families moving away from home-towns, and an affluence which allows Saudi couples to establish nuclear households, present painful challenges to patriarchal control over the extended family. However, it is not only men who respond positively, for women too are uncertain about the effects social change may bring. If they stay in school too long, will they be considered undesirable for marriage? Do they want to work at all, and if they did, would they choose to work in a mixed-sex situation which could be perceived by others as compromising?

Controlling things that women do appeals to a range of fears and concerns over the effects of Westernization. These effects include not only the demise of the extended patriarchal family, but secularization and the growing insistence on the right of the individual to make personal decisions about matters once held sacrosanct in custom and vital to communal well-being, such as the choice of a marriage partner, where one will live, or to whom one defers. These effects also include the destruction of familiar space, such as the demise of the old *suq*, and with it, the means for the small trader to do business, the traditional ways of conducting business, and the circle of life between *suq*, home and mosque. In its place are vast shopping malls and arcades, with foreign names, selling foreign goods, and staffed by Europeans or Asians who often don't speak Arabic. These are foreign spaces, inviting foreign behaviour, making people, especially those who cannot adapt easily, feel themselves foreigners in their own land.

The ideology of ideal Islamic womanhood has up to now allowed the monarchy to defuse opposition emanating from disparate conservative voices and at the same time negotiate between concerns about cultural erosion and the desire for change. Offering assurance that women will not be seen working in shops, or that the establishment of educational institutions for girls will not lead to their employment alongside men, curtailing scholarships to study abroad or denying women a right to travel without a male guardian's permission has mollified conservative feelings while the state has built its Westernized economic, educational and physical infrastructure and opened byways for women's access to it.

Because the ideology of ideal Islamic womanhood is so closely tied to monarchal power, women's issues have been subject to manipulation at particularly vulnerable points in time. Such was the case of the driving demonstration. From the point of view of the demonstrators, defying the ban on driving was about freedom from dependency: it was about being able to take a sick child for medical treatment, getting oneself to work, attending a social event, buying one's own groceries. The government's response, however, was about internal security. Had the incident occurred at another time, it is likely that, at worst, the women would have been stopped and taken home, at best they would have been ignored, and their determination rewarded with tacit approval of women' driving in the future. Instead, the demonstration became a way to appease the many voices rising in opposition to the monarchy over issues that has nothing to do with women's driving but with the conduct of monarchy during the Gulf crisis.

In Saudi Arabia, the political connection between gender, monarchy and national identity was vividly drawn out in a poem addressed to the King and circulated anonymously in Riyadh just after the demonstration. The poem begins,

the banners of secularism were raised in Najd.
I never thought I'd live to see
The daughter of the peninsula making light of principles
Attempting to remove the hijhab as though
She were a nation losing its might
Obvious to us as believers in an unswerving religion
In the shadow of which vice is not permitted
Sister, daughter of the peninsula thus have you done
As the trenches of aggression around you are dug?
Thus as the drums of war are beaten
Are you not ashamed to spread your call for throwing down the hijab?
Thus as the atheists have congregated round?
Your adherence to the hijab is devotion
And efforts to remove it are deterioration
I challenge the men of my tribe
Where is decency, was it lost in a culture
Which is Western, which buries decency as it enters ?
I wonder how the front can hold out
While behind it the sword of conspiracies is raised
I wonder how our soldiers can remain steadfast
While with the fires of apprehension their hearts burn
Afraid that the call of the uncovered women will destroy
And break what noble traits have been built into the home...
Oh servant of the Two Holy Shrines I fear that I shall see
The chain of cohesion in the peninsula shattered
Strike with the sword of righteousness the head of a vice
Whose trumpets are eating into us like decay...
Strike for God's sake, leave not in our land
A voice that calls openly for vice and blasphemy
A small mouse could destroy a mighty dam;
And one who is careless might destroy a nation[45]

The alignment of Saudi Arabia with the United States during the Gulf War and its aftermath is unlikely to produce any change in the political culture's construction of women. That alignment has in fact already given voice to young ultra-conservatives opposed to close relations with the United States. These groups oppose the Saudi discussions with Israel. They are opposed to the King's plan for a written constitution which would partially supplant the Shariah. They are opposed to the conservative civil-service religious bureaucracy whom they view as yes-men for the monarchy, and they are opposed to women working outside the home.[46] The rise in Islamic militancy suggests that the Gulf War alignment with the United States is, in effect, contributing to the unravelling of the cohesion of Saudi Arabia. Any further flirtation with the West will have to be countered by strong expressions of Islamic leadership on the home front: the instrument of proven success is the role of women.

NOTES

1. Broadsheet headed 'The names of the sluts who advocate vice and corruption on the earth', translated from Arabic to English, in possession of author. Unpublished, undated.
2. 'Letter addressed to Prince Salman bin Abdul Aziz, Prince of Riyadh', translated from Arabic to English, in possession of author. Unpublished, undated
3. 'From a report by a Mutawwa', translated from Arabic to English, in possession of author. Unpublished, undated.
4. *Arab News*, 14 Nov. 1990.
5. The following is an example of the way 'ideal Islamic woman' constructs a sense of religious-moral identity for the nation by constructing a sense of moral difference. 'A woman's role is no less significant than a man's, but it entirely differs from the man's role. It is only through a balanced coordination of their roles that a sound society is formed; when their roles get mixed up the result is invariably what we see and hear about moral degeneration, social corruption and family break-ups in Western societies. We would urge women to focus all their interest and attention on the task for which they have been created. A woman's task is essentially to work as a mother to bring up children and to prepare a noble generation.' *Al-Medina*, Saudi Arabia, January 1980.
6. Ad-Da wah no. 6036/19/1397 AH 1977, quoted from Hamad Muhammad Al-Baadi, 'Social Change: Education and the Roles of Women in Arabia.' Unpublished Ph.D. dissertation, Stanford University, 1982, pp. 133–4.
7. Valerie Hoffman-Laad, 'An Islamic Activist: Zaynab al-Ghazali', In Elizabeth Fernea (ed.), *Women and the Family in the Middle East, New Voices of Change* (Austin: University of Texas Press, 1985), pp. 231–54.

8. A discussion of this literature may be seen in Yvonne Haddad, 'Traditional Affirmations Concerning the Role of Women Found in Contemporary Arab Islamic Literature'. In *Women in Contemporary Muslim Societies*, ed. Jane Smith (Lewisburg: Bucknell University Press, 1980), pp. 61–86; see also Valerie Hoffman-Ladd, 'Polemics on the Modesty and Segregation of Women in Contemporary Egypt', *International Journal of Middle East Studies*, 19(1) (February 1987), pp. 23–50
9. Rema Hammami, 'Women, Hijab, and the Intifada', *Middle East Report*, 164/165 (May–August 1990), pp. 24–8; 'Gaza Journal: The Veiled Look. It's Enforced with a vengeance', *New York Times*, 22 August, 1991.
10. 'Divided House: Algeria Conflict Pits Father Against Son', *Wall Street Journal*, 23 January 1992.
11. William Darrow, 'Women Place and the Place of Women in the Iranian Revolution'. In Yvonne Haddad and Ellison Banks Findly (eds.), *Women, Religion and Social Change* (New York: State University of New York Press, 1985), pp. 307–19.
12. Polygyny is not only allowed but encouraged in one state-funded publication, which states that polygyny must be sanctioned because it is authorized by God in the Koran, and because polygyny assures a morally healthier society than is possible in the West. 'It is a fact that a healthy man has the ability to satisfy the sexual desire of four women. Should he restrict himself to only one wife as christians and others do and as muslim pretenders call for, this brings about many different kinds of corruption.' Abd Al-Rahman bin Hammad Al Umar, *Islam the Religion of Truth* (Kingdom of Saudi Arabia Supreme Head Office for Religious Research, Ifta, Call and Guidance, n.d.), p. 52.
13. This policy is rooted in social attitudes about women's protection, according to which a woman ideally never leaves her own house, and certainly not her own *dira*, her neighbourhood, without a male companion. A fatwa issued explaining the restriction states: 'A woman is not permitted to travel for purposes of a pilgrimage or otherwise except in the company of her husband or another mahram of hers. This is because the prophet (peace and prayers be upon him) said: A woman is not permitted to travel the duration of a day and a night without a mahram.' Ad-Dawah no. 767, 11/20/1400 A.H., 1980, quoted in Al-Baadi, p. 132.
14. Kingdom of Saudi Arabia, Labour Regulations. 'Employment of Juveniles and Women', Chapter X, Section 1, Article 160.
15. 'The Philosophy of Education in the Kingdom of Saudi Arabia', in Dr Abdulla Mohammed Al Zaid, *Education in Saudi Arabia* (Jeddah: Tihama Publications, 1981), p. 56.

16. 'Letter addressed to Prince Salman bin Abdul Aziz, Prince of Riyadh', translated from Arabic to English, in possession of author. Unpublished, undated.
17. *Arab News*, 5 September 1991.
18. In February 1991, for example, the General Presidency for Girls' Education announced a programme for the girls' colleges to be included in the next five year plan, a programme which is compatible with 'the aspirations of the state to qualify Saudi girls in the specialities appropriate to her nature and in harmony with Islamic Shariah, which preserves for women her dignity and her ability to take part in the advancement of Saudi women's society'. *Al-Jazira*, 28 February 1991, no. 6737.
19. Al-Baadi, p. 30.
20. Obedience to the Muslim ruler is a requirement emphasized in literature produced by the Department of Religious Guidance: 'Allah commanded the muslims to appoint from among themselves an Imam to be their ruler. Muslims should acknowledge to their ruler the rights of authority. They should also unite in one nation and never disperse. They are not allowed to disobey their rulers except in one case, when the ruler orders them to commit a sin or an action contrary to the commandments of Allah.' Abdul Rahman Al Omar, *Islam, the Religion of Truth* (Riyadh, 1401), p. 45.
21. Kingdom of Saudi Arabia, Ministry of Planning. Third Development Plan, 1980–85, p. 324.
22. John Habib, *Ibn Sa'ud's Warriors of Islam* (Leiden: E. J. Brill, 1978), p. 17.
23. Ibid., pp. 54–5.
24. Ibn Sa'ud revived the morality committees in 1903 after his conquest of the city of Riyadh, and with the conquest of the Hejaz, he established committees of Mutawwa in Mecca, Median and Jiddah, hiring a leading Meccan theologian to disseminate literature on the Wahhabi principle of enforcing good and preventing evil. See Ayman al-Yassini, *Religion and State in the Kingdom of Saudi Arabia* (Boulder and London: Westview, 1985), pp. 67–73
25. Ibid., pp. 67–73.
26. Ibid., p. 71.
27. Ibid., p. 70.
28. Ibid., p. 67.
29. *Wall Street Journal*, May 1991.
30. Al-Yassini, p. 67.
31. Ibid., p. 73.

32. See Christine Helms, *The Cohesion of Saudi Arabia* (Baltimore: John Hopkins University Press, 1981).
33. See, for example, Amin Rihani, *Maker of Modern Arabia* (Boston: Houghton, Mifflin, 1928).
34. Third Development Plan, p. 378.
35. In 1981, the King set up a 'Mehr' fund according to the announcement by Abd al-Aziz bin Baz, Director of the Department of Religious Guidance. 'In this way the poor class of native youth will be able to enter into the life of matrimony, protecting themselves from the vices of forbidden matters, and will ensure success for our social responsibility within the framework of Islamic Society.' The fund was to be administered by Shariah Court, and the prospective groom was to attest that he goes to the mosque five times a day. *Al Bilad*, June 1981.
36. Aisha Almana, 'Economic Development and its Impact on the Status of Women in Saudi Arabia', p. 204. 'This is a secret ruling,' Almana says. 'Previously Women in Saudi Arabia were entitled to separate identity or citizen cards.'
37. Almana, p. 204.
38. Circular issued by Saad ibn Mutrafi, Director, Haiat al-Amr bil Ma'roof, Jeddah, no. 1039, 9 January 1979; Circular issued by Abdullah ibn Muhammad al-Dubaikhi, General Supervisor, Haiat al-Amr bil Ma'roof, Eastern Province Branch, no. 178/6/T/129/1, 13 September 1982.
39. *Al-Jazirah*, no. 2738, 28 January 1980.
40. Ad-Da'wah, no. 767, 11/20/1400 (1980).
41. Interview with Ms el-Idris, ARAMCO employee and director of the clerical training programme (February 1981, in Dahran, Saudi Arabia).
42. Foreign Broadcast Information Service, 26 September 1990, p. 17.
43. 'The most important political document in the history of the kingdom of Saudi Arabia': *Al-Sha'ab* (Egypt), May 21, 1991; Clarification Document to King Fahd from Clergy, by Shaikh Abd al-Aziz bin Abd Allah bin Baz; no date, no place; in possession of author.
44. See Mai Yamani, 'Women in Saudi Arabia: Traditional roles and Modern Aspirations', unpublished paper presented at the Council on Foreign Relations, 23 January 1992.
45. 'An appeal from a girl to the servant of the Two Shrines', unpublished; no date; in author's possession.
46. Youssef Ibrahim, 'Saudi King Takes on Islamic Militants', *New York Times*, 30 January 1992.

Part III
Political Change and Militarization: the Impact of the Gulf War

10 Post-War Kuwait and the Process of Democratization: the Persistence of Political Tribalism

Paul Aarts[1]

Wars may have both destructive and integrative effects. It is a truism to say that the Second Gulf War had more than devastating results for the Arab world as a whole, Kuwait and Iraq obviously being the most affected. Less natural is the assertion that the Gulf War may also have had a *civilianizing* effect, comparable to earlier European experiences.[2] As Charles Tilly states, 'While we can not quite say that war caused democracy, bargaining over the means of war certainly involved European citizens in the creation of checks on arbitrary power.'[3] In a rather persuasible way, Tilly argues how the pursuit of war and military capacity, after having created national states as a sort of by-product, resulted in a kind of civilianization of government and domestic politics. This he dubs 'the central paradox of European state formation'.[4]

There are numerous indications that Third World states behave differently and do not follow the 'European road'. In the Middle East in particular the situation is anomalous. Here, in many cases, rulers have the capacity to find external sources with which to finance their expenditures (including war). Through distribution of rent income, legitimacy is bought and political stability enhanced. 'The availability of such resources made the rulers of the modern Middle East, at war or peace, far less attentive and responsive to domestic political and economic imperatives then their European counterparts at comparable stages of industrialization and administrative strength.'[5] At the level of international relations, this situation has been corroborated by US foreign policy, which sustainedly has been preoccupied with ensuring access to cheap oil, reinforcing conservativetendencies in the region and, concomitantly, withholding any support to democratic forces in the Gulf countries. In this respect, some even speak of an 'historic incompatibility of oil and democracy'.[6]

This might be an overstatement, however, because it is heedless of both divergent historical developments (i.e. Kuwait's idiosyncratic make-up) and recent traumatic events which shook several political systems to the core (notably Kuwait). In this article I will contend that Kuwait not only is an exceptional case among the oil-based rentier states, in which the state normally is fully autonomous *vis-à-vis* society, but also – and in more detail – that the trauma of occupation and liberation politicized the Kuwaiti people even further in a way that otherwise would not have occurred.

In that sense war continues to occupy a pivotal position, releasing societal diversity *vis-à-vis* state autocracy. The October 1992 elections brought a clear anti-government majority in parliament, widely seen as the beginning of a significant change in the relationship between the Kuwaiti public and its rulers. Although the wave of euphoria faded out sooner than anticipated, the ruling family's high-handed behaviour of the past can no longer easily be repeated.

THE EXPERIENCES OF THE PAST[7]

Two hundred years ago, the foundation was laid for what later would develop into a primitive form of political participation. Between the eighteenth century and the start of the oil age in the late fourties of this century, Kuwait's political power constellation was determined by an alliance of the Sabah dynasty, merchants (*tujjar*) and tribal shaikhs. The foundation of the alliance has to be found in the complementarity of interests between merchants (commanding economic power) and the Sabah family (controlling military and political matters). Their economic power procured the merchants important political clout, occasionally leading to frictions with the political elite.

After initial easy going together, the pro-British Mubarak al-Sabah (1896–1915) tried to break the economic power of these merchants by arbitrarily levying taxes on their commercial activities. He used this capital to buy off the so-called Utbi traders.[8] They were small, pro-British merchants deriving their income from the transit trade in primary commodities – coming for the most part from the British colonies – for the domestic market and other markets on the Arabian Peninsula. The eroded position of the Ottoman-oriented commercial elite, brought about by the fierce competition from British steamships in the regional trade, was helpful to Mubarak's efforts to eliminate its power. In 1909–10, the pearl merchants initiated a tax revolt against Mubarak after he had declared a ban on diving for the season. The major pearl merchants responded by 'voting with their feet (ships)' and migrated from Kuwait with their followers after the diving season.[9]

This internal discord among the Kuwaiti traders was to persevere until the twenties and thirties of this century. In 1938, a broad coalition of oppositional forces (including members of the ruling family and partisans of a closer co-operation with Iraq) extorted the creation of a National Legislative Council (*majlis al-umma al-tashri'i*). It proved a fleeting exercise in defying the ruler's absolute power. After a six-month spell the *majlis* was dissolved.

Oil had been struck in 1936, but it would still take until 1946 before exports from Kuwait went into gear. From that moment on, oil revenues enabled the ruling Sabah clan to detach itself gradually from the trade families' support. The merchants paid a political price, redeemed by economic indemnification. They lost immediate access to the ruling coalition, but that did not lead to their economic marginalization. On the contrary, they managed to get hold of enormous amounts of money, due, partially, to the Kuwaiti government's policy of large-scale land acquisition. In addition, representatives of the richer merchant families acquired leading positions in both state-founded undertakings, listed on the stock market, and the private sector, which the merchants considered their exclusive domain. In short, they forged an historic compromise: 'the merchants would forgo political participation in exchange for wealth beyond their wildest imagination'.[10] The ruler made a quiet promise to keep the Sabahs out of Kuwaiti business. In as far as the wealthy members of the ruling family had not invested their money abroad – as most of them were wont to do – they operated very discreetly in their own country, namely on the basis of cooperation with traders.

Gaining independence (1961) gave the desire for political participation a new impetus. Two years after independence, the first elections for 'parliament' were held.[11] Apart from Cabinet members of the ruling family, merchant notables, representatives of the intelligentsia, Shi'ites and Bedouin were delegated. The amir tried to balance the merchants with the other groups in parliament, in turn politicizing each community. Once politicized, however, these communities became harder to control.[12] The merchants' political clout gradually declined.

Intense debates about, among other things, whether or not to nationalize Kuwait Oil Company (KOC) led to the temporary dissolution of parliament in 1967. Relations between the new amir, Shaikh Sabah al-Salim (1965–77), and the parliamentary opposition had cooled considerably. This made the government look for new allies. By a massive naturalization programme, enfranchising tens of thousands of tribesmen, the ruling family assured itself of electoral loyalty. These select tribal groups were given low income housing and jobs in the police and the army. In the coming years their electoral power was to grow by leaps and bounds.[13] By rigging the 1967 election the government managed to have a far more docile Assembly than its predecessor, but as of 1973, nationalist sentiments again prevailed. In 1976, a new dissolution followed.[14]

Growing oil revenues gave the resources for expanding the state's role. Paradoxically, this has reduced state autonomy. As Richards and Waterbury forcefully argue, 'Part of the complexity and diversity that state intervention brought about lay in the creation of new class actors and interests that benefited from state policies or from state business. Over time, these groups have become entrenched in their economic niches, absorbing resources, saving and investing in such a manner that they developed some economic autonomy and the means to lobby effectively *vis-à-vis* the state.'[15] Although this statement certainly applies more to *non*-rentier states in the Middle East, there is more than some truth in it for Kuwait too, a rentier state *par excellence*.

A steadily growing bureaucratic and technocratic apparatus led to unintended (and undesired) consequences. It is common knowledge that bureaucracies never tend to be neutral. 'As these institutions grow in size and complexity, they are becoming less amenable to control through ruling kinship networks... Bureaucrats have the potential for developing their own centers of power, social relationships, and political ideals and goals.'[16] Once again, the old merchant families are taking centre stage. In particular, sons of the pre-oil era's commercial elite succeeded in permeating the highest levels of the bureaucracy. They were the first, after all, to be sent abroad for their education and to acquire the technocratic and financial skills the state needed. In this way, the merchants might gain in a different form what they had lost because of the oil extraction, even if through the 'back door' of the bureaucracy: political clout.[17] With regard to this, special attention has to be given to the national oil – refining industry. Here we find an exemplary, though unexpected, case of economic policy which has ramifications beyond the government's original intentions.[18]

It was self-evident that the bureaucrats and technocrats within the public sector routed their claims mainly through the ministries, whereas the entrepreneurs in the private sector lent weight to their demands through parliament. In 1981, elections for the National Assembly had again been called for. Mainly as a result of re-districting (favouring tribal candidates), and more subtle ways of vote – buying, the tribal deputies rose from 22 in 1975 to 27 in 1981 (out of a total of 50 seats).[19] The major opposition groups lost, but new groups had joined the Assembly: deputies who had run on a sectarian (i.e. religious, Sunni or Shia) basis.[20] Sunni Islamists became the leading opposition, at times joined by the Shia. The Sabah family was clearly apprehensive about the Assembly's influence; the numerous instances in which parliamentary pressures were nipped in the bud may serve as examples. Government was not always successful in this, however. The Islamists, for example, managed to get the liberal education minister ousted, and, together with other deputies, put the oil and finance ministers through the mill. After the 1985 elections, the government discovered to its dismay that the Islamists and the nationalists, rather than neutralizing each other, showed an unanticipated ability to coordinate their opposition. The financial and political aftermath of the Suq al-Manakh crisis,[21] emanations from the Iran–Iraq war (among other things, violent opposition by pro-Iranian Shia), but most of all, plummeted oil prices brought the amir in July 1986 to dissolve parliament indefinitely. Constitutional provisions for new elections were suspended.

In the ensuing non-parliamentary period Kuwait was not to be exempted from political turmoil. The pro-democracry movement, calling for restoration of constitution and parliament, gradually came into prominence and Islamist and nationalist forces displayed an even greater sense of pragmatism than before. At certain moments the Sabahs gave the impression of being willing to cave in. In April 1990, however, the amir announced the establishment of a National Council (*majlis al-watani*), with only advisory powers, comprising 50 elected and 25 appointed members. Most of the opposition disqualified the council as 'toothless' and decided to boycott the elections. As a result, the slates were dominated by 'taxi drivers', i.e. non-elite Kuwaitis from tribal backgrounds.[22] The National Council had barely started its yes-manning activities when Saddam's army, on 2 August 1990, put an end to its operation.

INSIDERS VERSUS OUTSIDERS

The Kuwaitis closed ranks. In October this was demonstrated during the three-day Popular Conference in Jiddah, though not without asking for a *quid pro quo*. This meeting of a thousand-odd Kuwaiti exiles, spanning the political spectrum, took place under the principle that 'If we don't hang together, we will surely hang separately.' The opposition and the crown prince hammered out an understanding: the ruler would promise restoration of the 1962 constitution while the opposition would stand loyally behind him. Liberalization would follow liberation.

Resistance inside Kuwait was mainly organized through the mosques, which became the centre of Kuwaiti gatherings, apart from the old system of (now secretly held) *diwanniyas*.

In here the Kuwaitis organized themselves into various committees (information and communication, food distribution, educational, medical, and cleaning). The Islamic movement, in particular the Social Reform Society (Muslim Brotherhood) and the Heritage Society (*salafi*), played a pivotal role in the food cooperatives. Many of the elected boards were controlled by these Sunni Islamists. They were also heavily represented in many of the other voluntary committees, but here their influence had to be shared with secular forces (former Baathists and Arab nationalists) and – last but not least – the Shiite Islamists of the Cultural and Social Society.[23] Not surprisingly, mainly Shia Kuwaitis took to arms and made sporadic small-scale attacks on Iraqi soldiers at night. Life under occupation obscured long-established differences between liberals and Islamists, and between Sunnis and Shia. In short, it led to a 'democratization of everyday life'.[24] Among those of Kuwait's nationals who stayed after the invasion – less than a third[25] – a strong feeling of solidarity grew, hitherto unknown in Kuwaiti society.

This led to a psychological division between 'insiders' (or remainees, called *al-samidoun*, the steadfast) and 'outsiders' (or, alternatively, returnees, called *al-hariboun*, the fleers), which was aggravated by the government's behaviour on the eve of the ground war. From Jiddah it was announced that immediately upon liberation the country would be placed under martial law. This was in flagrant contradiction with the promise made at the Popular Conference in Jiddah in October 1990. After liberation, the Kuwaitis faced the gigantic task of triply reconstructing their country: economically (the mere costs of repairing damaged infrastructure is estimated at $160 billion), socially (less reliance on foreign workers), and politically.

The amir put up a poor show by waiting two weeks before returning to his temporary palace, refurbished with golden taps. That stirred up bad feelings not only in circles of 'insiders', but also among those who had returned immediately, putting up with bad post-war conditions (no electricity, no adequate food and water). Late March 1991 the amir dissolved the pre-war Cabinet, but did neither announce the forming of a new, reformed Cabinet nor an early election date. The crown prince argued that reconstruction and security should take precedence over democratization. After another Cabinet was formed, there were no new faces in it. As far as the opposition was concerned, this was only more of the same, and by this time citizen–state relations had reached a nadir from an already remarkable pre-invasion low.

THE 1992–6 PARLIAMENT

Under the umbrella of a unified demand for (a) restoration of parliamentary life, and (b) protection and implementation of the constitution (both promises made at the Jiddah Congress), seven political groups formed the Political Alliance.[26] It was an unusual attempt at coalition politics, ranging from secularized pan-Arab nationalists to fundamentalist Muslims, from capitalist merchant elites to Western-educated professionals and intellectuals. The Alliance was representative of various classes, sects and social strata of Kuwaiti society and therefore could not be more than a loosely framed coalition. Four of the seven opposition groups were so well-organized that many observers believe they could form the potential nuclei for full-fledged political parties.

The results of the October 1992 elections – bringing in a marked majority of oppositional candidates (35 out of 50 members) – were hailed by some as 'a new dawn for a new Kuwait' and a 'clean sweep in the city'. Also the newly formed sixteen-man Cabinet, with six ministries going to newly elected members of parliament, looked like a clear improvement compared to earlier Cabinet formations. Although some fundamental complaints remained, e.g. about the persisting monopolization of top ministries by al-Sabah family members, the opposition accepted the trading of a hoped-for majority within the Cabinet against an actual majority in the Assembly.

Two years after the opposition groups in Jiddah had accepted the proposed deal, 'support us now and, come liberation, we will give you your parliament', this promise was now redeemed. The new Assembly took matters seriously and wanted new policies, not just new faces. Economic and financial issues were set to dominate politics in the years ahead. The resulting effect was supposed to be a substantial extension of parliamentary control and public debate of policy matters which previously had been the virtual prerogative of the ruling family (in particular with regard to oil and investment policies).

The seventh session of the National Assembly was full of lively debate and the MPs had an opinion on all major issues, many of which had a financial aspect. One of the most controversial, and protacted, issues has been the burden of *bad debts* arising from the Suq al-Manahk crash of 1982 and the Iraqi invasion of 1990. A sizeable amount of the bad debts date back to the collapse of the Kuwaiti unofficial stock exchange, after which the government had dug in its heels and refused to comply with the Assembly's demand for publication of the list of all debtors whose loans have been taken over by the government. Many of the major debtors come from the highest echelons of Kuwaiti society – including members of the royal family – which gives the issue an explicit political character. It is widely believed that these well-to-do Kuwaitis are well able to pay what they owe, but are secretly keeping funds abroad or understating their true net worth.[27] For a long time it looked like this topic was going to provide the first showdown between the Assembly and the al-Sabah family.

Arguments about the ways and means of settling the debts had been going on for many years, but finally in August 1993 a new law was passed that might settle the issue. Debtors were given a choice between repaying what they owed (minus a discount) immediately or rescheduling the whole amount over twelve years. Two years later, after the end of the second 'act' of the 'Difficult Debts Settlement Program' (DDSP2), an end to the bad debt problems was in sight. However, when a deadline was put off again and a further grace period was allowed, many analysts sensed that the government's commitment to the scheme and its willingness to take tough decisions against Kuwaiti citizens were in doubt. Less-sceptical observers, and local bankers, argued differently. According to their view the first deadline had been the most critical, and after that the process of settlement had developed a momentum of its own. The significance of the settlement supposedly lies in the fact that the process has started, rather than in the amounts settled. Moreover, by the end of 1995 more than 75 per cent of the debtors actually paid up. At last the world's longest-running financial soap opera is coming to an end and it seems that the National Assembly can claim at least one victory in its battle against vested interests.

Foreign investment allegations are not new in Kuwaiti politics, but could be traced back to about thirty years ago. During discussions in the 1992 Assembly, attention was drawn to the fact that most embezzlements in the past decade were committed in the wake of the dissolution of the 1985 National Assembly (which lasted from 1986 till October 1992). MP Ahmed Baqir said it was not surprising that such abuses of public money had occurred, since the amir had left the country without a 'watchdog'. Key players in the Kuwait Investment Office (KIO) scandal were Shaikh Fahd Mohammad al-Sabah, chairman for more than twenty years and a cousin of the amir; the ebullient and energetic oil minister, Sheikh Ali Khalifa al-Sabah (who also was finance minister between 1982 and 1985, and from June 1990 till April 1991), a cousin of the amir and a first cousin of KIO's chairman; and Fouad Jaafar, general manager of KIO. During the Iraqi invasion the investment office in central London had become Kuwait's treasury in exile. The management in London was granted total and unsupervised control of the country's foreign investments, much to the dismay of the opposition. Sheikh Ali Khalifa together with Sheikh Fahd started selling many of KIO's bluest-chip assets. In fact, no one knew where the cash was going. During one of the Assembly sessions in early 1993, Abdullah al-Nibari sighed: 'Those entrusted with our overseas investments acted on the assumption that Kuwait will not be liberated from Iraqi occupation. Had the occupation lasted longer, nothing would have remained of our money.'[28] The value of investments, estimated at $100 billion before the Iraqi invasion, had fallen to less than one quarter this figure, mainly because of reckless management. Meanwhile, bit by bit, revelations were made about KIO's 'fallen empire' in Spain. At the end of 1992, it became known that Kuwait's nearly $5 billion investments had a negative value of $400 million, a combination of industrial downturn, asset liquidation and alleged mismanagement and embezzlement. Here also no one seemed to know where the billions went.[29]

The National Assembly became fully convinced that it must get the bottom of it. Each new revelation had made it ever

Post-War Kuwait: Political Tribalism

clearer that a major scandal had been brewing, involving high-ranking Kuwaiti officials and a cast of dubious characters. Slowly but surely the oppositional deputies got a grip on the situation and Sheikh Ali in particular came under further attack, also because of his involvement in the alleged misappropriation of funds at the Kuwait Oil Tanker Co. (KOTC; see below). The Assembly seemed out for royal blood. Early in October 1993, the attorney-general finally imposed a travel ban on Sheikh Ali, followed by a few days of high drama (and the subsequent lifting of the ban on humanitarian grounds). In the meantime, the Kuwaiti government got very much embarrassed by the *Financial Times*'s allegations that KIO illegaly obtained tax refunds of over £600 million.[30] Fears were widespread that this affair might lead to other revelations about KIO's activities, which were worth tens of billions of dollars and might have given rise to other unjustified tax refunds. On top of all this came another report, commissioned by the 1992 Assembly, revealing more bad management of Kuwait's foreign investments between 1989 and 1992, resulting in more net losses of $640 million.[31] Gradually, attention shifted from one scandal to another, for some Kuwaitis raising the opportunity of finally chopping Sheikh Ali Khalifa's head off.

Late in 1992, a lot of commotion had been caused when it became known that former executives of the Kuwait Oil Tanker Company (KOTC) allegedly had misappropriated more than $100 million. During the tanker war at the height of the Iraq–Iran war, KOTC officials profited from tanker purchases in Korea, involving hefty commissions from South Korean shipyards. KOTC's former deputy president was held for questioning, while its former president managed to escape the country.

The fat was in the fire, however, when Sheikh Ali Khalifa's name too was mentioned in the KOTC embezzlement affair. For the first time in Kuwaiti history a member of the royal family; was formally charged with a criminal offence. According to most observers the ruling family was (and still is) likely to defend Sheikh Ali to the bitter end. The main explanation for this is not because he is an influential member of the royal family; far from that. The royalist cover he receives is rather made understandable by his extensive knowledge of intimate details of the family's finances and his easy access to the media (Sheikh Ali owns one of Kuwait's leading Arabic dailies, *al-Watan*). The National Assembly, however, took an unflinching position, the more so after the state Audit Bureau had labelled the 1981 takeover of Santa Fe as a 'hasty and controversial' decision, causing a loss of almost $3 billion between 1981 and 1990. Moreover, Assembly members accused the former oil minister of having accepted bribes in the course of KPC's takeover of Santa Fe.

The KOTC trial started early 1994, with only Sheikh Ali and KOTC's former deputy chairman, Hassan Qabazard, in the country. The other co-defendants were being tried *in absentia*. While Sheikh Ali denied all charges, he remained free throughout and – as expected – his trial became effectively tied up in knots by the ex-minister's legal team. The defence was able to exploit some ambiguity in the legal position to obfuscate the issue. After much bickering (around the alleged illegality of the trial court and the amir setting the stage for a constitutional crisis),[32] Sheikh Ali's case was separated from the other four and sent to the new Ministers Court. In exchange, twelve of the thirteen charges against him were dropped. Although Ali Khalifa's long-time opponents do not feel very confident about the special court's final verdict, they do consider the (ex-)minister's trial as a great achievement.[33] Mid-1996 a criminal court found three of his co-defendants guilty of corruption. They were sentenced to prison terms of 15–40 years and ordered to pay fines as well as reimburse the company for a total of $130.8 million.[34]

Another, related, achievement of the 1992 parliament took place in the wake of the KOTC scandal, when a new law to protect public funds was adopted in January 1993. It gave the National Assembly the right to scrutinize, reject or approve any transaction by a state-owned company, or any company in which the state has a stake of 25 per cent, involving an outlay of $330,000 or more. In the Assembly debate, neither the finance minister nor the prime minister could mount an effective campaign against the law.

One more success was booked in the field of *budgetary control*. In particular, as Kuwaitis were asked to tighten their belts (see below), there was a rising clamour for clean, more accountable and transparent government. It was in 1994 that the Assembly demanded, and won, the right to approve the budget on a line-by-line basis. That year was the first time that parliament was involved in detailed budget planning. As the *Financial Times* rightly stated, 'Indeed it is as financial watchdog of a government used to buy loyalty through patronage that the Assembly has made its biggest impact.'[35] Mid-1995, a parliamentary committee accused the defence ministry of corruption and incompetence, denouncing the misappropriation of several hundred million dollars through arms contracts. One year later a bill was drafted by the Assembly which obliged all military contracts to be subject to public tender.

An issue which for some time had stayed in the (parliamentary) background, but was gradually coming to the fore, is the widely shared anxiety about the country's fundamental economic weaknesses, and the required *economic policy* to cope with that situation. For the first time since Kuwait became a major oil producer fifty years ago, the ruling family was starting to realize that oil revenue alone cannot finance the comprehensive welfare state to which it had accustomed Kuwait's citizens and thereby secured their loyalty, most recently in the period after the liberation in 1991. Although official unemployment among Kuwaitis is very low, disguised unemployment is as high as 20–40 per cent, and it is estimated that up to 8,000 young Kuwaitis enter the job market every year.[36] The budget deficit began to look structural and permanent ways of dealing with that had to be found.

Here again, economist Jasem al-Sadoun acted as the unoffical spokesman of those critics who made no effort to disguise their feelings and argued strongly in favour of radical measures. To name a few, squeezing public expenditure (by reviewing direct and indirect subsidies and reducing defence outlays); instilling a greater work ethic in the national population; cuts in the public-sector wage bill; and the creation of a more market-oriented economy.

Early in 1994, in a keynote speech to the nation, Kuwait's crown prince and prime minister, Sheikh Saad Abdallah al-Sabah, announced belt-tightening and privatization measures. He was preceded by finance minister Nasir al-Rudhan, who had stressed the need to reduce the budget deficit by imposing charges for some public services, declaring that

Kuwaitis should be willing to give up 'some of the welfare state'.[37] Serious consideration should be given to the introduction of some form of general taxation. When the government finally submitted its proposals to the Assembly, combining all kinds of (hardly popular) cuts, together with an expansionary budget deficit, the Assembly's finance and economic affairs committee was infuriated. It accused the government of playing politics by shifting the burden of cost-cutting onto the Assembly. It clearly was an indication of the government's tactic of distancing itself as much as possible from unpopular measures, while – at the same time – creating divisions within the opposition's ranks.

This situation did not change in the period preceding the October 1996 elections. The resolve to match the rhetoric remained to be found. The debate on how to reduce the public-sector deficit continued unabatedly, however, focusing on how to develop a sustainable fiscal strategy. While the imposition of a personal income tax could be ruled out in the foreseeable future, there was much discussion on the introduction of *zakat* (at the rate of 2.5 per cent on the annual income of companies), and at the end of 1995 a draft law was passed in parliament. The implementation of the Islamic tithe, though, is also not without controversy as there are substantial differences of opinion between religious groups. In the meantime, deputies in the Assembly lobbied for more detailed responsibility in the budget-making process, arguing in favour of legislative budget limits, including areas where the government should and should not spend as well as limits on the size of the deficit. Some piecemeal attempts to cut spending were made by the government, but a masterplan was still not there. The election campaign in the run up to the October 1996 elections delayed even further any far-reaching economic reforms as parliament was much less prepared to take unpopular decisions. On top of that, oil revenue was well above the official target, thereby substantially reducing the deficit and apparently taking away the need to take drastic measures.

The government was still reeling from the impact on the Kuwaiti public of the Iraqi invasion. That is why the *'invasion file'* is one of those other issues which are less related to inance but none the less figured prominently in parliamentary debates. In the first weeks of the new Assembly's term, the crown prince had asked for assurances that the investigative committee would not embark on a witch hunt within the government and ruling family. The committee should limit itself to fact-finding, no blame to be apportioned. The always outspoken Abdullah al-Nibari, member on the committee, remarked in response that it had the authority to constitute itself as a judicial inquiry and prosecute whomever it thinks necessary.

For quite some time it looked not inconceivable that this issue too might lead to a clash with the al-Sabah family. A foretaste was given by the opposition's demand of the appointment of a commoner as chief-of-staff in lieu of Sheikh Jabir al-Khaled al-Sabah. Fear of having to appear before the investigative committee made him resign in March 1993. Furthermore, rumours were around that members of the royal family had enriched themselves since the war with commissions, usually in excess of 20 per cent, paid by foreign suppliers of military equipment (see above).

In mid-1996, the long-awaited National Assembly's 520-page report on the events leading to the Iraqi invasion was debated. The report criticized ministers for the handling of Iraq in the weeks before the invasion, but in essence it came to the conclusion that the government did not order the armed forces to mount defence of the country until the last minute. As expected, the government's reaction was furious, accusing the Assembly of bias in its investigation of the affair, triggering a walkout by 12 deputies from the Assembly hall. Needless to say, not all opponents of the regime were equally satisfied with the report's findings.[38]

Another political hot potato – though much less discussed in parliament than the other issues dealt with above – remained the *nationality question*. The Kuwaiti citizenship law is one of the most frequently amended of Kuwaiti laws. So far this happened nine times, as a result of which previously qualifying large groups of residents were stripped of their right to citizenship. This problematic is related to the state's peculair division into first-, second-, and third-class citizens. The Iraqi invasion had renewed the old question about Kuwaiti nationality, i.e. the status of the *bidun jinsiyyah* ('without nationality/citizenship'). The bidun are those Gulfians unable to prove Kuwaiti residency but lacking other nationality papers.

The government already had started a crackdown on the position of the bidun in the mid-eighties. After liberation this was intensified and all the bidun who had been employed by the Kuwaiti government were dismissed *en masse*, retroactively from 2 August 1990.[39] Since then their general condition has worsened deeply. The National Assembly has not been very active and appears to have deferred to the government on the bidun issue, although MPs regularly expressed concern about lack of progress in solving their case. Human Rights Watch/Middle East correctly remarks that few support granting citizenship in large numbers, even among opposition deputies.[40] The newly established National Assembly's Committee for the Defence of Human Rights – one of the opposition's achievements in the 1992 parliament – has also rarely addressed the issue of the bidun.

During the second half of the Assembly's eighth session, the deputies' attention tended to divert more and more into the direction of *cultural and moral issues*. Campaigns which had attracted popular support in the early days of the Assembly began to ran out of steam, and 'immature' debates, in particular between Islamists and secularists, gained the upper hand. Instead of addressing the wide spectrum of more pressing problems, the Assembly spend much of its time debating side-issues such as co-education at the university, the wearing of headscarves and amending the constitution in a more Islamic one.

Not only ahead of the elections in October 1996, but also much earlier, the Islamist fundamentalist faction had been anxious to thrust these issues higher up the policy agenda, followed by lengthy debates, drafting of bills, and one vote after another. Islamist policies were responsible for this 'culture war', and much of the paralysis afflicting the 1992 parliament resulted from that. One prominent issue was the draft bill which contained the banning of any contact between men and women in the university, as well as banning the contact between male and female students at applied education institutions and private schools. In the second round, the draft of a segregation law finally was adopted. As the elections were in sight, the deputies apparently would not risk losing votes if they objected to the segregation proposal. Kuwaiti women activists, though, are in disagreement on the likely implications of the adoption of this law.[41]

THE 1996 ELECTIONS: SHEIKHS AND BALANCES

The feeling of euphoria which had followed the 1992 elections faded out sooner than anticipated. Although some achievements were to be noted, the Kuwaiti public had all in all become disillusioned by an Assembly which had proven itself to be long on debate but short on action. The parliamentarians mainly had to look at home for the cause, but the negative role of the government was not to be sneezed at: not only did the regime help the Islamists a lot (believing that this might check the power of the secularist opposition), but it also regularly raised the threat of an Iraqi invasion to try to silence its opponents, of whatever political colour they might be.

That was the political climate in which the electoral campaign and the next elections took place. The electorate had always been restricted to men over 21 who could prove Kuwaiti ancestry, but for the 1996 election this had been relaxed to include children and descendants of naturalized citizens. The total number of eligible voters increased by one-third to 107,000, of which 82.5 per cent cast their vote.[42]

The elections on 7 October 1996 resulted in a clear shift in the parliamentary balance of power in favour of the government. The *Arab Times* spoke of 'one of the most conservative parliaments in the nation's short democratic history'.[43] Sixteen members of the 1992 Assembly who contested the elections were defeated – among whom were several prominent MPs. Nine others did not contest, thus making a total change of 50 per cent in the Assembly. Islamists and the government with its supporters emerged as the major winners, while liberals were handed perhaps their most crushing defeat ever. Seventeen full-blown pro-government candidates won a seat (as against 15 in 1992) and a good number of (Islamist) independents are likely to stand with the government on many issues. Moreover, the government can also count on the support of appointed Cabinet members who are *ex officio* Assembly members.

While the 1992 elections had been almost completely free of allegations of fraud, overt manipulation or vote-buying, the 1996 elections were far from unblemished. 'Service candidates', carrying the message 'vote for me and I will cut through red tape to secure the services you need', campaigned prominently and won a sizeable number of seats. Vote-buying was more open than before, and the amounts offered were larger than ever (up to KD5,000).[44] Jasem al-Sadoun commented that 'the government tried to buy everybody from everywhere', while MP Hassan Jawhar put forward an equally scathing criticism: 'Since 1961 the government wants to contain democracy, if not by suspending parliament then from within via service candidates. In 1992, the international atmosphere was not good for the government to openly interfere in the elections, but now there seemed to be no obstacle.'[45]

The new Cabinet sworn in was a clear reflection of the election results and, obviously, elicited heavy criticism from opposition circles. Abdullah al-Nibari, of the Kuwait Democratic Forum, denounced the inclusion in the Cabinet of members who have 'unclean records against democracy and the Assembly', and vented his anxiety that Kuwait was heading towards 'another period of immobility and muddling'.[46] This assessment looks correct. Although the new parliament is more to the government's liking than its predecessor, it might make things worse. Paradoxically, the more conservative Assembly is likely to make it more difficult for the government to undertake necessary economic reforms, since the pro-government deputies were largely 'service candidates', who made promises that the government cannot afford to keep. The fact is that they were elected just because they were opposed to belt-tightening. On political issues, however, the government now has a more or less free hand. Instead of regular confrontations with the Assembly – as was the case in the 1992 parliament – the future might lead to more open conflict with institutions of Kuwaiti civil society.

CONCLUSION

'Political development is shaped by war and trade.' This maxim – thought of by Peter Gourevitch in 1978[47] – applies emphatically to the rentier state of Kuwait. Both dimensions have been discussed above: 'trade' in a more implicit way and rather briefly, 'war' explicitly and more extensively. The second Gulf War may prove a blessing in disguise from a democratization standpoint. The trauma of invasion, war and liberation has politicized the Kuwaitis in a manner that otherwise might not have occurred. It opened the way toward more pluralist politics, although one should be careful not to overstate the argument, as recent developments have shown.

In most Arab countries there is neither a well-developed concept of citizenship nor of public responsibility of the state. Kuwait is no exception to that, albeit there is a vast difference between the Kuwaiti experience of limited political liberalization and those of the other Arab states in the Gulf region. 'Political tribalism' still is the basic form of social organization of the states in the Arab Peninsula.[48] But, as with all authoritarian forms of organization, the system of political tribalism also has its built-in limits and leads to economic, political and cultural stagnation. On top of that came the Gulf crisis, proving the inability of the Kuwaiti regime to guarantee external security, which seriously (further) undermined the government's legitimacy.

As Salamé writes, Kuwait has been oscillating between a tribal authoritarianism and an oligarchic republicanism.[49] Under clear pressure the ruling family has reluctantly submitted to several demands of the opposition. Political developments in Kuwait look like pointing in the direction of more openess and away from the familiar patterns of monocracy. Seeing no way out, the regime has 'chosen' to broaden rather than contract the democratization process. Note that this policy has the appurtenant benefit of 'sharing the burden' and relieving the regime from having directly to shoulder the full blame for all problems. Moreover, as a result of shifting the burden of cost-cutting onto the Assembly, divisions within its opposition ranks might deepen. Nevertheless, all this has certainly widened the space for interest-group leaders to display their aptitude for broadening all kinds of mixed commissions (of government and group leaders) into power-sharing arrangements that encompass a wider range of views about economic, political and social reform. With some hesitancy it could thus be argued that Kuwait's post-war political system is showing the contours of a 'mid-intensity democracy'. To be sure, its tentative democracy is a small, male preserve, but the Gulf War toughened the sinews of a people (m/f) already more politicized than any other Gulf Arabs. Much will depend on the role played by the Third Estate, dubbed as 'the leaven of civil society'.[50] Indubitably the ruling family will not willingly give up anything of importance, but its high-handed behaviour of the past cannot easily be repeated.

NOTES

1. This article is a revised and updated version of the author's 'Les limites du "tribalisme politique". Le Koweit d'après-guerre et le processus de démocratisation', *Monde arabe/Maghreb-Machrek*, no. 142, October–December 1993, pp. 61–79.
2. Charles Tilly, *Coercion, Capital, and European States, AD 990–1992* (Oxford: Blackwell, 1992) and Tilly, 'War and State Power', *Middle East Report*, July–August 1991, pp. 38–40. Also Dietrich Rueschemeyer, Evelyne Huber Stephens and John D. Stephens, *Capitalist Development and Democracy* (Cambridge: Polity Press, 1992), pp. 70–1 and p. 279.
3. Tilly, 'War and State Power', p. 38.
4. Tilly, *Coercion, Capital, and European States*, p.206.
5. Lisa Anderson, 'Remaking the Middle East: The Prospects for Democracy and Stability', *Ethics and International Affairs*, vol. 6 (1992), p. 167.
6. MERIP Editors, 'The Democracy Agenda in the Arab World', *Middle East Report*, January–February 1992, p. 47.
7. This section draws upon earlier work. Paul Aarts, Gep Eisenloeffel and Arend Jan Termeulen, 'Oil, Money, and Participation: Kuwait's *Sonderweg* as a Rentier State', *Orient*, 32 no. 2 (1991), pp. 205–16.
8. Jacqueline S. Ismael, *Kuwait: Social Change in Historical Perspective* (New York: Syracuse University Press, 1982), p. 55, and *Kuwait: Dependency and Class in a Rentier State* (Gainesville: University of California Press, 1993), pp. 57–8.
9. Ismael *Kuwait* (1982), p. 58; and Mary Ann Tétreault, 'Autonomy, Necessity, and the Small State: Ruling Kuwait in the Twentieth Century', *International Organization*, 45, 4 (Autumn 1991), p. 574.

10. Fareed Mohamedi, 'State and Bourgeoisie in the Persian Gulf', *Middle East Report*, November–December 1992, p. 35.
11. The quotation marks indicate the parliament's limited degree of representation. Its fifty members could only be elected by 'first-class' citizens, i.e. adult males whose families had lived in Kuwait since 1920. The actual number of voters is always a tiny fraction of the total population. To some extent this type of 'democracy' recalls Athenian democracy. As one observer noted: 'Like the Athenian democracy described by David Held, Kuwait was "a tyranny of citizens", with the *demos* consisting entirely of male adults of incontestable Athenian (Kuwaiti) descent' (Ghassan Salamé, 'Small is Pluralistic: Democracy as an Instrument of Civil Peace', in Salamé (ed.), *Democracry without Democrats? The Renewal of Politics in the Muslim World*, London/New York: I. B. Tauris, 1994, p. 100). None the less, the Assembly's importance should not be underestimated, which may become apparent from the above exposé.
12. Jill Crystal, *Oil and Politics in the Gulf: Rulers and Merchants in Kuwait and Qatar* (Cambridge: Cambridge University Press, 1990), p. 83.
13. Nicolas Gavrielides, 'Tribal Democracy: the Anatomy of Parliamentary Elections in Kuwait', in Linda L. Layne (ed.), *Elections in the Middle East* (Boulder/London: Westview Press, 1987); and Crystal, *Oil and Politics in the Gulf*, pp. 88–9.
14. For more details, see Crystal, *Oil and Politics in the Gulf*, pp. 91–3; Crystal, *Kuwait: The Transformation of an Oil State* (Boulder: Westview Press, 1992), p. 97; and Essa Al-Sa'di and Richard U. Moench, 'Oil Prices, State Policies and Politics in Kuwait', *Arab Studies Quarterly*, 10 no. 2 (1988), pp. 220–1.
15. Alan Richards and John Waterbury, *A Political Economy of the Middle East: State, Class, and Economic Development* (Boulder: Westview Press, 1990), p. 236.
16. Crystal, *Oil and Politics in the Gulf*, p. 174.
17. Crystal, 'Coalitions in Oil Monarchies', pp. 438–9; and Crystal, *Oil and Politics in the Gulf*, p. 175. For a comparison of the predominant role of Kuwait's old merchant class as a client group with other ('capitalist' and 'socialist') oil states, see among others Crystal, *Oil and Politics in the Gulf*, pp. 112–70 ('Qatar'); and Kiren Aziz Chaudhry, 'Economic Liberalization in Oil-Exporting Countries: Iraq and Saudi Arabia', in Iliya Harik and Denis J. Sullivan (eds), *Privatization and Liberalization in the Middle East* (Bloomington: Indiana University Press, 1992), pp. 145–66.

18. For more detail, see Aarts et al., 'Oil, Money, and Participation', pp. 210–12.
19. Different sources give different figures, but the general trend is clear: pro-government Bedouin were the big winners in the 1981 elections. See among others, Gavrielides, 'Tribal Democracy', pp. 165–70; Crystal, *Kuwait: The Transformation of an Oil State*, p. 98; and Said Zahlan, *The Making of the Modern Gulf States*, p. 43.
20. Zahlan, *The Making of the Modern Gulf States* (London 1989), p .43.
21. The crash of the unoffical stock market took place in 1982. The affair continues to affect Kuwaiti politics and economy up to now. Interpretations differ on the cause of the crisis. See Gavrielides, 'Tribal Democracy', p. 175; Haider Hassan Al-Jumah, *The Kuwaiti Stock Market Crisis* (Kuwait, 1986); Crystal, *Kuwait: The Transformation*, pp. 105–8; and Crystal, *Oil and Politics in the Gulf*, pp. 97–100.
22. Tétreault, 'The Crisis in the Gulf: The View from Kuwait' (Revised version of paper prepared for a conference held at the University of Masachusetts, Amherst, April 1991), p. 7.
23. Shafeeq Ghabra, 'Voluntary Associations in Kuwait: the Foundation of a New System?', *Middle East Journal*, 45, no. 2 (Spring 1991), pp. 213–14; and Shamlan Y. al-Essa, 'The Political Consequences of the Crisis for Kuwait', in Ibrahim Ibrahim (ed.), *The Gulf Crisis: Background and Consequences* (Washington: Center for Contemporary Arab Studies, 1992), pp. 172–6. It seems that al-Essa underestimates the role of the secular forces in the voluntary work during the occupation.
24. Tétreault, 'The Crisis in the Gulf', p. 21. Others maintain that 'lifestyles and social taboos' were broken among Kuwaitis in late 1990. 'For example, during the occupation Kuwaiti women stopped wearing the veil, worked alongside males in hospitals or in the resistance, and openly drank whisky supplied from Iraq.' *Energy Business Review*, 'Kuwait's Recovery Strategy & Future Business', 2, no. 3 (1990–1), p. 41; also *Middle East Times*, 'Kuwaitis Mixed over New Social Freedoms', 24–30 September 1991.
25. This is a ball-park estimate. Compare Crystal, *Kuwait: The Transformation*, p. 156 and p. 166; Dilip Hiro, *Desert Shield to Desert Storm: The Second Gulf War* (London: HarperCollins, 1992), p. 249, p. 413; *The Economist* Intelligence Unit (EIU), *Kuwait: Country Profile 1992-3* (London, November 1992), p. 8; and *Middle East Economic Digest* (*MEED*), 31 July 1992, p. 15

26. The Kuwait Democratic Forum (KDF), The Islamic Constitutional Movement, The Islamic Popular Alliance, the Islamic National Alliance, the Constitutional Block, the Parliamentarian Group, the Independents.
27. Interviews with Kuwaiti economists Jasem al-Sadoun, Amir al-Tamimi and Yusuf al-Ibrahim (Kuwait, October 1992). Also *MEES*, 'Kuwaiti Assembly Sets Bold Agenda for Economic Change', 8 February 1993, pp. B1–B3; *Arab Times*, 'Manakh Crisis Debts KD7.5b', 30 November 1992, and 'Kuwait Buys $20b in Bad Debt', 21 October 1993.
28. *Mideast Mirror*, 'Investigation into Suspected Fraud at KOTC Follows Seizure of Assets over KIO Irregularities', 8 February 1993, p. 13.
29. Sources: interviews with Kuwaiti economists in October 1992; *Financial Times*, 'KIO in Spain: Where Did the Billions Go?', 30 November 1992, p. 15; and *Wall Street Journal*, 'Fallen Empire: A Fortune Disappears in Demise of Holdings Kuwait Had in Spain', 25 November 1992, pp. 1 and 7.
30. *Financial Times*, 'KIO, BP and the $5bn Shell Game', 24 September 1994, p. 9; *Arab Oil & Gas*, 1 October 1993, p. 11, and 1 November 1993, pp. 11–12. Earlier research had already indicated the KPC connection of the Kuwait Investment Office; see Paul Aarts, Gep Eisenloeffel & Arend Jan Termeulen, 'The KPC Connection of "Kuwait Inc."', *Amsterdam International Studies*, Working Paper no. 10, 1989.
31. *Arab Oil & Gas*, 1 February 1994, pp. 25–6.
32. For more details, see Mary Ann Tétreault, *Stories of Democracy: Politics and Society in Contemporary Kuwait* (forthcoming).
33. Interviews with Jasem al-Sadoun, general manager of Al-Shall Economic Consultants, and Abdul-Wahab al-Wazzan, director at Kuwait Chamber of Commerce and Industry, Kuwait, December 1996.
34. *Arab Oil & Gas*, 1 August 1996, p. 3; *EIU Kuwait Country Report*, 3rd quarter 1996, p. 10.
35. *Financial Times Survey, Kuwait*, 23 May 1995, p. viii.
36. *EIU Kuwait Country Report*, 1st quarter 1996, p. 11; *Financial Times Survey, Kuwait*, 23 May 1995, p. vi.
37. *MEES*, 8 November 1993, p. B4, 24 January 1994, p. B1, 11 April 1994, pp. B1–B3, 9 May 1994, pp. B8–B9; *EIU Kuwait Country Report*, 1st quarter 1994, pp. 10–11; and *Arab Oil & Gas*, 16 November 1993, p. 10.
38. For example, note the difference between, on the one hand, Jasem al-Saqr (former chairman of the Assembly's foreign affairs committee) and Jasem al-Sadoun, who are explicitly

positive and, on the other hand, political scientist Ahmad al-Baghdadi, who criticized the invasion file as 'badly tackled and a great disappointment' (interviews, December 1996).
39. From the time Kuwait gained its independence, bidun had formed the backbone of its military and police forces. The total number of bidun is about 300,000, nearly half of which reside in Kuwait while the rest are languishing in exile, mainly in Iraq, because Kuwait blocked their return after the war (Human Rights Watch/Middle East, *The Bedoons of Kuwait*, New York, August 1995). Other sources give different numbers, usually less. See among others *EIU Kuwait Country Profile 1995–1996*, p. 9, and material gathered from interviews in Kuwait, December 1996. Mid-1996, Kuwait's population stood at 2.016 million, of whom Kuwaitis formed only 35.7 per cent, i.e. almost 720,000 (*Arab Times*, 26 November 1996).
40. The highest number (30,000) was given by former independent Shi'a MP Abdul Mohsen Jawad (interview, Kuwait, December 1996).
41. Interviews with Haya al-Mughni, author of *Women in Kuwait: The Politics of Gender* (London: Saqi Books, 1993), Fatima al-Abdaly of the Women's Cultural and Social Society (WCSS), and Lubna Saif Abbas, one of the coordinators of a small but influential group of women activists.
42. *EIU Kuwait Country Profile*, 1995–6, p. 4; *Arab Times*, 9 October 1996.
43. *Arab Times*, 9 October 1996.
44. Examples abound, as I found out during interviews in Kuwait with Ahmed al-Khatib, Kuwait's longest-serving MP, who recently retired from active politics, Abdul-Muhsin Jamal, Jasem al-Sadoun, Ahmad al-Baghdadi, and Hassan al-Jawhar (an independent Shi'a MP). See also *Kuwait Times*, 26 August 1996, 'Diwaniyas play an important role in electoral campaign; vote-buying phenomenon also exists'.
45. Interview, December 1996.
46. *Arab Times*, 17–18 October 1996.
47. Peter Gourevitch, 'The Second Image Reversed: the International Sources of Domestic Politics', *International Organization* 32, 4 (Autumn 1978), p. 883.
48. The concept of 'political tribalism' was coined by Khaldoun Hasan al-Naqeeb in his *Society and State in the Gulf and Arab Peninsula*. I interviewed the author in October 1992 and December 1996 in Kuwait. Much of what follows is derived from those interviews. Al-Naqeeb speaks of 'political tribalism' in at least three senses: (a) it provides the bases of group

cohesion (*asabiyya*); (b) it serves as an organizing principle, that is, allocating group resources and specifying charters of categorical inclusion/exclusion in the group; and (c) it represents a general (or popular) mentality, which governs all forms of political relation. The state apparatus, in being the private property of the ruling elites, channels all benefits and advantages through a network of tribal-sectarian corporate arrangements. Naqeeb typifies political tribalism as a 'Middle East version of corporatism'. Also see Eric Davis, 'Theorizing Statecraft and Social Change in Arab Oil-Producing Countries', in Eric Davis and Nicolas Gavrielides (eds), *Statecraft in the Middle East: Oil, Historical Memory, and Popular Culture* (Miami: Florida International University Press, 1991), pp. 1–35.
49. Salamé, 'Small is Pluralistic', p. 101.
50. Ibid., pp. 100–4.

11 Arms, Oil and Security in the Gulf : a Tenuous Balance

Serge Herzog

As the world prepares to enter the twenty-first century, nations are grappling to comprehend the challenges of a newly unfolding global order. The search for peace and stability in and around the Gulf region in many ways serves as a litmus test in gauging the chances for a new post-Cold War beginning that may usher in the next millennium without the tension and conflict that marred the international system of centuries past. The sources of instability in the Gulf are many and their regional impact rarely follows a concentric pattern. Challenges to the security of the area are often precipitated by a composite of domestic, regional and international factors that encompass ideological, economic and social grievances which both evoke and respond to the involvement of extra-regional actors.

While alliances have shifted and issues have changed, the security of the Gulf littoral states has always been tied to outside interests. At a time when ideological bipolarity has been replaced by global economic interdependence as the hallmark of the new world order, the Gulf, with its massive hydrocarbon reserves and energy production capacity, is no less important to international stability today than it was during the Cold War. The 1991 Gulf War is a stark reminder of how local conflicts can rapidly escalate into large-scale conflagrations. Unfortunately, as much as the US-led coalition succeeded in dislodging Iraqi forces from Kuwait, Gulf security continues to be defined by the Iran-Iraq rivalry and the threat both countries pose to their Arab neighbours to the south. The latter, including Bahrain, Kuwait, Oman, Qatar, Saudi Arabia and the United Arab Emirates (UAE), face a vexing security predicament: Individually they all lack the capability or resources to muster sufficient military strength to defend themselves against Iran or Iraq; collectively as members of the Gulf Cooperation Council (GCC) they fail to foster the requisite unity to turn the organization into a preferred vehicle for regional defence. Instead, they depend on Western, primarily US, power projection capabilities to deter and, if necessary, fight an outside aggressor, even though doing so invites domestic political pressure and criticism from other Arab and Muslim states.

Predicated on the commitment by the West (and acquiescence, if not support, by Russia) to defend the area in an emergency, the GCC states have elected to acquire some of the most sophisticated weapons in an effort to strengthen their defences, to solidify bilateral security agreements with supplier states, and to promote foreign investment through contractual obligations imposed on suppliers. Though the large quantities of advanced military technology are rarely absorbed by indigenous forces in an operationally effective way, they can be ear-marked for foreign troops in an emergency and, hence, serve as an added deterrence. The careful allocation of arms purchases with UN Security Council member states is a principal foreign policy instrument by the Gulf states to ensure a measure of outside protection. In addition, members of the ruling circles in the Gulf have a vested interest in the purchase of arms due to the collection of middlemen commissions.[1]

The GCC countries are among the world's largest arms importers, with Saudi Arabia, Kuwait and the UAE ranked in the top ten.[2] Between 1987 and 1994 Saudi Arabia was the leading recipient of high-tech weaponry, based on the dollar value of arms transfer agreements signed. The kingdom allocated $75.9 billion over that period, out-distancing second-ranked Iran by some $63 billion.[3] In an attempt to beef up their defences after having been greatly outgunned during Iraq's invasion of Kuwait, GCC states intensified their acquisition of conventional arms. GCC military spending rose by 50 per cent between 1992 and 1993 and accounted for 9.35 per cent of the gross domestic product (GDP) on average; in Kuwait, Oman and Saudi Arabia that figure was more than 12 per cent. Not counting the tiny island state of Bahrain, GCC countries have the highest per capita military expenditures in the world, save Israel, which spends slightly more than Saudi Arabia and Oman but less than Kuwait, the UAE and Qatar when measured on a per capita basis.[4] GCC defence spending between 1993 and 2000 is estimated to exceed $70 billion, while spending on procurement, military construction, and local production of arms in the Gulf region (excluding Iraq) may surpass $225 billion during that timeframe.[5]

Although officially designed to deter further aggression by its larger neighbours to the north, acquisition of modern military hardware by the GCC countries entails a host of problems that compromise the quest for greater security. The introduction of more arms into these countries is financially taxing at times of depressed oil-based revenues; it exacerbates structural economic weaknesses associated with demographic and educational constraints; it introduces incalculable exposure to the politics of supplier states due to the globalization of the arms industry; and it subjects these countries to prolonged dependence on supplier states because of the lengthy operational life of modern weapons. These factors are further magnified by a lack of GCC coordination in defence planning and weapons procurement.

ARMS AND SECURITY: AN UNWIELDY RELATIONSHIP

The GCC was established in 1981 largely in response to fears of a spillover of the Iran–Iraq war and concerns over the 1979 Soviet invasion of Afghanistan and the Islamic revolution in Iran. Though the Iraqi invasion of Kuwait has heightened the interest in tighter GCC military planning, lingering territorial disputes pitting Qatar against both Saudi Arabia and Bahrain, uneasiness about Saudi domination, and little unanimity on how or what constitutes the primary threat are preventing the organization from taking decisive steps toward a unified posture. Hence, military procurement suffers from massive diseconomies of scale, costly duplication, and non-standardization. Similarly, there is little operational integration, and plans to substantially boost the joint Peninsula Shield force beyond its symbolic size of 4,000 troops have been foiled by disagreements over the extent of the actual expansion, the basing arrangement of this force, and concerns by some member states that it will conflict with military manpower demands at home. The lack of determination to ensure some means of collective self-defence again surfaced at the 1994 GCC summit meeting: Oman's proposal for a 100,000-strong rapid deployment force was quickly dismissed in favour of a modest 25,000-men mechanized brigade, while calls for an integrated air defence system have resulted in little more than the siting of one more radar in Bahrain to extend Saudi air surveillance.

Without substantive progress for collective defence, GCC states will find it exceedingly difficult to develop a viable indigenous military capability sufficiently effective against emerging threats in the region. In particular, they face several challenges: the build-up of adequate air and naval defences to protect the Gulf coast, offshore oil and gas facilities, nearby desalinization plants and the shipping infrastructure; the establishment of an integrated command, control, communication and intelligence (C^3I) system in conjunction with centralized area-wide early-warning sensors; the construction of survivable basing and support facilities; investment in tactical mobility to ensure rapid mutual reinforcement across all countries; the procurement of interoperable equipment to maximize the effectiveness of joint-force operations and to ease the deployment of extra-regional forces; and the provision of advanced training and adequate logistic support to optimize and sustain the use of high-tech equipment in combat.

Given the geography of the Gulf and the fact that the GCC states share a common culture, language and ethnicity, banding together for the purpose of mutual security would seem to come easily. Even Saudi Arabia, which geographically and militarily overshadows the group, is unable to fashion an effective defence without cooperation of its smaller GCC neighbours. Should one of them experience a hostile takeover, the defence of the peninsula (not to mention the safety of Gulf shipping) would be greatly complicated. Yet, divergent threat perceptions and the fear that an effective regional defence may provoke Iran or Iraq, or lessen external commitments to the security of the Gulf, appear to supersede the drive for unity. Instead, with the exception of financially strapped Bahrain and Oman, GCC states acquire large stocks of military hardware; they all engage the principal Western powers in broadly formulated bilateral agreements, eschew political over-identification with any one of them, and shy away from encumbering multilateralism.

To varying degrees the GCC states face domestic political and economic challenges that render the current approach to security – awarding big defence contracts in return for Western security commitments – increasingly untenable. The combination of depressed oil revenues, constraints on economic diversification and privatization, and demographically driven expansion of government spending on wages, subsidies, public services and social programmes limit the amount of affordable military investment. Between 1980 and 1995 the GCC population grew by 50 per cent while total oil income dropped in real terms.[6] Expanding hydrocarbon production to meet the expected growth in global oil and gas consumption is hampered by limited financial resources to develop the energy sector and by output expansion of other energy exporters. Government tapping of domestic capital markets inhibits enlargement of the private sector due to the capital shortage, while a sell-off of government assets may result in risky maldistribution of income and unwelcome hikes in domestic prices. Borrowing from international lenders is equally unpalatable, as it exposes GCC states to mounting financial scrutiny that may raise politically uncomfortable questions.

Heavily dependent on oil and gas earnings, GCC government revenues are highly susceptible to swings in energy prices. Considering the period from 1989 to 1996, Bahrain, with only a modest and steadily falling oil production, derived an average of 58.4 per cent of its revenues from hydrocarbon receipts. Kuwait, Oman and the UAE depended on it for over 80 per cent of their government revenues, while equivalent figures for Saudi Arabia and Qatar are 75 per cent and 66.4 per cent respectively.[7] The paucity of revenue diversification, the high level of non-discretionary spending, the accelerated depletion of monetary reserves, and the need to finance infrastructure and hydrocarbon sector expansion put unprecedented pressures on the government budget of GCC states. Acquisition of costly military equipment designed to yield a force-multiplier effect may mitigate the GCC's deficit in recruitable manpower *vis-à-vis* Iran or Iraq; however, such a capital-intensive strategy is irreconcilable with budgetary demands of the cradle-to-grave welfare system that exists to varying degrees in GCC states. High birth rates and longer life expectancy generate demographic pressures that increasingly outpace the ability of governments to meet public expectations for social services and employment opportunities. Hence, the GCC states will be hard pressed to sustain the current level of military expenditures without fuelling domestic tensions associated with falling living standards.

Similarly, the purchase of high-tech weapons compounds the shortage of technically skilled people in GCC countries, a critical resource for economic diversification and to assuage foreign labour dependence. Though the application of high technology in military hardware may have reduced the total number of people required to carry out a given combat mission, the sophistication of modern weapons increases the demand for specially trained operating and support personnel. Historical evidence confirms a steady rise in the proportion of technical to administrative and clerical workers due to the growth in electronics-related occupations.[8] Since the operational utility of advanced weapons is contingent upon the fielding and mastery of associated support systems (e.g., C^3I, warning, targeting, battle-damage assessment systems), the technical complexity of modern military hardware puts a premium on highly skilled professionals. As a result, the introduction of high-tech weapons aggravates both the problem of economic diversification and efforts at reducing the dependence on foreign labour.

A corollary effect of costly arms imports is the mounting difficulty in establishing effective war planning and operations. Large-scale acquisition of new weapons keeps a significant portion of the military personnel in a prolonged state of reorganization and retraining. The almost constant phasing in of new equipment generates significant churning in logistic support (e.g., spare parts management), while the politically inspired retention of multiple suppliers complicates contract management and equipment inventory integration. Frequent personnel rotation, lack of adequate skills and overstretched manning, as well as insufficient infrastructure and ancillary support are some of the prevalent factors that inhibit the formation of effective military forces.

The acute imbalance between available resources and nominal inventory strength in the area of combat aircraft epitomizes the problem GCC states face. Combat aircraft incorporate the cutting-edge in military technology and normally require a multilayered support system that relies heavily on sophisticated maintenance and repair equipment. Unfortunately, such equipment suffers from its own malfunctions, rendering accurate diagnosis and expeditious repair of defective weapons exceedingly difficult. A 1990 report by the US General Accounting Office on the Apache helicopter – operated and ordered by several GCC states – concluded that

> [t]he on-board fault detection and location system has not proven dependable in locating valid faults...the system does not accurately find the component that is the root cause of a particular fault indication...[and] about 40 per cent of the time the system detects faults that do not actually exist....Troubleshooting is further hampered by the fact that maintenance manuals lack wiring diagrams, are vague, and do not provide continuity between subsystems of different manufacture.[9]

The latter point is important, for many weapons that are ordered by the GCC states are customized, incorporating non-standard components to handle the unique climatic conditions of the Gulf and the surrounding desert. Skilled technicians, ample spares provisioning, and tailored basing facilities are crucial to aircraft operability; so are sufficient attention to life-cycle costing, downstream support requirements and operational suitability. However, GCC states almost invariably under-emphasize these dimensions due, in part, to a preoccupation with the political and symbolic importance of possessing such weapons. Many end up purchasing more aircraft than simple arithmetic warrants. For example, France and Germany respectively employ roughly 95,000 and 93,000 personnel in support of their land-based air forces, which include some 545 and some 439 combat aircraft respectively.[10] Although the GCC states, with the exception of Saudi Arabia, field far fewer combat aircraft, the available manpower per aircraft is sharply smaller in comparison to France or Germany. This ratio differential is further magnified by the fact that the two European air forces enjoy economies of scale that favour the more efficient use of military personnel.

Of the GCC states only Saudi Arabia has the demographic base to muster enough manpower to sustain a meaningful military force without relying on foreign nationals, without unduly drawing on locals needed to run the economy, or resorting to a militia-based system of part-time soldiering. The paucity of eligible nationals of serving-age in the other five GCC states limits the total number of recruitable men and women and, hence, severely circumscribes staffing of multi-service armed forces encompassing air, land and sea units. This situation is compounded by concurrent efforts to diversify the economy away from the hydrocarbon-based sector to more labour-intensive service industries (e.g., tourism) and to augment the proportion of nationals serving in the military. As if the numerical constraints would not be formidable enough, the GCC states also face political and social obstacles that complicate a military manpower expansion commensurate with the size of their equipment inventories. Imposition of a military service obligation, whether through conscription of full-time or militia soldiers, challenges the social contract in GCC states which, to various degrees, rests upon the provision of benefits *to* citizens, not the extraction of resources *from* them.[11] Though the GCC states are benevolent autocratic monarchies, which secure the citizen's political loyalty through generous government benefits, committing nationals to military service may well fuel the pressure for greater popular voice in government. More importantly, perhaps, the expansion of a professional military corps introduces an element of potential instability should it abandon its support for the rulership. Existence of the 50,000-man Saudi National Guard – a tribal force, under the command of the crown prince, formed to check any domestic challenge by the regular armed forces – illustrates the problem of raising large military forces. Finally, rivalries among tribes and their position in the social strata come into conflict with the institutional hierarchy of a professional military.

Counting on the political willingness and military readiness by the West to project their forces into the Gulf in order to ensure the stability of the area and the free flow of oil, the GCC states are unlikely to push for serious collective defence any time soon. Similarly, there are no reasons to expect a change in arms import policy, though the volume of transfers is likely to drop in coming years due to the gestation of massive agreements signed in the aftermath of the Gulf War, persistently flat oil prices, and mounting strains on government budgets. However, arms imports may no longer be as straightforward an instrument in cementing the political commitment of the seller to the security of the buyer. For one, the defence industry in the West is rapidly shrinking as cuts in military spending continue unabated. Second, the remaining economic and commercial benefits that accrue from the sale of arms are spread over a growing number of countries due to the globalization of the weapons manufacturing industry. As a result, the contribution of the defence industry to the economic well-being of any given country has diminished, reducing the influence of arms agreements on bilateral relations between supplier and recipient.

In search of lower costs and new markets, globally operating defence firms raise other pertinent issues. Internationalization of the development, production and marketing of arms is spurred on by a sharp rise in cross-border subcontracting, licensed manufacturing and multinational co-development and co-production. These arrangements often result in the establishment of joint-venture companies and lead to industry consolidation through international corporate takeovers and mergers.[12] The ensuing diffusion of advanced military technology and production capability erodes the quality lead enjoyed by Western manufacturers and undermines efforts to stem the proliferation of arms.

Implications for the GCC states are apparent: Acquisition of costly high-tech weapons is more likely to contribute to a regional arms race and may not guarantee an edge in equipment quality, nor may it strengthen the commitment of the West to defend the Gulf given the diminishing importance of arms sales to the economic prosperity of any single country. Moreover, globalization of the defence industry introduces greater uncertainty about the political ramification of arms imports. Without an arms industry of their own, GCC states are entirely dependent on supplies from the outside.

Arms, Oil and Security in the Gulf 247

Considering the multinational origin of components that go into modern weapons, the GCC states may come to depend on politically sensitive countries for the supply of spare parts and maintenance equipment. The potential impact would be long-term due to the extended operational life of new weapons. (For general data see Tables 11.1 and 11.2.)

THE ROLE OF OIL

However flawed their current arms import policy, the GCC states have little incentive to measure up militarily, and ensure defence expenditures are translated into meaningful investments and weapons are operated by seasoned professionals, as long as Gulf oil resources are tied up with Western strategic interests. Several developments must be considered: GCC states no longer dominate global oil production, as in the years following the 1973 Arab oil embargo when prices were high and non-OPEC production resided largely in the

Table 11.1 Geographic/demographic data of GCC states

Country	Area (km^2)	Land Border (km)	Coastline (km)	Population (1,000s) [% Citizens]	Population Growth (%)
Bahrain	620	0	161	590 [68]	2.27
Kuwait	17,820	462	499	1,950 [39]	6.65*
Oman	212,460	1,374	2,092	2,186 [73]	3.50
Qatar	11,000	60	563	547 [25]	2.39
Saudi Arabia	2,149,690	4,415	2,640	19,400 [69]	3.45
UAE	75,581	867	1,318	3,057 [24]	4.33

Note: Demographic figures are July 1996 estimates. *Reflects return of nationals and expatriates after the 1991 Gulf War.
Source: CIA, *The World Factbook* (Washington, DC: USGPO, 1996); IISS, *The Military Balance 1995–1996* (London: Brassey's, 1995); 'World Defence Almanac 1994–95', *Military Technology* 21 (January 1995); *Economist* Intelligence Unit, *Country Profile 1995–96* (GCC states); Gulf Organization for Industrial Consulting, *Gulf Statistical Profile 1995* (Doha, Qatar: Dar Al Kotob Al Qataria, 1995).

Table 11.2 Economic/military data of the Gulf states

Country	GDP per Capita 1994 ($)	Defence Budget ($billion) [% GDP, 1995]	Active Military Manpower	Main Battle Tanks	Combat Aircraft	Major Combat Ships
Bahrain	8,100	.25 [6]	10,700	120	24	8
Kuwait	16,800	3.5 [12.8]	16,600	245	71	2
Oman	10,000	1.82 [13.7]	39,700	76	38	4
Qatar	15,800	.30 [3.4]	11,100	24	18	3
Saudi Arabia	10,100	12.1 [8.5]	105,500	770	314	20
UAE	20,400	1.59 [4.3]	70,000	130	68	10
Iran	4,780	n/a [n/a]	513,000	750	286	20
Iraq	2,000	n/a	382,500	2,000	150–180	1

Note: Budget figures are for 1994 and exclude procurement expenditures; Iraq's figures are estimated; inventory figures are for 1994; main battle tanks excludes *light* tanks; combat aircraft includes *recce*, but not training planes; combat ships counts frigates, corvettes and fast-attack craft.

Source: CIA, *The World Factbook* (Washington, DC: USGPO, 1996); IISS, *The Military Balance 1995–1996* (London: Brassey's, 1995); 'World Defence Almanac 1994–95', *Military Technology* 21 (January 1995).

United States and the former Soviet Union. The past twenty years have seen a dramatic rise in output among other non-OPEC countries. Mexico, Norway and the United Kingdom raised their combined level (including natural gas liquids) from less than 700,000 barrels per day (b/d) in 1974 to 9.5 million b/d in 1997 – an increase surpassing Saudi Arabia's average production since the 1991 Gulf War, when the kingdom sharply augmented its output to make up for the loss in Kuwaiti and Iraqi oil. While it once produced more than 60 per cent of all the oil consumed, OPEC's share of the world market is down to less than 40 per cent, in spite of years of declining US and Soviet/Russian production.[13]

Although US imports of oil are greater than ever – over half of what the country consumed in 1995 came from overseas, with Saudi Arabia being the biggest single supplier – the seeming risk of incalculable energy dependence is conditioned by several factors which were largely absent twenty years ago. First, the United States is supplied by 57 different countries – no single one responsible for more than 16 per cent of total imports – and its economy is sufficiently cushioned to endure an abrupt cut-off from foreign oil for several months due to the accumulation of 592 million barrels in its strategic reserve. Second, having massively invested in refineries, service stations and downstream petrochemical industries in consumer countries, Gulf oil producers have vested interests in uninterrupted exports to these clients.[14] Third, effective cartellization in the free-trade 1990s of a commodity as fungible as oil is virtually impossible; the recent withdrawal of Gabon and Ecuador from OPEC underlines the desire to be free of production quotas. Equally important, the emergence of a sophisticated crude futures market has introduced a highly responsive mechanism for risk spreading to mitigate the possibility of a sustained surge in oil prices. The latter are constantly monitored and subjected to electronic arbitraging, due to the use of global telecommunications, which keeps price volatility at a minimum. Furthermore, the criticality of oil is mostly limited to the transportation sector, where commercial viability of alternate fuels is still years off. However, a California law mandating that 2 per cent of cars sold in the state in 1998 must be free of emissions and the mounting use of ethanol and compressed natural gas are harbingers of likely changes in transportation fuels.

Yet, these developments have scarcely marginalized the role played by the GCC states in global energy security. According to an OPEC study, oil's diminishing share of the world energy supply – a drop of 5 per cent is projected by the year 2020 – is compensated for largely by a rise in gas production, which the GCC is rigorously expanding to make use of its large reserves (estimated at almost 14 per cent of the world total). But oil will remain the preeminent source of energy over the projected timeframe, accounting for an estimated 34 per cent of the global output by 2020. In turn, the study postulates, world oil demand could reach 72 million b/d by 2000, 80 million b/d by 2010, and 86 million b/d by 2020, based on steady crude prices for the remainder of the decade and annual increases of up to 3.5 per cent thereafter as the market starts to tighten up.[15] These figures compare with a forecast by the International Energy Agency (IEA) which projects a faster growth in energy consumption, whereby global demand may reach 77.3 million b/d by 2000 and 93.9 million b/d by 2010.[16] Average annual growth in global demand for oil over the next twenty years is generally believed to reside somewhere between 1.5 per cent and 3.5 per cent, resulting in a rise in world consumption of at least 5 to 7 million b/d between 1995 and 2000, a figure that could swell to almost 26 million b/d by 2010, according to the prognosis by the IEA.

Whether such increases in oil consumption will elevate the importance of the GCC states depends on a host of factors. For one, actual energy consumption is a function of many variables influencing both consumer demand – including economic growth, fuel efficiency, viability of alternative fuels, changes in consumer behaviour, and environmental and tax laws – as well as production capacity – such as upstream investment, Iraq's entry into the market, the future of the oil industry in the former Soviet Union, and liberalization of oil industry ownership, to name a few. Though the GCC states enjoy the lowest exploration and production costs, ongoing technological advances such as three-dimensional seismic surveying and horizontal drilling continue to narrow that advantage.[17] Also, a capital shortage may constrain production capacity expansion and, hence, limit the GCC share of the oil market. Barring a significant boost in production elsewhere, however, the ensuing hike in the utilization rate may effect an upward pressure on prices which, in turn, may generate the requisite cash to enlarge production. Moreover, much of the expected growth in oil consumption will come from Asia, where production of low-sulfur crude, the type suitable for Chinese refineries and available in the Gulf, is steadily diminishing. China, which turned into a net importer of oil in 1993, is registering double-digit increases in energy consumption and may import up to two million b/d of oil by 2005 – enough to exhaust Kuwait's entire production in 1995.[18] Burgeoning demand in the economically vibrant Far East may usher in a global trend of mounting dependence on Gulf oil and reverse the decline of the region's share of the energy market. In anticipation, Saudi Arabia has stepped up efforts in China Japan and the Philippines to secure joint ventures in refining exploration, and downstream operations.

Most importantly, though, GCC states are likely to steadily recapture lost market share and embark on a sustained production expansion due to high reserves and low depletion rates. Based on 'proven' reserves, those recoverable in the future from known reservoirs, the GCC states sit atop close to half of the remaining oil in the world. In contrast to other major oil producers whose aggregate production has peaked in 1991, Gulf states are unlikely to reach that level until the turn of the century, after which their production will decline at a slower pace compared to the rest of the world.[19] Using OPEC numbers as a surrogate measure, it is apparent that GCC states – they make up 60 per cent of the cartel's proven reserves, but generate less than half of its production – have the greatest capacity to meet long-term energy demands. For example, the dramatic rise in North Sea output has been matched by a sharp drop in residual reserves, as production has quickly outpaced new discoveries in the area. Meanwhile, OPEC oil has been depleted at only one-third the rate sustained in the North Sea, and the cartel enjoys a reserves-to-production ratio more than twice that of any other area.[20] Moreover, Gulf states enjoy the most productive oil wells in the world, averaging annually around 3,700 barrels per well, or roughly 53 times the global average.[21] Precluding major finds of recoverable crude elsewhere, or notable reversals of declining production in the former Soviet Union and the United States, chances are GCC relations with the West will be no less dominated by energy security over the next 15 years as hitherto.[22]

THE 'OFFSET' FACTOR

Amid the host of issues that govern GCC military spending, one of mounting saliency is the contractual obligation imposed on arms suppliers to invest a stipulated proportion of the value of the contract into the economy of the recipient country. Such offsets, which are normally realized through the setup of corporate partnerships, are designed to broaden the GCC's industrial base, boost private-sector activity, promote non-oil Gulf exports, and assist with the global integration of their economies. Although offsets have been introduced decades ago as part of arms sales between industrialized nations, and are largely integral to the arms trade of the 1990s, they engender potentially pernicious effects on the development of economically monochromatic states such as the Gulf monarchies. The problem is twofold: GCC economies offer limited investment opportunities due to the paucity of private-sector businesses, skilled labour, and restrictive conditions that govern the approval of offset proposals; accordingly, funds may not be invested in oil refining or production, in projects that are labour-intensive, or result in higher prices or lower quality for products or services that already exist. Secondly, the flowback of billions of dollars into projects that are highly derivative of the defence industry thwarts balanced economic development and thereby perpetuates, if not magnifies, structural deficiencies.

Started first in Saudi Arabia in 1985, and now pursued also in the UAE and Kuwait, offset projects thus far established are centred predominantly on providing maintenance and ancillary services for the military or existing infrastructure. In Saudi Arabia joint ventures between foreign contractors and local partners have been formed to furnish personnel training and logistic support for armoured vehicles, tanks, aircraft, air-traffic control, naval vessels and missiles. Other projects involve reinvestments in the petrochemical sector and plants for water-purification and car-oil recycling. Notable exceptions to purely military-related activities or those typical to the Gulf are the setup of a tire production facility, investment in a truck assembly plant, manufacturing of navigation devices and pharmaceuticals, and telephone maintenance service. Still, ten years of offsets have created no more than a few hundred jobs in the kingdom, even though the government relaxed the offset obligation from 30 per cent of contract value to 25 per cent in order to enlarge the number of bidders. Similarly, Kuwait, which approved a compensation project for the maintenance of its M-1A2 tanks, has seen a dearth of offset activity in spite of allowing locally registered joint ventures to operate outside the country.[23] To ease offset obligations in the UAE, which were introduced in 1990, defence contractors have the option to discharge their obligation after paying into an investment fund without having to wait until a joint ventures materializes. Major offsets thus far include privatization of a desalination and thermal powerplant, maintenance of avionics for commercial airliners and construction of a naval shipyard. There are also projects to set up a medical equipment firm, to invest in environmental protection and to provide overseas scientific training to UAE students.[24] The $1 billion investment fund indeed gives defence contractors greater flexibility in identifying UAE partners and in structuring offsets to diversify the country's industrial base.

Nevertheless, without more vigorous local human resources development, joint ventures are likely to increase the demand for foreign labour. The Gulf states' penchant for migrant workers may be difficult to break. They contribute to corporate profitability, since the bulk of them work for little money and raise few management problems due to the more tenuous legal standing expatriate labour is accorded (although they do pose the risk of absconding). Also, GCC nationals tend to eschew technical fields in favour of social sciences and arts, while manual jobs in the private sector that impart some technical experience are passed over for less demanding government employment.[25] Furthermore, the channelling of offsets into defence-related activities, such as maintenance and logistic support for military equipment, siphons technically skilled labour away from commercially more promising ventures. Though the nature of offset business depends on a defence firm's size, product lines and ability to tie in subcontractors in other industries, many of the prime contractors that supply the Gulf states are heavily military-dependent with a propensity to stay close to their trade. Used to operating in a monopsonistic market, such firms find it difficult to branch out into civilian-oriented areas where product marketing, distribution and support pose different challenges. To spur economic development and enlarge employment opportunities for nationals, GCC states are better off concentrating on consumer-related products and services. Military-related investments are notoriously government-centred, contradicting the Gulf's enunciated goal for private-sector expansion.

FEW INCENTIVES FOR CHANGE

Table 11.2 (above) shows that the GCC states in the *aggregate* are by no means hopelessly outgunned by either Iran or Iraq and will further improve their standing due to the vigorous modernization that followed the 1991 Gulf War. Together, if not individually, they are an economic powerhouse that can afford to purchase, for the most part, the latest military equipment and best product support available on the market. Of course, numerical comparisons of arms do hardly translate into meaningful measures of military *capability* without assessment of a host of factors, including respective concepts of operations, manpower skills and basing infrastructure. As Desert Storm so compellingly illustrated, the employment of modern weapons entails a complex web of associated support and battle-management systems to conduct concurrent large-scale multi-service (i.e., air, land and sea) combat around the clock, in any weather, and over large distances away from main operating bases. This puts a premium on technical competence, realistic training and, above all, professionalism.

These qualities are easily neglected, however, amid the glitter of highly sophisticated weapons purchased to symbolize the commitment of suppliers to the security of the recipients. Moreover, the politically inspired distribution of military procurement money across all major arms suppliers impedes integration of GCC forces and offers little prospect for a harmonized collective acquisition policy. Years of uncoordinated decision-making in this area have led to distinct country- specific organizations and forces. As Oman's Secretary-General for Foreign Affairs points out: 'The idea of unifying things is not really acceptable because there is a great waste in it. Who is going to change their complete structure for a new structure, and from a security point of view, is it really healthy to do so?'[26]

The Gulf's enduring, and perhaps mounting, role as the world's key hydrocarbon energy supplier, which continues to guarantee Western protection of the area, is arguably the single most important reason behind the ostensible reluctance among GCC states to go beyond public declarations of unity that highlight the council's annual meeting and, instead, initiate substantive steps toward collective military defence. Wary of potential consequences that may ensue from tighter collaboration – no one wants to provoke Iran or Iraq, give in to Saudi domination, or encourage a lessening of outside help when needed – GCC members invest in bilateral security agreements with countries of the UN Security Council and bank on their rapid response should one of them be threatened by an unruly neighbour. The US commitment to safeguard the area is central to this strategy, since Washington alone has the wherewithal to quickly counter an Iranian or Iraqi military foray.

GCC leaders may comfort themselves over the soaring US military presence in the Gulf, which mitigates pressures to seek collective solutions among regional states to the security dilemma of the area. The number of regularly deployed US troops (most of them afloat with the Fifth Fleet) has reached some 20,000 by 1995, compared to a paltry 450-personnel permanent contingent in early 1990. The same period saw a 200 per cent rise in the US capability to launch sea-based stand-off weapons from its deployed vessels, while the number of regionally based US combat aircraft carrying precision-guided munitions has increased by 50 per cent since the Gulf War.[27] To compensate for loss of year-around naval air presence in the area due to cuts in the US Navy carrier force, periodic force augmentation will occur, such as the deployment of 30 aircraft and 800 military personnel to Bahrain in the fall of 1995.[28] Meanwhile, prepositioning of equipment for two mechanized brigades in Kuwait and Qatar is part of an ongoing effort to form one full army division from stocks stored in the area.

US commanders have compelling reasons to further pursue prepositioning in the GCC states. According to US Central Command calculations, it takes six days and $26 million to get a prepositioned brigade fully operational – roughly 22 days faster and $319 million cheaper compared to one airlifted from overseas.[29] More importantly, prepositioning could be the only option to compensate for the current shortfall in air and sealift as mapped out in the 1995 update to the US military mobility roadmap.[30] The post-Cold War pullback of US forces from Europe and Asia coupled with steep cuts in the US defence budget puts further pressure on a forward-basing strategy centred around prepositioning and intermittent deployments.

Yet, a rise in the politically and socially discomfiting presence of foreign troops could quickly outweigh the advantage associated with Western security guarantees. And although forward-basing would save some money, the defence of the

Gulf is a costly enterprise, especially in times of fiscal austerity. In spite of large financial contributions from the Gulf states and Western allies, the US government still ended up paying $7.4 billion for Operation Desert Storm and $390 million to rush in 35,000 troops in response to Iraq's escapade near the Kuwaiti border in October 1994.[31] In addition, the spectre of domestic unrest befalling any of the Gulf states could render US military presence a thorny liability, for both local rulers and Washington, due to the propaganda value it offers to those seeking to fuel internal dissent.

Clearly, bilateral security agreements are fraught with drawbacks that ultimately compromise the stability of the region. None the less, the potential military threat from either Iran or Iraq looms large and can scarcely be met by the GCC states alone. Collectively they do possess formidable resources, but lack the political will to pool them in ways that would minimize their dependence on outside assistance. Instead, they individually engage in large arms purchases that exacerbate their shortage in skilled manpower, complicate interoperability among their forces, and potentially hinder even economic development and diversification away from the hydrocarbon sector. Though these factors alone may not prompt a reorientation in military procurement policy, the financial savings that would accrue from coordination in this area almost certainly will move into sharper focus as the drain on government revenue multiplies. As it is, few fiscal policies are in place to help pay for the wages, subsidies, public services and social programmes that will balloon as the GCC population doubles between 1995 and 2020.[32] Rationalization of procurement policy, stressing GCC coordination to realize greater economies of scale, may also serve as the nucleus for selected cooperation in functional areas (e.g., joint field exercises, integration of early-warning sensors, coordination of over-the-horizon and cross-country reinforcements) that are specifically designed to enhance military readiness in response to threats anywhere along the periphery of the member states. Incremental steps in this direction bear measurable benefits for all countries and are more easily accomplished than the formation of a substantial supranational rapid-reaction force that is politically sensitive and operationally taxing given the limited manpower of GCC forces.

NOTES

1. Middlemen commissions are a notorious part of global arms transactions but are rarely focused on for fear of jeopardizing job-generating business. See e.g. Michael White, 'Tories Braced for Sweeping Reforms under Fowler', *The Guardian*, 11 May 1992; John Mintz, 'Korean Legislator Alleges Bribery in Sale of F-16s', *Washington Post*, 26 October 1995.
2. In 1995 the value of arms transfer deliveries to Saudi Arabia amounted to $8.6 billion, to Kuwait $0.9 billion, and to the UAE $0.875 billion. US Arms Control and Disarmament Agency, *World Military Expenditures & Arms Transfers* (Washington, DC: USGPO, 1996), Table III.
3. Jeff Erlich, 'Russia, France Hike Arms Sales to Developing Nations', *Defence News*, 21–7 August 1995, 10. Figures are always current-year values unless noted otherwise.
4. US Arms Control and Disarmament Agency, *World Military Expenditures & Arms Transfers 1996* (Washington, DC: USGPO, 1997); the following 1996 per capita military expenditure figures were taken from the agency website (www.acda.gov) prior to publication of its *WMEAT 1996* and adjusted for GCC states to count their citizen population only: Kuwait ($4,920), UAE ($2,679), Qatar ($2,468), Saudi Arabia ($1,332), Oman ($1,126), Bahrain ($696). By comparison, Israel ($1,646), United States ($1,056).
5. 'GCC Arms Market Is Expanding But Sellers Will Face Tough Competition', *APS Diplomat: News Service*, 13–20 March 1995, 177.
6. Patrick Clawson, 'US – GCC Security Relations, II: Growing Domestic Economic and Political Problems', *NDU Strategic Forum* 40 (August 1995): 1.
7. Computed from data in Petroleum Finance Company, *Focus on Current Issues: Finances of the Gulf Cooperation Council Members* (Washington, DC: Petroleum Finance Company, January 1995), 10–44.
8. Martin Binkin, 'Military Technology and Army Manpower: Do Smart Weapons Require Smart Soldiers?' in *Marching Toward the 21st Century*, eds Mark J. Eitelberg and Stephen L. Mehay (Westport, CT: Greenwood Press, 1994), 169–71.
9. Quoted in Binkin, 179–80. The debate over operational suitability of sophisticated weapons, especially aircraft, has animated the discourse on military procurement and manpower requirements for some time. See e.g. Binkin's *Military Technology and Defense Manpower* (Washington, DC: Brookings, 1986); Serge Herzog, *Defense Reform and Technology* (Westport, CT: Praeger, 1994).

10. Data from CIA, *The World Factbook* (Washington, DC: USGPO, 1994); IISS, *The Military Balance 1994–1995* (London: Brassey's, 1994); 'World Defence Almanac 1994–95', *Military Technology* (January 1995).
11. Steeped in the rentier-state literature, this argument is advanced in F. Gregory Gause III, *Oil Monarchies: Domestic and Security Challenges in the Arab Gulf States* (New York: Council on Foreign Relations Press, 1994), 123.
12. See Richard A. Bitzinger, 'The Globalization of the Arms Industry', *International Security* 19 (Fall 1994): 170–98.
13. Figures computed from data in 'World Oil Production', *Petroleum Economist* 64 (July 1997): 52.
14. Rick Wartzman and Ann Reifenberg, 'Oil's Well: Big Energy Imports Are Less of a Threat Than They Appear', *Wall Street Journal*, 17 August 1995.
15. Rilwanu Lukman, 'Policy Implications of the World Energy Outlook', *OPEC Bulletin* 26 (July–August 1995): 4.
16. Cyrus Tahmassebi, 'The Changing Structure of World Oil Makets and OPEC's Financial Needs', *OPEC Bulletin* 26 (March 1995): 8.
17. The Saudi National Commercial Bank estimates the cost of developing new offshore fields in the UAE to be no more than 60 per cent compared to the North Sea during peak production; onshore costs in Saudi Arabia are a mere 25 per cent. Andrew Rathmell, 'The Struggle for Control of Gulf Oil', *Jane's Intelligence Review* 7 (August 1995): 355.
18. 'Benefit Seen in China's Dependence on Mideast Oil', *Oil & Gas Journal*, 28 August 1995, 105.
19. Jean Laherrere, 'World Oil Reserves – Which Number to Believe?' *OPEC Bulletin* 26 (February 1995): 12–13.
20. The use of reserves-to-production ratios is intended to convey the *comparative* advantage in production sustainability by the Gulf states *vis-à-vis* others; the ratios do not yield the years of supply remaining at current production levels, since output naturally diminishes over time with all oil fields. See Laherrere, 9–12; C.J. Campbell, 'Proving the Unprovable', *Petroleum Economist* 62 (May 1995): 27–30.
21. Only Norway, with an estimated annual 6,500 barrels per well after its recent North Sea expansion, surpasses the Gulf states in oil well productivity, though at the expense of faster well depletion. 'The Need for Low Producers', *Petroleum Economist* 64 (February 1997): 2.
22. Russia's oil industry shows signs of recovery on the export side due to price deregulation and abolition of export quotas. But a

decrepit energy infrastructure and oil fields that are past their prime production are unlikely to permit a sustained turnaround anytime soon. See Steve Liesman, 'Russia's Oil Industry Is Ripe for Rebound', *Wall Street Journal*, 18 September 1995.
23. 'Country Briefing: Saudi Arabia', *Jane's Defence Weekly*, 6 May 1995, 33–5; William Maclean, 'Firms Chasing Kuwait Work Face Offset Challenge', *Reuter News Service*, 3 January 1994; *idem*, 'Hughes Venture Seeks Kuwait Defense Work', *Reuter News Service*, 28 July 1994.
24. 'Regional Briefing: UAE', *Jane's Defence Weekly*, 18 March 1995, 53–9.
25. Robert E. Looney, *Manpower Policies and Development in the Persian Gulf Region* (Westport, CT: Praeger, 1994), 172; 'Traditions Built on Shifting Sands', *Financial Times*, 19 April 1995.
26. 'One on One', *Defense News*, 22–8 May 1995, 46.
27. Caryle Murphy, 'Engulfed in a War that Won't End', *Washington Post*, 30 July 1995; James Bruce, 'Iraq Warned, U.S. 5th Fleet Firepower Has Increased', *Jane's Defence Weekly*, 9 September 1995, 23.
28. Philip Finnegan and Robert Holzer, 'Bahrain Seeks Support for USAF Presence', *Defense News*, 23–9 October 1995.
29. Barbara Starr, 'USA Seeks a Division's Pre-Positioning in Gulf', *Jane's Defence Weekly*, 25 February 1995, 8.
30. Projections are that the US Army will have to wait until 1998 to receive 16 roll-on–roll-off, container and heavy-lift vessels, while the air force will be short of airlift assets until the turn of the century due to continued retirement of cargo aircraft from its fleet. Both shortfalls are tied to the 1995 update of the Pentagon's Mobility Requirement Study, which calls for sufficient lift capacity to respond to a major regional crisis in less than three weeks. Theresa Hitchens, 'C-17 Buy Is Top Question in U.S. Military Lift Strategy', *Defense News*, 3–9 July 1995, 9; Jason Glashow and Robert Holzer, 'US Military Emphasizes Vital Role of Prepositioned Gear', *Defense News*, 10–16 April 1995; *idem*, 'Pentagon Review Reaffirms US Mobility Stance', *Defense News*, 6–12 March 1995, 3, 28.
31. Murphy, 'Engulfed'.
32. The population forecast is based on 1993 UN figures and taken from Gulf Organization for Industrial Consulting, 209.

Index

Abdul-Fadil, M. 5, 51, 52
Abdulla, A. 88
Abu Lughod, L. 165, 167, 175, 180
Addleton, J. 37
Agricultural sector 8, 120, 125
Al-Kuwari, A. K. 76
Al-Maojil, H. A. 123–4
al-Misnad, S. 42, 155, 158
Al-Qudsi, S. S. 155
Al-Tuhaih, S. M. 42
Aluminium industry
  Saudi Arabia 111
  UAE 86, 95
Arab migrants 33, 35, 36–7, 38
  population policies 134–7, 138–9, 140–1, 144
Arab Oil and Gas Directory (AOGD) 14, 105, 110, 111, 113
Ardener, E. 165, 176, 180
Asians
  migrant labour 33, 36–7, 38, 39
  population policies 135, 137, 138–9, 141–2, 147
  women in labour force 43
Azzam, T. H. 6, 111, 113, 118, 128

Bahrain 15
  attitudes to work 155
  dependence on oil 31, 57–8, 59, 66–7, 77
  education and training 39, 40, 41, 42, 43, 158
  emergence of oil industry 58
  foreign grants 61
  geographic data 247
  GNP per capita 30
  government employment 64, 65, 69–70
  government expenditure 62–3, 67–9, 77
  health development 44, 45

internationalization of economy 31
military spending 46, 248
non-national labour force 32, 35, 37, 38, 64–5
oil production levels 25, 57–8
as oil rentier economy 5–6, 57–72
oil reserves 27, 58, 66
oil revenues 61, 65–71, 72, 75–6, 77
political structures 13, 15, 61
political unrest after overthrow of Shah 136
population data 34, 140, 247
population policies 135, 142, 143
privatization 70–1
security issue 238–9
sponsorship system 64–5
state allocation of oil rents 64–5, 69
state as entrepreneur 63, 70–1, 78
state exploitation 62
state role before oil 59–60
taxation 67
US military personnel in 255
women in labour force 152, 153–4
Bahraini migrants 137–8
Beblawi, H. 28, 51, 53–4, 55
Bedouin migrants 134, 140, 144
Bedouin women, gender relations 11–12, 164–81
Bhardwaj, J. S. 111
Birks, J. S. 32, 36, 42, 138–9

Cement industry
  Saudi Arabia 112–13, 120
  UAE 93, 96
Central Statistical Organization 68, 69

260

Index

Chatty, D. 165, 167
Class, rentier economies 56–7, 62

Defence spending *see* Militarization
Delacroix, J. 57
Democracy 12–13
  Bahrain 13, 15, 61
  impact of war 213–14
  Kuwait 13, 16–17
  see also Kuwait, political change since Gulf War
Devine, P. 90
Diversification, military spending and 14, 243
  see also Industrialization
Doumato, E. A. 167

Economist Intelligence Unit (EIU) 6, 14
  educational development 41, 42
  health development 45
  labour force 38, 39
  Saudi industrialization 105, 108, 109, 110, 111, 114, 115, 123, 125
  Education and training 10, 39–44, 157–9
  ideal woman ideology 189, 190, 199
  migrant workers 146–7
  or military spending 46
  women teachers 153
Egypt, migrants from 134, 137, 147
Eikleman, D. 164, 167
El Sadaawi, N. 167
Employment *see* Labour force
Etatisme 56
Europa 25, 26, 27, 29
  Saudi industrialization 105, 109, 113, 114, 116
Expatriate communities, policies 133, 134–42, 227–8
  see also Migrant workers

Fertilizer industry 111–12, 119–20

Fisheries sector 8
Foreign investment, Saudi Arabia 115–16, 123–4, 128
Foreign population, policies 133, 134–42
  see also Migrant workers

Gender ratios, migrant communities 140–2
Gender relations 11–12
Islamic womanhood in Oman 166–7, 177–8
Islamic womanhood in Saudi Arabia 12, 167; controls on men 201–3; driving demonstration 184–6, 189, 194, 200–1, 205–6; economic dependence 196; education and training 189, 190, 199; government assistance 196; Gulf War and 200–1, 205–7; the ideology 186–91; legitimation of political system 191–7, 203–4, 205–6; marriage 196–7; morality committees 194–5, 198–9; national identity 187, 197, 203, 205–6; political stability through 197–201; religious doctrines 192–3; religious institutions 193–5, 198; segregation 187–9, 190, 191, 193, 198–200, 203; the tribal family 195–7; utility of 'ideal woman' ideology 203–7; work 184–5, 188–90, 198–9, 201
Kuwait 228–9
Oman 164–81: attitudes to weaving project 169–71; citizenship 167; masks 165, 167, 172; patriarchy 176–80, 181; seclusion of women 165–6, 167; segregation 164–5, 166, 172–6, 180–1; space 165, 166, 173, 174–6, 180–1; subordination of women 166–7, 179–80, 181; weaving centres as place of

(Gender relations *Contd.*)
 work 171–4; weaving project set up 168–9
Ghanem, S. M. A. 126, 127, 154, 160–1
Ghoussab, M. 166
Gourevitch, P. 230
Governments
 and attitudes to work 155–6
 employment by 55, 64, 65, 69–70, 155
 impact of oil 5
 Islamic womanhood 12, 177–8
 labour force structure 9
 oil revenues 28–30
 patriarchy 176–9, 180
 see also Political policies and systems; Public sector; Rentier economies; Rentier states
Guest workers *see* Migrant workers
Gulf, definition 3
Gulf Cooperation Council (GCC) 3
 security 238–56
 see also Bahrain; Kuwait; Oman; Qatar; Saudi Arabia; United Arab Emirates
Gulf War 3
 impact on political systems 13–14; civilianizing effects 213; Kuwait 13, 17, 213–37
 Islamic womanhood 12, 200–1, 205–7
 migration after 35–6
 militarization after 13–14, 238–59
 oil production levels 26–7, 106
 population policies after 135, 137

Health development 44–5
 or military spending 46
 population policies 142
Human resource
 development 10–11, 39–46, 151–62
 education and training 39–44, 46, 157–9

 health 44–5, 46
 ideal woman ideology 189, 190, 199
 or military expenditure 45–6
 Omani weaving project 168
 population policies 142
 Saudi industrialization 117, 126, 129
 social attitudes to work 154–7
 technology transfers 126–7, 159–61
 UAE industrialization 86–7, 98–9, 101, 102
 women in labour force 152–4

Immunization rates 44
Industrialization 6–8
 military problems and 14, 243
 offsets 252–3
 Saudi Arabia 7–8, 104–5;
 agricultural sector 120, 125;
 aluminium 111;
 cement 112–13, 120;
 competition 127; difficulties with 123–9; domestic market size 124–5; export costs 128;
 export-orientation 107–8, 110; exports 119–20, 127–8;
 external problems 127–9;
 fertilizers 111–12, 119–20;
 foreign investment 115–16, 123–4, 128; gas liquefaction 110, 115; genesis of 107; government ownership 115; growth of 107–9; import substitution 107–8, 125;
 imports 120–2, 128; incentive programs 117; industrial zones 114; internal problems 123–7; investment patterns 115–19, 123–4, 128;
 iron 113; joint ventures 109, 111, 117–19, 126–7, 128, 159–60, 250;
 labour force 122–3, 126, 129;
 light industries 113–14, 125;
 manpower shortage 126;

Index

marketing 119, 127–8;
minerals 108, 112, 119, 120;
need for 105–7; oil
refining 109, 115;
outcome 122–3;
petrochemicals 110–11, 115,
119, 120, 127–8; planning
problems 123–4; private
ownership 116–17, 125;
production costs 124–5;
protectionism 127–8;
steel 113; technology
transfers 126–7
UAE 7–8, 79–80; authoritative
bodies 85–6; domestic
market 87, 95, 96, 98;
efficiency 96–9; by
emirate 92–3, 94;
export-oriented 86–7;
goals 83–4; hydrocarbon-
based 86, 95, 97, 98, 99;
import substitution 87–8;
incentive policy 88–90;
investment distribution 92–3,
94, 95–6; investment
strategy 85,
99–100; labour force 86–7,
96, 97, 98–9, 101, 102;
manufacturing sector 90–9;
metallic industries 86, 95, 97;
need for 80, 82;
objectives 83–4;
outcome 98–9, 100–1;
outlook 99–100, 101–2;
performance 96–9;
plans 84–5; policies 84–5;
private sector 88–9, 99, 100,
101; strategies 85–8, 101–2
Infant mortality 44, 45
International Energy Agency
249–50
International Monetary Fund (IMF)
Bahrain 58, 78
UAE 81, 87
Internationalization
defence industry 246–7
Gulf economies 31–2
Iran
after overthrow of Shah 135–6

military data 248
oil production 58
as oil rentier economy 52
oil reserves 58
threat to Gulf states see
Militarization
Iraq
invasion of Kuwait see Gulf War
military data 248
oil production 26, 27, 58
oil reserves 58
threat to Gulf states see
Militarization
Iraqi migrants, population
policies 135, 136, 137, 140,
141, 144, 147
Iron industry
Saudi Arabia 113
UAE 86
Islamic womanhood in
Kuwait 228–9
Islamic womanhood in
Oman 166–7, 177–8
Islamic womanhood in Saudi
Arabia 12, 167
controls on men 201–3
driving demonstration 184–6,
189, 194, 200–1, 205–6
economic dependence 196
education and training 189,
190, 199
government assistance 196
Gulf War and 200–1, 205–7
the ideology 186–91
legitimation of political
system 191–7, 203–4, 205–6
marriage 196–7
morality committees 194–5,
198–9
national identity 187, 197, 203,
205–6
political stability through
197–201
religious doctrines 192–3
religious institutions 193–5,
198
segregation 187–9, 190, 191,
193, 198–200, 203
the tribal family 195–7

(Islamic womanhood *Contd.*)
 utility of 'ideal woman'
 ideology 203–7
 work 184–5, 188–90, 198–9, 201

Joint ventures 159–60
 offsets 252–3
Saudi Arabia 109, 111, 117–19,
 126–7, 128, 159–60, 250

Kabeer, N. 165, 166
Kandiyoti, D. 181
Katozian, H. 72
Keely, C. B. 36–7
Keynesian multiplier–accelerator
 mechanism 62–3
Kritz, M. M. 36–7
Kuwait 16–17
 attitudes to work 154–5
 dependence on oil 30, 31, 32
 education and training 40, 42,
  43, 158, 228–9
 geographic data 247
 GNP per capita 30
 health development 44, 45
 internationalization of
  economy 31
 Islamist fundamentalism 228–9
 militarization 238–9; arms
  purchases 46, 239, 248;
  offsets 252; US
  presence 255
 non-national labour force 32,
  35–6, 137, 145, 146–7
 oil production 26–7, 58
 oil reserves 27, 28, 58
 oil revenues 29–30, 216
 political change since Gulf
  War 13, 17, 213–37; 1992–6
  parliament 220–9; 1996
  elections 229–30; cultural
  issues 228; economic
  policy 225–7; financial
  management issues 221–7;
  historical background
  214–18; insiders vs
  outsiders 219–20; invasion
  report 226–7; mid- intensity
  democracy 232; moral
  issues 228–9;
  nationality 227–8; oligarchic
  republicanism 231; political
  tribalism 231; resistance
  movement 218–19;
  women 228–9
 political structure 16–17
 political unrest after overthrow of
  Shah 136
 population data 34, 140–1, 247
 population policies 134;
  citizenship 140, 144, 227–8;
  dependence on migrant
  workers 147; gender
  ratios 140–1; health
  services 142; housing
  programmes 143; internal
  security 135–7, 144–5; public
  opinion 138; social
  allowances 143; social
  services 146–7
 as rentier economy 55, 155
 segregation of women 228–9
 strategic importance 5, 28
 women in labour force 43, 44,
  152, 153, 154

Labour force 8–11, 32–9
 after Gulf War 137
 attitudes to work 154–7
 citizenship for migrant
  workers 144, 227–8
 dependence on
  non-nationals 37–9, 122, 126,
  147, 148, 151–2
 government employment 55,
  64, 65, 69–70, 155
 inter-state political
  relations 137–8
 legislation on migrants 145–6
 local–migrant group
  relations 138–9
 migrants' access to social
  services 146–7
 migrants' gender ratios 140–2
 migrants' origins 36–7
 migration phases 33–6
 military problems 243–5, 253,
  254

Saudi industrialization 122–3, 126, 129
skill development *see* Human resource development
sponsorship system 145
UAE industrialization 86–7, 96, 97, 98–9, 101, 102
women 10–11, 43–4, 152–4; Saudi Arabia 184–5, 188–9, 198–9, 201
Lancaster, W. 169
Life expectancy 44–5
Literacy rates 39, 40, 41–2, 43
Longuenesse, E. 56
Looney, E. R. 8, 10, 32
 attitudes to work 156
 foreign labour 151
 Saudi industrialization 108, 111, 122, 123, 124, 128
Lunciani, G. 28

Mahdavy, H. 5, 28, 51, 52
Manufacturing sector, UAE 82–3, 90–9
Marxist class analysis 56, 62
Masood, R. 107, 126
McHale, T. R. 119
McLachlan, A. 12–13, 28, 31
McLachlan, K. 12–13, 28, 31
Mernissi, F. 166, 167
Middle East Economic Digest (MEED) 123
Middle East Research Institute (MERI) 108, 125, 127
Migrant workers
 access to social services 146–7
 after Gulf War 137
 attitudes to work 155, 156
 dependence on 37–9, 122, 126, 147, 148, 151–2
 economic factors 139, 148
 gender ratios 140–2
 legislation 145–6
 migration phases 33–6
 military joint ventures 253
 naturalization 144, 227–8
 origins 36–7
 political determinants 148

political relations between Gulf states 137–8
public opinion 138–9, 142–3
quota systems 146
sponsorship system 145
Militarization 13–14, 238–59
 arms purchases 239–40, 246–7
 collective self-defence 240–2, 245–6, 254–6
 combat aircraft 244–5
 defence industry internationalization 246–7
 dependence on US 255–6
 incentives for change 253–6
 manpower problems 243–5, 253, 254
 offset projects 251–3
 oil revenues and 242–3
 problems of 14, 240–7
 role of oil 247–51, 254–5
 the security problem 238–9
 vs social development 45–6
Mohyaddin, B. 90
Montague, C. 114
Montana, P. J. 154
Muntarbhorn, V. 159
Muslim society, women in *see* Islamic womanhood

Najjar, A. 82
Neutral Zone
 oil production 26
 oil reserves 27
Non-oil GDP (NOGDP), rentier economies 62–3
NTDB 122

Oil 3–4
 dependence on 30–2, 58; Bahrain 31, 57–8, 59, 66–7, 77; Saudi Arabia 31, 32, 105–7; UAE 30, 31, 80–2
 diversification from 6, 14, 79; *see also* Industrialization
 government revenues 28–30; Bahrain 61, 65–71, 72, 75–6, 77; UAE 29–30, 80–2
 militarization and 242–3, 247–51, 254–5

(Oil *Contd.*)
 population structure 8–9
 production 25–7, 57–8, 65–6
 reserves 27–8, 58, 66
 strategic importance 5, 28
 see also Rentier economies;
  Rentier states
Oman 17–18
 attitudes to work 155
 dependence on oil 31
 education and training 40, 41, 43, 158
 fisheries sector 8
 gender relations 11–12, 164–81
 geographic data 247
 GNP per capita 30
 health development 44, 45
 internationalization of economy 31
 militarization 46, 239, 248, 254
 non-national labour force 32, 35, 38–9
 oil production levels 26
 oil reserves 27
 political system 18
 population data 34, 140, 247
 security issue 238–9
 weaving project 168–81
 women in labour force 152
Organization of Arab Petroleum Exporting Countries (OAPEC) 58
Organization of Petroleum Exporting Countries (OPEC) 58, 106
 oil and security 248–51
Ortner, S. 167

Pakistan, migrants from 134, 137
Palestinian migrants 134–5, 137, 141, 147
Patriarchy 176–80, 181, 196–7, 204
Petrochemical industry
 Saudi Arabia 110–11, 115, 119, 120, 127–8
 technology transfer 160
Political policies and systems 12–13

Bahrain 15, 61
constraints on change 12–13
in Kuwait since Gulf War 13, 17, 213–37
migrant labour 36–7
Oman 18
Qatar 21
Saudi Arabia 12, 20; controls on men 201–3; ideal woman ideology 186–91; legitimation of 191–7, 203–4, 205–6; stability 197–201; utility of ideal woman ideology 203–7
UAE 22
see also Population policies
Population policies 8–9, 133–4
 expatriates 133, 134–42;
  citizenship 140, 227–8;
  economic factors 139;
  fifty-fifty formula 135; gender ratios 140–2; intercountry relations 137–8; internal security 135–7, 144, 145, 148; local-migrant group relations 138–9; pressures to raise numbers 134–5, 138; public opinion 138–9, 142–3
 fertility rates 142–3
 health services 142
 housing programmes 143
 legislation on migrant labour 145–6
 marriage 143, 196–7
 national population 142–7
 naturalization 140, 144, 227–8
 quota systems 146
 social allowances 143
 social services 146–7
Population structure 8–10, 32–9
 dependence on migrant workers 37–9
 migrants' origins 36–7
 migration phases 33–6
 military problems and 243
 see also Population policies
Private sector 6
 rentier economies 56, 63, 70–1, 72

Index

Saudi industrialization 116–17, 125
UAE industrialization 88–9, 99, 100
Protectionism, Saudi industrialization 127–8
Public sector population policies 143
rentier economies 56, 62–3, 72; employment 55, 64, 65, 69–70, 155
Saudi industrialization 115
UAE industrialization 88–9, 99–100, 101

Qatar 21
attitudes to work 155
dependence on oil 31
education and training 39, 40, 42, 43, 158
geographic data 247
GNP per capita 30
health development 44
internationalization of economy 31
militarization 46, 240, 248, 255
non-national labour force 32, 35, 37, 38
oil production levels 26
oil reserves 27
oil revenues 29–30
political structure 21
population data 34, 140, 247
population policies 135, 137–8, 143
security issue 238–9
women in labour force 43, 44, 152, 153

Raffer, K. 45
Religious right in Saudi Arabia *see* Islamic womanhood in Saudi Arabia
Rentier aristocracy 56
Rentier economies 5, 51–4
Bahrain 57–72
definitions 52, 53–4
state role 54–7; Bahrain 59–71; classical view 60–1; as entrepreneur 63, 70–1, 78; *étatisme* 56; falling rents 65–71, 72; fiscal policy 56, 67; government employment 55, 64, 65, 69–70, 155; infrastructure development 55–6, 63, 67, 69; pre-oil era 59–61; rent distribution 55, 56, 64–5, 69–70, 155; social stratification 56–7, 62; tribal traditions 55; welfare policies 10, 64, 225–6
Rentier states 5–6, 51, 52–3
attitudes to work 155–6
definitions 52, 53
Kuwaiti state autonomy 216
private sector 6
see also Rentier economies
Richards, A. 216
Roukis, S. G. 154
Roy, A. D. 42, 44

Salamé 231
Salih, M. 45
Saudi Arabia 18–20
agricultural sector 8
attitudes to work 155
dependence on oil 31, 32, 105–7
education and training 40, 43, 44, 158, 189, 190, 199
geographic data 247
GNP per capita 30
health development 44, 45
industrialization 7–8, 104–5; agricultural sector 120, 125; aluminium 111; cement 112–13, 120; competition 127; difficulties with 123–9; domestic market size 124–5; export costs 128; export-orientation 107–8, 110; exports 119–20, 127–8; external problems 127–9; fertilizers 111–12, 119–20; foreign investment 115–16, 123–4, 128; gas

(Saudi Arabia *Contd.*)
liquefaction 110, 115; genesis of 107; government ownership 115; growth of 107–9; import substitution 107–8, 125; imports 120–2, 128; incentive programs 117; industrial zones 114; internal problems 123–7; investment patterns 115–19, 123–4, 128; iron 113; joint ventures 109, 111, 117–19, 126–7, 128, 159–60, 250; labour force 122–3, 126, 129; light industries 113–14, 125; marketing 119, 127–8; minerals 108, 112, 119, 120; need for 105–7; oil refining 109, 115; outcome 122–3; petrochemicals 110–11, 115, 119, 120, 127–8; planning problems 123–4; private ownership 116–17, 125; production costs 124–5; protectionism 127–8; steel 113; technology transfers 126–7
internationalization of economy 31
Islamic womanhood 12; controls on men 201–3; driving demonstration 184–6, 189, 194, 200–1, 205–6; economic dependence 196; education and training 189, 190, 199; government assistance 196; Gulf War and 200–1, 205–7; the ideology 186–91; legitimation of political system 191–7, 203–4, 205–6; marriage 196–7; morality committees 194–5, 198–9; national identity 187, 197, 203, 205–6; political stability through 197–201; religious doctrines 192–3; religious institutions 193–5, 198; segregation 187–9, 190, 191, 193, 198–200, 203; the tribal family 195–7; utility of 'ideal woman' ideology 203–7; work 184–5, 188–90, 198–9, 201
militarization 14, 245; military spending 46, 239, 248; offsets 252
non-national labour force 32, 35, 36, 37–8, 137; industrialization and 122, 126; population policies 137, 138–9, 146, 147
oil production 26–7, 58, 105–6, 107
oil reserves 27, 28, 58
oil revenues 29–30, 105–6
political structure 12, 20; ideal woman ideology 191–7
population data 34, 140, 247
population policies 134, 137, 138–9, 143, 146, 147
religious right *see* Islamic womanhood *above*
security issue 238–9
state subsidies to private sector 6
strategic importance 5, 28
women, ideal *see* Islamic womanhood *above*
women in labour force 44, 152–3, 184–5, 188–9, 201
Seikaly, M. 153
Serageldin, I. 36, 64, 152–3, 155, 158
Sex composition, migrant communities 140–2
Shah, N. M. 154, 155, 156
Shia communities 134–5, 136
Sinclair, C. A. 32, 36, 42, 138–9
Social allowances, population policies 143–4
Social attitudes to work 154–7
Social class, rentier economies 56–7, 62
Social development *see* Human resource development

Stauffer, T. 28
Steel industry
　Saudi Arabia 113
　UAE 86
Subsidies
　to private sector 6
　in rentier economies 55, 64, 70
　Saudi industrialization 127, 128
　UAE industrialization 88–90
Sudanese migrants 135, 137, 147

Tabari, A. 167
Technical training 42, 157–8
Technology transfers 126–7, 159–61
Tilly, C. 213
Trade
　history of 4–5
　internationalization of Gulf economies 31–2
　see also Rentier economies
Training see Education and training
Tribal traditions
　Islamic womanhood ideology 195–7
　population policies 134
　rentier economies 55
Turnma, E. H. 160

UN-ESCWA 34, 35, 151, 158
UN Industrial Development Organization (UNIDO), Saudi industrialization 107, 108–9, 116, 117, 120
UNDP reports
　attitudes to work 155
　education 40, 43, 158
　health 44
　military spending 46
　weaving project 168
　women in labour force 43, 152, 153, 154
United Arab Emirates (UAE) 21–2
　attitudes to work 155
　dependence on oil 30, 31, 80–2
　economic structure 80–2
　education and training 40, 41–3, 158
　geographic data 247

GNP per capita 30
health development 44, 45
industrialization 7–8, 79–80;
　authoritative bodies 85–6;
　cement 93, 96; domestic market 87, 95, 96, 98;
　efficiency 96–9; by emirate 92–3, 94;
　export-oriented 86–7;
　goals 83–4; growth of manufacturing 90–3; hydrocarbon-based 86, 92–3, 95, 97, 98, 99; import substitution 87–8; incentive policy 88–90; investment distribution 92–3, 94, 95–6;
　investment strategy 85, 95–6, 99–100; labour force 86–7, 96, 97, 98–9, 101, 102;
　manufacturing sector 90–9;
　metallic industries 86, 95, 97;
　need for 80, 82; objectives 83–4;
　outcome 98–9, 100–1;
　outlook 99–100, 101–2;
　performance 96–9;
　plans 84–5; policies 84–5;
　private sector 88–9, 99, 100, 101; strategies 85–8, 101–2;
　structural change 90–6
internationalization of
　economy 31
　manufacturing sector 82–3, 90–9
militarization 46, 239, 248, 252–3
non-national labour force 9, 32, 37, 139, 140
oil production levels 26
oil reserves 27
oil revenues 29–30, 80–2
political structure 22
population data 34, 140, 247
population policies 134, 135, 139, 140, 143, 148
security issue 238–9
women in labour force 43, 44, 152, 153

270   Index

Villie, P. 56
Vocational training 42, 157–8

Waterbury, J. 216
Weaving project, Oman 168–81
Webster, R. 11, 152
Welfare policies
  Bahrain 64
  Kuwait 225–6
  labour force structure and 10
Wells, A. D. 122
Wikan, U. 167
Winterford, D. 111, 128
Women
  educational development 41, 42–4, 189, 190, 199, 228–9
  gender ratios of migrant communities 140–1
  in labour force 10–11, 43–4, 152–4
  see also Gender relations
Workforce *see* Labour force; Migrant workers
World Bank
  Bahrain oil exports 59
  UAE industrialization 86, 88, 92
  World Development Reports 30, 31, 40, 44
  World Tables 1991 31
World of Information 31, 38

Yemeni migrants 135, 137, 140

Zahlan, A. B. 160
Zahlan, R. S. 4